CRAFTS

MADE EASY

200 PROJECTS

Hundreds of beautiful things to make, plus home decorating
ideas, all shown step-by-step with 1750 stunning photographs

SIMONA HILL

southwater

Contents

Humans are naturally creative and there is nothing quite so satisfying as making beautiful items to use in our homes. The basic knowledge, skills and inspiration are easily acquired.

Introduction

For anyone wishing to create lovely things with which to beautify their homes, this book is a veritable compendium. With 200 fantastic projects grouped into 13 craft areas, it provides the ideal taster for beginners, as well as inspiration for experienced craftspeople wishing to explore new disciplines.

Each craft begins with a full explanation of the materials and techniques involved and all the projects are fully illustrated with a detailed step-by-step approach. Templates are provided for many projects where necessary. You can either follow the projects exactly as they appear or adapt them to your own designs and ideas. Once you have mastered the techniques you can then create virtually anything you want.

Decorating Fabric shows how to paint, stamp and stencil different types of cloth. There are lots of exciting suggestions for decorating table and bed linen, towels, soft furnishings, lampshades and even a floorcloth.

In *Silk Painting* you will understand the affinity between silk and paint, and learn how to transform plain items into gorgeous and desirable possessions, from parasols, fans and seat covers to personal clothing. Or, you can use painted silk to make framed 'paintings', translucent panels and greetings cards.

For an individual look to home furnishing, try the wax-resist dyeing method revealed in *Batik*. It can be applied to cotton or silk table linen,

cushion covers, sarongs and scarves. Or dye a piece of plain material for use as a stunning hanging. More unusually, you might like to try out the technique on leather to make a rather special book cover.

Diverse effects can be achieved by dyeing cloth using the simple traditional methods shown in *Fabric Dyeing*. You can use these to create unique designs for table linen, shower curtains, cushions, throws and lampshades as well as more unusual items like glasses cases, hot water bottle covers, lavender bags, and even a co-ordinated desk set.

Ribbonwork reveals how to add a touch of luxury to all sorts of items – pillowcases, gift boxes, table mats,

Below: Beads have a delightful charm and can be fashioned into many useful and decorative accessories.

Below: Wire is a ubiquitous material and yet wonderfully versatile with a very decorative history.

Below: Once an essential material around the home, tinware has now become ornamental in value.

Above: Inspiration for picture frames can come from many everyday materials.

Above: Stained glass techniques are now easier to master and fun to do.

Above: Mosaic as a craft has stood the test of time and is enjoying a revival.

lampshades, curtains, tie-backs, coat hangers, a roll-up needlework case, an evening bag or even a bridal headdress. It also shows how to weave ribbon to make a sumptuous waistcoat.

Beads have regained some popularity recently, and the techniques described in *Beadwork* will enable you to make or decorate all sorts of home accessories from jug covers and candle holders to window dressings and trims for cushions and lampshades. Items for personal use include bags, belts, old-fashioned hatpins that can be used as brooches, and other jewellery.

Making enamelled jewellery requires the use of more specialized materials and a certain amount of skill, but if you follow the projects in *Enamelling* carefully you will soon be making some fine decorative items.

Wire is cheaply available and easy to work with surprisingly sophisticated results. *Wirework* shows how you can fashion almost any item. There is a fly swatter, monogrammed clothes hangers, candle sconces, lanterns, desk accessories, place mats and a toasting

fork. There is also a range of holders for toothbrushes, rolling pins, bottles, vegetables and spices.

The section on *Tinwork* shows how to work a variety of metal sheets and foils as well as recycled cans and tins into a miscellany of objects. There are pretty decorations for greetings cards, a jewel box, spice racks, coat racks, picture frames, doorstops and chandeliers. For outdoors you can make a birdhouse, a weathervane and house number plaques.

In *Picture Framing* you can learn the art of making frames as well as how to decorate them in many different ways to make each unique and stylish.

The section on *Decorating Tiles and Ceramics* enables you to create beautiful designs based on a wide range of styles. Apart from the paint, you will probably have most of the necessary tools at home. For those who want to try their hand at tiling with their own creations, instructions are included.

Glass is another hard material that lends itself to artistic expression, and in *Decorating Glass* you will find some

impressive suggestions. Transform plain bottles, vases or bowls, even a glass-fronted cabinet into imaginative and colourful works of art. Use the stained or leaded glass techniques to create decorative hangings and plaques. Even a plain glass jar can be transformed into a magical lantern for the garden.

Finally, in *Mosaic* you will discover how to beautify a range of surfaces both indoors and outside, including making a real mosaic floor! You can buy tesserae (the little coloured bits of glass or ceramic that are used to make up the pattern), but it can be more satisfying to use broken pieces of pretty china or glass, especially if they have sentimental value.

Whether you wish to make useful decorative items for your home or to give as presents, this book is sure to satisfy your creative instinct. Use it to hone your skills in a particular craft or to try out new ones that you might not have considered before. You may surprise yourself by discovering hidden talents and developing new passions.

Decorating
Fabric

Painting and printing on fabric offer unlimited scope for your creative skills and the chance to turn a blank piece of cloth into a unique item. Minimal artistic skills are required for the projects that follow. All can be made with simple freehand strokes, or using the templates provided to make a range of decorative stamps and stencils. There are plenty of styles to try your hand at, from fresh modern floral prints to Mexican-inspired designs.

Fabric paints are available in various forms from solid oil sticks and powders to felt-tipped pens, and are ideal for painting a range of designs and surfaces. Household paints are useful for larger projects.

Materials

Acrylic paint

Use for large wall hangings or floorcloths that do not need to be washed.

Embroidery thread (floss)

Available in a wide range, so choose thread (floss) to suit the weight of fabric you are working with.

Emulsion (latex) paint

Use to paint floorcloths or wall hangings that will not need to be washed.

Fabrics

Natural fabrics provide the best surface for hand painting, and there is a wide variety to choose from. The fabrics used in this chapter include linen, velvet and cotton duck canvas as well as delicate fabrics such as chiffon and organza. Pre-wash washable fabrics.

Always protect the work surface. Insert thin cardboard inside cushion covers to prevent the paint from spreading through to the other side.

Fabric medium

Use to thicken fabric paint.

Fabric paints

The wide range of permanent fabric paints available includes metallic colours such as gold, bronze and silver. Many are fixed (set) by ironing with a warm dry iron, but always read the manufacturer's instructions. Paints are also available in pen form, which makes drawing designs very simple.

Gum thickener or anti-spread

Use to thicken fabric paint.

Oil pastel sticks

Use like crayons to draw on to surfaces that will not need to be washed. Available in a wide range of colours.

Powder pigments

Use to colour substances. Can be mixed with malt vinegar and sugar to make a traditional glaze.

Ribbons

Ribbons and braids are used to add textural interest. Attach with fabric glue or machine stitching.

Varnish

Use gloss, matt (flat) acrylic or polyurethane varnish to seal floorcloths. Use separate brushes to apply varnish.

Choose paintbrushes and other equipment to suit the size of your project, whether it be a large canvas floorcloth or a delicate chiffon scarf. Larger projects require larger equipment and work space.

Equipment

Masking tape/Carpet tape

Use to temporarily mask off areas of background fabric. Leave the paint to dry before removing the tape.

Needles

Choose a size of needle to suit the thread (floss) used. Use an ordinary needle for hand sewing.

Paintbrushes

Use a fine artist's paintbrush to paint a precise design, and to add details. Use larger paintbrushes for large items.

Pens and pencils

Use a soft pencil to trace templates and a sharp pencil or felt-tipped pen to draw lines with a straight edge.

Plate or palette

Use to hold paint and to mix various colours together.

Ruler/Straight edge/Tape measure

Use to mark out large designs.

Sponges

Small natural sponges give a mottled paint effect. Use a larger household sponge to cover large areas of fabric.

Vanishing fabric marker

Available in pen form. Use to trace or draw designs directly on to fabric.

Carbon transfer paper

Use to transfer designs on to fabric. Place the paper chalk-side down underneath a tracing. Using a large embroidery needle, prick through both layers of paper, making a close line of holes to transfer the design on to the fabric.

Craft knife

Use to cut cardboard. Use a sharp blade and work on a cutting mat.

Silk pins (Push pins)

Use to secure fabric when stretched taut on a wooden frame.

Dressmaker's pins

Use to temporarily hold pieces of fabric together.

Fabric glue

Use to attach ribbon and braid to projects that do not require washing. Use sparingly or the glue will mark.

Different painting tools will make a different mark on different types of fabric, and the consistency of the paint will also vary the effect. Experiment with new tools on paper before starting a project.

Fabric Techniques

Paint effects   A paintbrush is not a requisite to create different paint effects – use your fingers, sponges, rags, cotton buds (swabs) and toothbrushes.

Gently dab on paint with a small natural sponge to give a mottled effect. The amount of paint loaded on the sponge will vary the effect.

Use a larger household sponge to cover large areas of fabric with paint.

A fine artist's paintbrush is ideal for painting a precise design, as well as for adding details.

Paint applied to wet fabric will "bleed" slightly as it mixes with the water to make a soft, feathery edge.

Paint applied very sparingly with a large decorator's paintbrush makes light, open marks. Used vertically, then horizontally, it creates a cross-hatched effect.

To create a light, speckled effect, dip a toothbrush in paint, shake off the excess, then flick the surface of the bristles with your thumb.

Colourwashing This is a simple method of applying colour to a background. Wonderful effects can be achieved as colours merge together.

1 Wash the fabric to remove any dressing. Watered-down paint can be applied directly on to damp fabric with a brush. The effect will be random as moisture helps the paint to spread and diffuse over the fabric surface. This method will dilute the paint colour. Alternatively, apply several colours of paint to dry fabric without waiting for the first to dry. The colours will blend into each other on the fabric surface.

2 Use a brush in proportion with the design you are creating. Load with paint and apply to the fabric.

3 Apply the next colour by painting directly over the edge of the previous colour, to allow the colours to merge.

Using an embroidery hoop

For painting designs on a small scale you may need to stretch the fabric to get the best result. A wooden embroidery hoop is the most popular method of stretching fabric.

 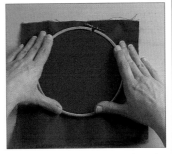

1 To protect the fabric wrap a length of 5mm/¼in-wide seam tape round the inside ring at a slight angle so that the tape overlaps all the way round. Fold the raw edge to the inside of the hoop and hem stitch.

If you are using an embroidery hoop for painting, wrap the inside ring with masking tape to protect the frame from the paint dyes.

2 Remove the outer frame. Place the required area of the fabric, right side up, over the inner hoop. Loosen the tension ring slightly. Hold the outer ring in place and push it down to secure the fabric between the rings. Pull the fabric taut in all directions and tighten the screw slightly. Use a screwdriver to tighten the outer hoop to keep the tension taut.

Masking

Adhering masking tape to fabric will prevent paint from penetrating defined areas of the fabric.

1 Stick strips of masking tape to dry fabric that has been stretched taut. Ensure that there are no gaps in the tape or the paint will seep through. Ensure that the tape is firmly adhered to the fabric to prevent paint from seeping underneath. Leave the paint to dry before removing the tape.

Rubber stamps and laminate stencils are widely available in many craft and department stores, but it is much more rewarding to make your own using one of the following simple techniques.

Stamps and Stencils

Polystyrene (Styrofoam)

This is easy to cut and gives good clean edges. Always mount it on to hardboard before cutting your design.

you will need
sheet of polystyrene (Styrofoam), approximately 1cm/½in thick
piece of hardboard, the same size as the polystyrene
wood glue or PVA (white) glue
felt-tipped pen
craft (utility) knife

1 Stick the polystyrene and hardboard backing together, using wood glue or PVA (white) glue. Without waiting for the glue to set, draw a design with a felt-tipped pen. The pattern will be reversed when printed.

2 Cut around the outline of the design using a sharp craft (utility) knife. If this is done before the glue has set, these pieces will pull away easily. Remove unwanted pieces of polystyrene as you cut them out.

3 Make shallow, angular cuts to scoop out the details. Use a new blade for this, so that the cuts are sharp and you do not accidentally lift pieces that are only partially separated.

Potatoes

Most of us learn this technique as school children, but potato prints are amazingly effective and should not be overlooked.

you will need
medium-sized raw potato
sharp kitchen knife
fine felt-tipped pen
craft (utility) knife

1 Make a single cut right through the middle of the potato, using a sharp kitchen knife. This will give a smooth surface for printing.

2 Draw the motif on the sliced potato using a fine felt-tipped pen. The design will be reversed when printed.

3 Use a craft (utility) knife to cut the outline, then undercut and scoop out the background. Cut out any details.

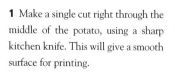

Foam High-density foam such as good-quality upholstery foam is recommended. Foam comes in many shapes, so a visit to a specialist foam outlet will give you inspiration for new patterns.

you will need
piece of foam
hardboard, cut to the same size as the foam
wood glue or PVA (white) glue
felt-tipped pen
ruler
craft (utility) knife
small block of wood

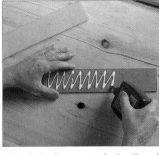 

1 Stick the foam on to the hardboard by applying wood glue or PVA (white) glue to the rough side. Without waiting for the glue to set, draw the pattern on to the foam using a felt-tipped pen and ruler.

2 Use a craft (utility) knife to define the outline of the sections to be cut. Using wood glue or PVA glue, stick the wooden block in the middle of the stamp back, to act as a handle. Leave to dry thoroughly.

Linoleum Cutting lino is a simple technique using special lino-cutting tools. You will be delighted with the intricacy of the motifs you can create.

you will need
tracing paper and pencil
lino block
sheet of transfer paper
masking tape
sharp pencil
craft (utility) knife
lino-cutting tools – a "U"-shaped scoop and a "V"-shaped gouge

1 Make a tracing of your chosen motif, the same size as the lino block. Slip a sheet of transfer paper (chalky side down) between the tracing and the lino, then tape the edges with masking tape. Draw over the pattern lines with a sharp pencil. The tracing will appear on the lino block.

2 Remove the transfer paper and cut around the outline with a craft (utility) knife. Cut any fine detail or straight lines by making shallow, angular cuts from each side, then scoop out the "V"-shaped sections.

3 Cut the rest of the pattern using the lino tools – the scoop for removing large areas of background, and the gouge for cutting finer curves and details. Hold the lino down firmly.

Designing with stamps

Explore the full potential of the thousands of ready-made stamps now available, by using them in interesting and unusual ways to give individual style to your hand-printed fabrics.

Rows

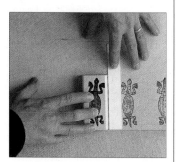

To create neat, regular rows, good spacing is vital. Decide on the space you want between prints and cut a strip of paper to that width. Use another paper strip to measure the distance between rows. Each time you make a print, place the strip against the edge and line up the edge of the printing block with the other side of the strip. Check right angles and corners with a set square (t-square).

Zigzags

Positioning a stamp at an angle will give a design extra interest. Make a print, then flip the shape over and repeat. Align the shape with the bottom edge of the fabric, or a line marked with tailor's chalk and a ruler.

Making large motifs

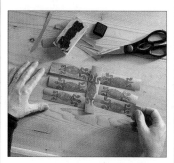

Stamps are usually quite small, but you can create a larger design by repeating a stamp, for example in the formation shown here. Use cut-out paper prints and experiment by placing them in spirals, circles and triangles, to create quite different effects.

Paper cut-outs

To help you visualize how a repeat pattern will look, make several prints on paper. Cut out the shapes and arrange them until you are satisfied, securing them with small pieces of masking tape if necessary.

Irregular patterns

If your design doesn't fit into a regular grid, plan the pattern on paper first. Cut out shapes to represent the spaces and use these to position the finished pattern.

Working with stencils

A wide range of stencil designs is available from craft suppliers, but it is very easy to make your own. Fabric paints used for stencilling should have a creamy consistency.

you will need

paper and pencil
tracing paper (optional)
fine felt-tipped pen
stencil card, Mylar film or stencil acetate
craft (utility) knife and cutting mat
spray adhesive (stencil mount)
fabric paints
stencil brush or small sponge
iron

1 Draw your design freehand on paper or if you prefer trace one of the templates at the back of the book. Using a fine felt-tipped pen, trace the design on to stencil card, Mylar film or stencil acetate.

2 Cut out the design using a craft (utility) knife and working on a cutting mat. It may be necessary to cut more than one stencil for the design to build up patterns and colours.

3 Apply spray adhesive to the back of the stencil to hold it in place on the fabric.

4 Remove excess paint from the stencil brush or sponge by dabbing on to paper or spare fabric. Hold the stencil brush vertically and dab on paint gradually to build up colour. With a sponge, use a light painting movement. Apply the paint sparingly.

5 Carefully remove the stencil and leave the paint to dry. Fix (set) the fabric paint according to the manufacturer's instructions. Repeat step 3, placing the second stencil on top of the painted area. Repeat step 4, remove the stencil and leave to dry.

Paint exuberant dots, circles and swirls on the front of this cushion, then decorate it with simple stitches and buttons in contrast colours. Finish with a row of buttons along the back.

Polka Dot Cushion

you will need

scissors

40cm/16in of 90cm/36in-wide white linen fabric

30cm/12in of 90cm/36in-wide coloured linen fabric

dressmaker's pins

sewing-machine

matching sewing thread

fabric paints in various colours

paint palette

medium artist's paintbrush

iron

embroidery thread (floss)

embroidery needle

assortment of coloured buttons

2m/2yd of 4cm/1½in-wide contrast fabric, for the piping

2m/2yd piping cord

tacking (basting) thread

Velcro

cushion pad, to fit the finished cover

1 From the white linen cut a 40cm/16in square for the cushion front, and 41 x 23cm/16½ x 9in rectangle for the back. From the coloured linen, cut a 41 x 30cm/16½ x 12in rectangle for the back. Fold over 1cm/½in of one 41cm/16½in edge on each back piece to make a hem. Pin, tack (baste), then machine stitch in place.

2 Place the front of the cushion on a flat, covered surface. Using fabric paints and a paintbrush, paint free-hand circles, dots and swirls. Leave the fabric to dry between each colour so that the paint does not smudge and discolour. Allow to dry, then fix (set) the paints following the manufacturer's instructions.

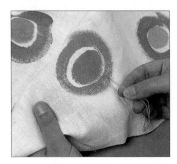

3 Decorate the painted design with circles of running stitches in contrast-coloured embroidery threads.

Left: The back of the cushion is finished with different size buttons in bright colours.

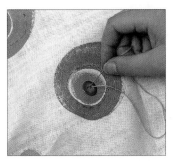

4 Sew a different colour button in the centre of each circle.

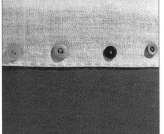

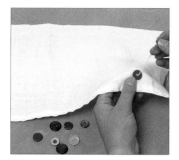

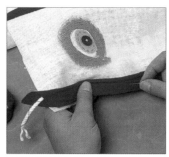

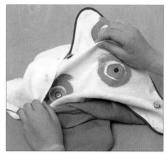

5 Using embroidery thread, work running stitch along the hemline of the white cushion back. Sew a line of buttons above the stitching.

6 Fold the piping over the cord and stitch. Pin to the cushion front, raw edges aligned. Place the cushion backs on the front, right sides together.

7 Using a zipper foot, stitch close to the piping. Turn the cover right side out. Press. Sew Velcro to each side of the opening. Insert the cushion pad.

Varnished floorcloths were introduced to America by European settlers, as a means of adding colour to the home. Artist's suppliers sell canvas in a wide range of sizes, pre-primed, or you can prime it yourself.

Stars-and-stripes Floorcloth

you will need
natural-coloured artist's canvas
ruler and pencil
craft (utility) knife and cutting mat
5cm/2in-wide double-sided carpet tape
white acrylic primer (optional)
medium decorator's brush
masking tape
acrylic paints in scarlet, cobalt blue
and white
plate
tracing paper
spray adhesive (stencil mount)
stencil card
stencil brush
clear or antique tinted matt (flat)
polyurethane varnish
varnish brush

1 Draw a 10cm/4in border on all four sides of the back of the canvas. Using a craft knife, cut diagonally across the corners. Stick double-sided carpet tape along the drawn border. Peel off the backing, then fold the raw edge in to create a neat edge.

2 If the canvas is unprimed, apply two coats of acrylic primer. Leave the primer to dry between coats. Using the pencil and ruler, mark vertical stripes 7.5cm/3in wide down the length of the canvas. Outline alternating stripes with masking tape.

3 Paint the alternating canvas stripes with scarlet acrylic paint.

4 Leave the paint to dry, then peel off the masking tape.

5 Trace the star from the back of the book and enlarge as required. Spray the back lightly with adhesive and stick on to stencil card. Accurately cut out the star template, using a craft knife.

6 Place the stencil on a white stripe, 5cm/2in from one end. Using a stencil brush, apply blue paint, working in from the points of the star. Wipe the back of the stencil to avoid smudging. Space the stars 10cm/4in apart.

7 Repeat with white paint on the scarlet stripes, positioning the white stars to fall halfway between the blue ones. Apply at least three coats of varnish. An antique tinted varnish will mellow the bright colours.

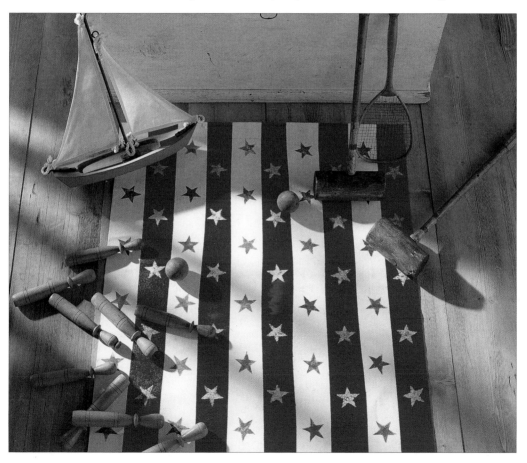

Paint this colourful sofa throw freehand so that all the flowerpots are different and the result looks spontaneous and creative. Decorate it with simple machine and hand stitching to add to the textured effect.

Flowerpot Throw

you will need
paper and pencil
tailor's chalk
large piece of thick cotton cloth
cardboard
fabric paints in dark blue, light blue,
olive green, pink, red and mauve
palette and sponges
wide masking tape
medium artist's paintbrush
sewing-machine
sewing thread
embroidery thread (floss) in
contrast colours
embroidery needle
iron

1 Plan your design on plain paper first, so that you know how many flower pots will fit along the length of the fabric. Using tailor's chalk, draw a large, simple flowerpot shape on the fabric. Alternatively, cut one out of paper and draw around it if you prefer. Position it at a jaunty angle.

2 Position a piece of cardboard underneath the fabric to protect the work surface. Empty a small quantity of fabric paint into a palette, and dilute as required. Using a sponge, apply dark blue fabric paint to fill in the flowerpot, taking care not to splash outside the outline.

3 When the paint has dried, stick strips of wide masking tape across the flowerpot in bands to mark out the stripes on the flowerpot. The stripes do not need to be parallel.

4 Using a smaller sponge, apply light blue fabric paint to colour the stripes, between the strips of tape. Allow to dry, then carefully remove the masking tape.

5 Using a paintbrush, paint an olive green vertical line for the flower's stem. Add some freehand leaves using the same colour.

6 Paint the flower centre pink, red or mauve, then paint the petals. Leave all the paints to dry thoroughly.

7 To define the shape, decorate the flower pot with machine embroidery using a complementary colour.

8 Machine stitch details on the stem and leaves, and around the petals in the same way.

9 Using contrast embroidery thread, hand embroider French knots in the flower centre. Repeat all over the fabric, placing the flower pots at different angles.

10 Press under a narrow double hem around all sides of the throw. Using thick embroidery thread or several strands in the needle, work large running stitches around the hemline to secure the hem in place.

The humble potato is one of the best printing tools and is inexpensive. A cut potato exudes a starchy liquid that blends into the ink and adds translucence. Print a set of napkins to match your new tablecloth.

Potato-printed Tablecloth

1 Pin the blanket to the work surface, using drawing pins. Arrange the cotton tablecloth on top. With a sharp knife, cut through the potato on a cutting board in one smooth movement to give a flat surface.

2 Practise painting the clover leaf on paper, drawing the shape freehand. When you are confident, paint the shape on the potato using ink.

3 Using the craft knife, cut around the outline, cutting away the waste potato to a depth of about 5mm/¼in.

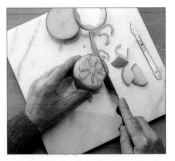

4 Using a kitchen knife, trim the potato into a square. Then cut a groove all around, about halfway down, to make it easier to hold.

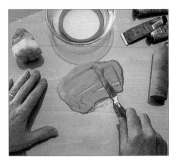

5 If you are using primary colours, mix green from yellow and blue. Then mix two parts green ink with one part blue and one-quarter part red.

6 Blend the colours thoroughly on a sheet of glass to achieve a consistent colour, using a palette knife.

7 Run the small paint roller through the ink until it is thoroughly coated.

8 Apply an even coating of ink to the surface of the potato stamp.

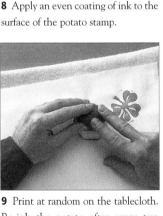

9 Print at random on the tablecloth. Re-ink the potato after every two prints to vary the intensity of the colour. Leave to dry, then fix (set) the paints using a warm dry iron, following the manufacturer's instructions. Hem the raw edges of the tablecloth by hand or machine.

Jazz up a plain fabric lampshade with hand-drawn stripes of colour, using oil pastel sticks, then decorate the bottom edge with oversized cotton pompoms for a completely new look.

Striped Pompom Lampshade

you will need

pencil

white lampshade

oil pastel sticks

cardboard

pair of compasses (compass)

scissors

cotton yarn, in 5 colours

selection of 5mm/¼in-wide ribbons

large needle

ceramic paints

fine or medium artist's paintbrush

white ceramic lamp base

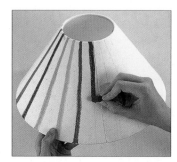

1 Using a pencil, draw 20 lines from the top edge of the shade to the bottom, spacing them evenly around the bottom circumference. Draw thick lines over the pencil marks, using different shades of oil pastels. Leave for at least 24 hours to dry.

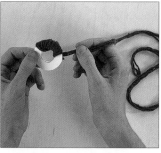

2 To make the pompoms, draw two circles each 6.5cm/2½in-diameter on a piece of cardboard. Draw a 2.5cm/1in diameter circle inside the centre of each one. Cut around the outer and inner circles. Holding the two circles together, wrap cotton yarn around them until the central hole is full.

3 Place one blade of the scissors between the two pieces of card and cut the yarn. Tie a length of ribbon around the centre, between the two cards. Pull one side of the pompom through the holes to remove the cards. Fluff out the yarn. Make ten pompoms, using different colours.

4 Using a large needle, punch ten holes around the bottom of the shade to correspond with alternate stripes. Thread one end of the ribbon around each pompom through a hole from the outside. Knot the ends. Paint stripes of colour around the lamp base, using ceramic paints. Leave to dry.

These Mexican-inspired bold lino-printed motifs, stamped in pale ink on a dark-coloured fabric, create a very striking effect. Interlaced satin ribbons divide the design into a grid.

Mexican Motif Place Mats

you will need

ruler

scissors

1.2m/4ft plain-weave cotton

bodkin

tracing paper and pencil

linoleum

linoleum-cutting tools

carbon paper

medium artist's paintbrush

cream fabric paint

paper

18m/19½yd of 1cm/⅜in-wide satin ribbon in two colours

1 Cut the fabric along the weave into six rectangles, each 50 x 35cm/20 x 14in. Pull out the threads along all four edges of each mat to make a fringe about 1.5cm/⅝in deep. Using a bodkin and scissors, draw out a 1.5cm/⅝in-wide section of vertical threads 2.5cm/1in from each short side, and two sections each 6.5cm/2½in from the vertical centre.

2 Following the same measurements, draw out three sections of horizontal threads from the mat at the top, centre and bottom. At the point where the lines of withdrawn threads cross will be a complete square. Trace the motif at the back of the book. Cut linoleum to the size of the motif and, using carbon paper and a pencil, transfer the motif on to the lino.

3 Using a fine V-shaped lino-cutting tool, carefully cut along the outline of the motif. Using a broader U-shaped blade, gouge out the excess lino. Make a few test prints with paint on some scrap paper. Using a paintbrush, apply just a small amount of fabric paint to the raised motif. Firmly press the loaded stamp on the mat and apply even pressure.

4 Remove the stamp and repeat until the pattern is complete. Leave the paint to dry. Using a bodkin, thread lengths of satin ribbon through the drawn-thread sections. Tidy the ends of the ribbons.

A simple grid of horizontal lines, drawn with a pencil and ruler, makes a very effective base for a stylishly modern pattern. Print it in varying tones of three different colours to give the design plenty of interest.

Block-printed Chair Pad

you will need

cotton-covered chair pad

strong scissors

felt-tipped pen

cardboard

newspaper

pencil

ruler

polystyrene (Styrofoam) tray

piece of wool blanket

plastic spoon

plastic gloves

fabric printing inks in yellow, green and blue

small block of 2cm/¾in wood

fine artist's paintbrush

iron

1 Remove the pad from the cushion cover. Cut a piece of cardboard to fit snugly inside the cover. Draw around the cardboard on a folded newspaper and cut this out about 5mm/¼in smaller than the cardboard. Cut about two newspapers for each side of the cushion. Slide half the sheets into the cover on top of the cardboard.

2 With a pencil and ruler, draw very light horizontal lines across the cover as a guide for printing. Space the lines a ruler's width apart. The lines could be drawn diagonally depending on the effect you wish to achieve.

3 Make a printing pad by lining a polystyrene tray with a piece of blanket. Using a plastic spoon and wearing plastic gloves, put small amounts of the fabric printing inks on the pad. Replace the lids on the jars to stop the inks from drying out.

4 Practise printing first on a spare piece of fabric. Dip the block of wood into each of the inks, combining the colours on the block, then press down firmly on the fabric. You may get a second print from the block before reloading with ink.

5 Print the cushion cover, starting from the middle and working downwards in horizontal lines. Use the pencil guidelines to help you to keep the printed rows straight.

6 When the first half of one side is complete, turn the cover round to print the rest. Experiment with different printing blocks to achieve a range of designs.

7 Retouch the edges and any piping, using a fine paintbrush, combining the colours as before. Print on one side of the cushion ties. Leave to dry for 48 hours.

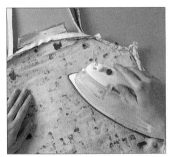

8 Empty the contents, and turn the cover inside out. Insert the cardboard. Press to fix (set) the inks. Remove the cardboard and turn right side out.

9 Turn the cover over, reinsert the cardboard and unused newspaper. Mark out the design lines on the second side. Print as before, finishing with the ties. Dry and fix, as before.

Fresh yellow gingham borders make an attractive background for this horse and foal, printed with foam rubber sponge. The squares on the gingham will help you to space and position the motifs accurately.

Sponge-printed Gingham Bed Linen

you will need

tracing paper and pen

spray adhesive (stencil mount)

24 x 24cm/9½ x 9½in thick cardboard

scissors

24 x 24 x 1cm/9½ x 9½ x ½in high-density foam rubber

ballpoint pen

iron

2.1m/7ft of 90cm/36in-wide yellow gingham fabric

tablespoon

base medium

fabric paints in red, ultramarine blue, jade green and white

2cm/¾in decorator's paintbrush

fine and medium artist's paintbrushes

flat white single-size bed sheet

dressmaker's pins

sewing-machine

white sewing thread

white pillowcase

1 Trace the two horses from the back of the book. Using spray adhesive, mount the tracing paper on to a piece of cardboard. Leave the adhesive to dry, then cut out the horses.

2 Place the templates on the foam rubber, trace around them with a ballpoint pen and cut out. Iron the fabric. Cut strips of fabric the sheet width by 21cm/8½in deep plus 3cm/1¼in seam allowances. For the pillowcase, cut a strip 21cm/8½in deep by the pillow width, plus seam allowances.

3 Add a loaded tablespoon of base medium to each pot of red, blue and green paint. For light blue, mix white paint into the ultramarine. Using the decorator's paintbrush, apply red paint to one side of a foam horse. The foam will absorb some of the paint; so dab it on until the paint sits on the surface.

4 Test the print on a fabric scrap. Place the back hoof 3cm/1¼in from the bottom edge, with the front of the horse prancing up. Press the foam firmly. Lift the foam. Print the sheet strip, working across from one end, and alternating the horse and the foal. Leave to dry.

5 For the pillowcase, print the first horse and foal, then wash the sponge thoroughly, squeeze out all the water and allow the sponge to dry. Apply red paint to the other side of the sponge in the same way and print so that the last horse faces the horse and foal. Leave to dry.

6 Using jade green paint and a fine artist's paintbrush, add tufts of grass in short strokes between each horse. Leave to dry. Using light blue, paint the hooves and manes, and add a stripe of colour to the tops of the tails. Leave to dry for several hours. Fix (set) the paints following the manufacturer's instructions, pressing on the wrong side with a warm, dry iron.

7 Press under a 1.5cm/⅝in hem at the bottom edge and sides of the printed sheet strip, and around the pillowcase slip. Pin the sheet strip with the printed side facing the wrong side of the bed sheet, and pin the edges together. Stitch 1.5cm/⅝in from the edge. Press the seam open. Flip the printed gingham edge over and press flat.

8 Pin the bottom and sides of the gingham into position on the top of the sheet. Top stitch the printed gingham along the top, bottom and sides of the sheet. Press under a 1.5cm/⅝in seam allowance around the pillowcase. Place the gingham strip for the pillowcase on the open edge, face up. Pin all around the edges, matching the hems with the existing hems and seams. Top stitch, keeping the stitching close to the hemmed edges so that it does not interfere with placing the pillow into the casing.

Decorate a tie-on seat pad with stylized leaf motifs. Trace the motifs on to linoleum and mount them on small wooden blocks. Print the leaves at random or plan out a design using tailor's chalk.

Lino-printed Leaves

you will need

soft pencil and paper
tracing paper
linoleum
linoleum cutting tool
wooden blocks
handsaw
hammer and nails (optional)
strong adhesive
scissors
wild silk fabric, pre-washed
tape measure
iron
masking tape
absorbent cloth
dressmaker's pins
opaque iron-fix (-set) fabric paints
in 3 colours
paint palette or separate plates
medium artist's paintbrushes
ribbon
sewing-machine
matching sewing thread
wadding (batting) cut to size
needle

1 Trace the leaf shapes provided on to a piece of paper. Trace them and transfer to the linoleum, one motif per lino piece. To do this, rub over the back of the tracing paper with a soft pencil, place the tracing right side up on the lino and re-trace over the drawn lines. If the lines appear faint, go over them with a pencil.

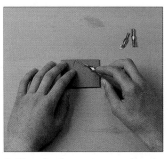

2 Use a linoleum cutting tool to cut away the areas that you don't want to print. Cut a wooden block to fit the design. If you like, nail a smaller cube to the back to act as a handle. Using a strong adhesive, glue the lino design to the flat side of the wood block. Make up several blocks with different designs in this way.

3 Cut two squares of silk to fit the chair seat, plus a 2.5cm/1in seam allowance all round. Wash one square and iron flat while still damp. Tape an absorbent cloth to the work surface, then pin the silk square to it.

4 Mix up the paints. Using a paintbrush, coat the first block with paint and press it firmly on to the silk. Repeat, using different blocks and colours, then leave to dry. Remove the silk. Fix (set) the paints, following the manufacturer's instructions.

5 Pin the back and front right sides together. Inside the back edge place four ribbon ties. Stitch around the edge leaving a gap. Turn right side out. Place the wadding inside the cover, fold in the seam allowance and pin. Hand stitch the open side.

A combination of stencilling and sponging is used to print this ready-made duvet cover. The light-coloured sponging creates a loose, painterly effect, while the stencils look precise and sharp-edged.

Summery Duvet Cover

you will need

absorbent cloth

pale-coloured, ready-made cotton duvet cover, pre-washed

seam ripper

dressmaker's pins

iron

tracing paper and pencil

Mylar film or stencil card

marker pen

craft (utility) knife and cutting mat

tailor's chalk

string

fabric paints in various light colours

plates

household sponge

spray adhesive (stencil mount)

small sponges or stencil brushes

sewing-machine

matching sewing thread

1 Cover the work surface with an absorbent cloth. Carefully unpick the sides of the duvet cover and open it out into a large rectangle. Roll up the underside of the cover and pin it so that it is out of the way. Iron flat the upper side of the duvet area to be painted.

2 Enlarge the templates at the back of the book to the required size. Transfer on to Mylar film or stencil card using a marker pen. On a cutting mat, accurately cut out the stencils with a craft knife.

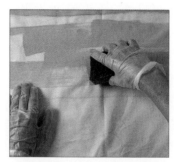

4 Dilute the background paint with water to the consistency of ink. Using a sponge, fill in the stripes. When each section of paint is dry, move on to the next; do not move the fabric while it is wet as this may cause smudging. When the duvet is painted, leave it to dry. Fix (set) the paints with a warm, dry iron following the manufacturer's instructions.

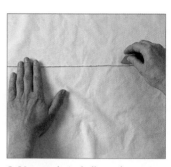

3 Using tailor's chalk, mark stripes at the duvet edge, deep enough for the stencils to fit inside. Mark the mid-point on each stripe. Stretch and pin a piece of string across the duvet from side to side. Rule across these lines.

5 Coat the reverse of one of the stencils with spray adhesive. Place it on the midpoint of a stripe and apply contrasting colours, using a small sponge or stencil brush. Carefully remove the stencil.

 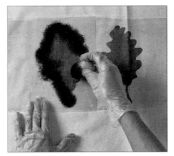 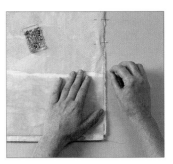

6 Continue along the stripes adding motifs, keeping them evenly spaced. After removing the stencil from the fabric, wipe away the excess paint to keep the colours clear and prevent paint from seeping on to the fabric.

7 Try blending colours to give the motifs a textured look. When your stencilling is complete and the paint is dry, fix (set) the paints according to the manufacturer's instructions, by pressing the wrong side with an iron.

8 Pin, then machine stitch the side seams to remake the duvet cover. The fabric may be stiff, but washing the duvet cover should ease this; follow the paint manufacturer's instructions for washing temperatures.

Print a jaunty sailing boat on to cotton fabric, decorate it with simple embroidery stitches, then appliqué it on to a hand towel as a novel decoration for your bathroom.

Foam-printed Boat Towel

you will need

high-density sponge, e.g. upholstery foam (foam rubber)

craft (utility) knife and cutting mat

metal ruler

stiff cardboard

PVA (white) glue

paper

scissors

felt-tipped pen

plain light-coloured cotton fabric

masking tape

fabric paints

plate or palette

paintbrush

embroidery hoop

stranded embroidery thread (floss)

embroidery needle

dressmaker's pins

hand towel

8 pearl buttons

1 Cut a 15cm/6in square and a 15 x 5cm/6 x 2in rectangle of sponge to make the stamps. Cut a piece of cardboard for each piece and glue one on to each sponge. Scale up the design at the back of the book as required. Make paper templates and cut them out. Draw around the boat and wave designs on the square sponge, using a felt-tipped pen.

2 Carefully cut away the excess sponge using a craft knife and metal ruler. Repeat on the rectangular sponge, positioning the waves so that they will fall between the first set. Cut a 17cm/7in square of cotton and tape it to the work surface, pulling the fabric taut.

◀ **3** Load the boat stamp with paint. Centre the stamp over the fabric and press. Remove the stamp. Leave to dry. Load the waves stamp with paint and stamp another set of waves between the first set. Re-load the wave stamp with paint and position it 1cm/½in from the bottom edge. Apply the stamp, aligning it with the bottom edge. Print the birds at a 45° angle above the waves. Stamp on to the fabric and leave to dry.

4 Fix (set) the paints by pressing on the wrong side with a warm, dry iron. Insert the panel in an embroidery hoop and work running stitch in stranded embroidery thread to pick out the clouds and details on the sails and boat.

5 Press under a small hem all round and centre at one end of the towel. Blanket stitch the panel in place.

6 Stitch a pearl button to each corner of the panel, and one in the middle of each side.

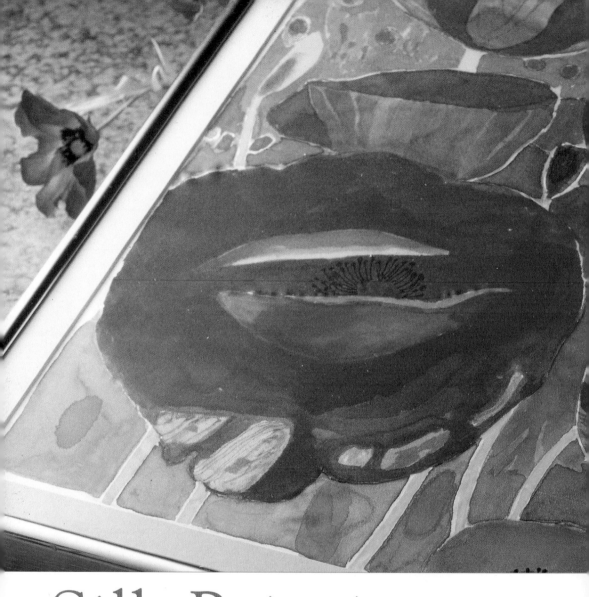

Silk Painting

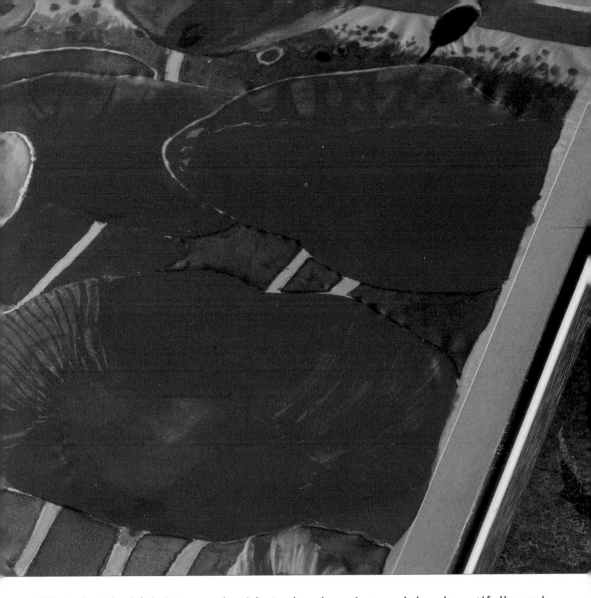

Silk is the ideal fabric to work with. It absorbs paints and dyes beautifully, and special transparent paints designed to give lovely clear colours are now widely available. Create finely drawn designs by tracing a pattern using gutta – an outline that creates a barrier to prevent the paint from spreading – or experiment with abstract effects by adding unusual materials such as salt and bleach to make fabulous cushions, throws, paintings and accessories.

Although any fabric paint can be used on silk, specially formulated silk paints are the best choice. Many weights and types of silk can be used, with medium-weight habotai silk a good choice for beginners.

Materials

Anti-spreading agent
Starch-like liquid applied to fabric to prevent the paints from spreading. Remove by hand washing.

Batik wax
Can be used to resist silk paints. Heat the wax in a double boiler or wax pot.

Bleach
Apply to pre-dyed fabric to remove the colour. Wash out immediately.

Gutta
Gel-like substance used with an applicator to draw a design on silk. It acts as a barrier to the paint. Remove transparent gutta by hand washing.

Iron-fix (set) silk paints
These paints are specially designed for use on silk. They are fixed (set) by direct heat, such as an iron or a hairdryer. Steam-fix dyes are also available, and are fixed with steam.

Paper
Silk paints can be fixed by placing each painted area between sheets of paper and ironing.

Powder dye
Fabrics can be pre-dyed using hot or cold powder dyes.

Salt
Add to damp silk paint to distort the colours. Brush off after use.

Silk
Available in different weights. Crêpe de chine, chiffon and georgette are ideal for lightweight items. Habotai or pongee silk varies in weight and has a smooth, soft sheen, as does silk-satin.

Sticky-backed plastic (Contact paper)
Attach to thin cardboard stencils and cut out to stick temporarily on to fabric to resist the paint.

Thickener
Mix into silk paints to prevent them from spreading. Thickened paint is used for painting details.

Watercolours or coloured inks
Useful for preparing designs on paper as they have the same quality as transparent silk paints on silk. Their strong colours can easily be seen through silk.

Silk painting does require specialist equipment, but most of it is quite inexpensive. The most important pieces you will need are a wooden painting frame and silk pins to hold the delicate fabric on the frame.

Equipment

Paint palette
Use to hold and mix paint colours.

Paintbrushes
Use a decorator's paintbrush to paint large areas. Use a medium paintbrush to paint a design, and a fine paintbrush for details. Use a sponge brush to dampen silk before painting and to apply paint or anti-spreading agent. Use a toothbrush to spray paint.

Pens and pencils
Use a black marker pen to draw on the acetate sheet. Use a soft pencil to trace templates.

Silk-painting frame
Make your own small- or large-scale wooden frame to stretch silk taut ready for painting.

Silk pins (Push pins)
Use special flat-headed pins with three points to attach silk to a frame.

Sponge
A natural sponge can be used to apply paint, e.g. around stencils.

Staple gun
Use to mount a picture in a frame.

Tailor's chalk and fabric marker
Use to temporarily mark designs on to the fabric.

Craft (utility) knife
Use to cut stencils. Always use with a cutting mat.

Double boiler or wax pot
Use to melt batik wax.

Gutta applicator
Fitted with various-size nibs (tips) for drawing a design on to silk to resist the paint. Fill no more than three-quarters full for even, flowing paint.

Hairdryer
Use to fix (set) iron-fix silk paints.

Iron
Use to press the fabric, and to make iron-fix silk paint permanent.

Masking tape
Use to mask off areas of the design.

Needle
Use for hand stitching.

Silk fibres normally contain dressing that looks slightly oily. It needs to be removed from the silk before painting or dyeing so that the colours can penetrate the fibres. To remove the dressing, hand wash the silk in warm, soapy water, using a mild detergent. Dry it by hanging it on a line, or roll it in a towel to remove excess water. Press while damp. Some objects, such as fans and umbrellas, are unwashable, and these should be painted by incorporating a thickener into the paint. Start with a simple project and practise with the silk paints first.

Silk Painting Techniques

Making a frame

Several different kinds of silk-painting or batik frames are available for purchase, the adjustable ones being the most useful.

1 Cut four pieces of planed timber or battening to make a frame. The frame should be slightly larger than the finished piece, to allow for trimming untidy fabric edges. Using wood adhesive, glue two pieces together to form a right angle. Repeat with the remaining two pieces and leave the adhesive to dry.

◀ **2** When the adhesive has set, glue the two right angles together to form the frame. Leave the glue to dry, then tap a panel pin (brad) into each joint to hold it firmly.

Pinning silk to a frame

Silk should be pulled taut on a frame and be springy to the touch before it is painted on, to ensure an even coverage of paint.

1 Use three-pronged silk pins to attach the silk to the frame. Place the first pin in the centre of one edge and work out towards each corner.

2 Space the pins an equal distance apart. Pull the silk over the frame and pin the opposite edge, placing the pins directly opposite each other.

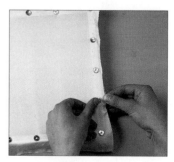

3 Pin down one of the sides, pull the silk taut across the frame, and then pin the final side. The silk should be springy, without being too tight.

Paint effects Iron-fix (set) silk paints are available in a wide range of colours and are specially designed for use with silk.

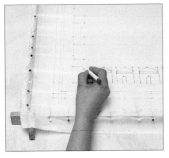

1 On fine silks place a traced design underneath the frame and copy over it with a vanishing marker pen.

2 Or, turn the frame upside down and trace the design with a pencil. On the right side, trace the lines with gutta.

3 Mix paints together to achieve the exact shade required. Ensure you have enough of each for the whole design.

4 A single paint colour mixed with white produces a delicate pastel tone. Continue adding white until you achieve the desired colour.

5 Paints can be diluted with water to make a wash. This is most often used to fill a background. Use a large brush to apply the diluted paint quickly over a large area.

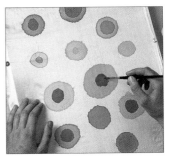

6 Paints will bleed into each other if applied quickly before they dry. Use a soft brush and flowing movements.

7 If a colour is applied over another, while the first paint is damp, they will merge and give a soft, blurred effect.

8 When using gutta, dot paint in the centre of each outlined shape and it will quickly spread to the gutta lines.

9 Use a large brush to fill large areas quickly (sponge brush or paint brush). This will stop watermarks from appearing. Use a fine brush for details.

10 Use a cotton wool ball held between tweezers or a clothes peg (pin) to create a softer tool where no definition is required.

Using gutta

Gutta is a thin, gel-like substance that acts as a barrier against paints, isolating areas of colour. It is applied to the fabric using an applicator that can be fitted with a detachable nib (tip) according to the fineness of line required. Do not fill the applicator more than three-quarters full and squeeze gently. Alternatively, purchase gutta in ready-to-use tubes.

Gutta is available in various colours, as well as transparent. Transparent guttas wash out, but coloured ones need to be fixed (set) and remain as part of the finished design. When working with gutta, it is essential to use special silk paints, as ordinary fabric paints contain binders that leave the colour opaque and can stiffen the fabric.

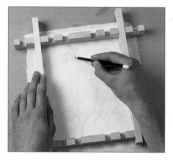

1 Place the covered frame upside down on the design and trace the pattern on to the back of the fabric, using a soft pencil. This will reverse the design; if you wish the design to be the original way round, transfer it first on to tracing paper.

2 Working on the right side of the silk, go over the design outline with gutta. It is important to maintain a continuous line, otherwise the paints will be able to seep through. Turn the silk over from time to time to check the back. Here, the applicator is fitted with a fine detachable nib (tip). Leave to dry.

3 When the gutta is dry, apply the silk paints in the centre of each defined area. Keep the brushstrokes light, allowing the colour to bleed from the brush outwards to the gutta lines. If the paint breaks through the gutta line there is no way to remedy the situation, except by washing the silk and starting again.

Fixing (setting) silk paints

Iron-fix (set) silk paints are made permanent by the use of heat, either by ironing the fabric or by using a hairdryer.

1 When the painting is complete, leave the paints to dry.

▶ **2** Remove the finished piece from the frame and fix the paints, following the manufacturer's instructions, usually by pressing with a warm, dry iron on the wrong side.

3 Alternatively, use a hairdryer set on a high setting to fix a piece of silk that is still mounted on a silk-painting frame, or if the object would be difficult to iron.

4 Wash out transparent guttas by hand, using a mild detergent.

Using thickeners

There are two types of thickener, both of which are used to prevent the silk paints from spreading into unwanted areas of the design. Thickener allows you to paint without flooding the fabric. It is used on objects that cannot be pre-washed, or where you are working with a stencil and do not want the paint to seep underneath. Thickened paint is mostly used for painting small areas and to add details to some designs. Mix thickener into the paints by placing both together in a screw-top jar with a lid and shaking vigorously.

1 Use thickener for painting small areas and to add details.

2 Alternatively apply anti-spreading agent to the silk before painting.

Using salt

Designs can be created by sprinkling salt or dabbing bleach on to the surface of the fabric while the paints are damp. Adding salt to damp silk paint will distort the paint, giving a lovely mottled effect. Different salts will produce different results, so experiment with different kinds. It is important that the paint is still damp when you add the salt, so alternate painting and applying salt. Leave the finished design to dry naturally, then gently rub off the salt crystals.

Using bleach

Remove the colour from pre-dyed silk by bleaching using a brush.

Dye the silk as desired, following the manufacturer's instructions. Apply the bleach a little at a time until you get the desired effect. Wash the silk immediately to remove the bleach, otherwise it will rot the fabric.

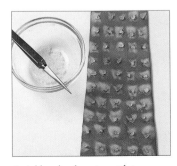

1 Add rock salt grains with tweezers.

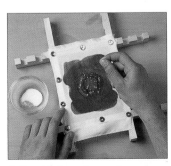

2 Sprinkle fine salt over the surface.

Transform a small silk umbrella into an exquisite parasol by adding a freehand design outlined with dots of metallic fabric paint. Open the umbrella while you are working so that the silk is stretched taut.

Summer Parasol

you will need
small plain silk umbrella
sponge brush
fabric paints in 4 colours, including metallic
hairdryer
tailor's chalk
fine artist's paintbrushes

1 Apply a background colour to some or all of the umbrella panels. Dampen the silk using a sponge brush soaked in water then apply the paint using the sponge brush. Fix (set) the paint with a hairdryer used on a high heat.

2 Using tailor's chalk, draw your choice of design on to the umbrella. Refer to the template provided. Using a paintbrush, apply dots of metallic paint along some of the tailor's chalk outlines. Allow to dry.

3 Paint a line along one edge of some of the chalked leaves. Paint in the details of the leaves in a contrasting colour. Add simple stylized flowers as desired. Leave to dry. Remove the tailor's chalk by brushing the surface lightly. Fix the paint using the heat of a hairdryer.

Decorate a plain silk fan with a lovely floral design in paint and gold gutta. In case adhesive has been used in the manufacture of the fan, add thickener to the paints to prevent them from spreading.

Painted Fan

you will need

pencil

plain silk fan

paper

tracing paper

masking tape

vanishing fabric marker (optional)

gold gutta

gutta applicator fitted with a

fine nib (tip)

thickener

iron-fix (set) silk paints

small bowls

fine artist's paintbrushes

1 Draw around the open fan on to a piece of paper, marking a dotted line where the fabric starts on the fan's handle. Trace the template from the back of the book, and transfer it to paper, within the outline of the fan.

2 Secure the open fan on top of the design with masking tape. Trace the flowers lightly on to the fan, using a soft pencil or vanishing fabric marker. Trace over the design with gold gutta. Leave to dry.

3 The gum used to make the fan may prevent the gutta from acting as a barrier, so mix thickener into the paints to keep them from spreading. Paint the design, using light brushstrokes. To keep the colours clean, use a different brush for each colour. If you need to wash a brush, make sure it is dry before using it again, to prevent the paints becoming too watery.

Trace this pretty flower motif on to a delicate silk camisole or pyjama top, then paint it in a soft pastel colour. Simple machine embroidery stitches complete the fresh, natural design.

Flowery Camisole

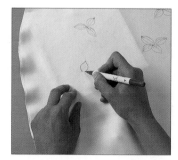

1 Trace the floral motifs from the back of the book on to a sheet of paper. Separate the two sides of the camisole by placing a shallow cardboard box inside. Insert the paper on top of the box and trace several flowers on to the outside of the camisole, using a vanishing fabric marker.

2 To make the silk taut, pin the camisole to the sides of the box, through the seams or hem only, using silk pins. Smooth out any wrinkles. Apply transparent gutta along the outlines of the design, making sure there are no gaps in the line. Leave the gutta to dry thoroughly.

3 Using a fine artist's paintbrush and a paint palette, mix the coloured paint with white until you achieve the desired tone. Apply the paint within the gutta outline. Allow the paint to dry thoroughly, then unpin the silk from the box.

4 To fix (set) the colour, place each painted area between two sheets of white paper and press using a warm, dry iron, following the manufacturer's instructions. Hand wash the camisole to remove the gutta.

5 Thread a sewing machine with metallic thread. Holding the fabric taut with your hands, stitch two curving lines as a stem for each flower. Add any other details you like.

Paint stripes of colour, then spoon on lines of salt while the silk is still damp to create a soft, watery effect. Alternate the painting and the salt, rather than painting the whole area first.

Abstract Picture Frame

you will need

silk pins (push pins)

at least 30cm/12in square lightweight plain-weave silk, pre-washed

silk-painting frame

iron-fix (set) silk paints

small bowls

fine artist's paintbrushes

small spoon

fine table salt

iron

pencil and ruler

graph paper

craft (utility) knife and cutting mat

PVA (white) glue

mounting board

wadding (batting)

scissors

adhesive tape

dressmaker's pins

needle

matching sewing thread

4 small ribbon rose decorations

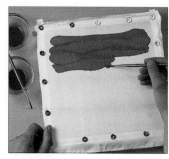

1 Pin the silk to the frame, pulling the fabric taut. Paint a few stripes of alternate colours, making the stripes at least 2.5cm/1in wide.

2 While the silk is damp, spoon lines of salt grains along the stripes. Continue alternating paint and salt until the surface is covered. Leave to dry. Brush off the salt, remove the silk from the frame and iron to fix (set) the paints.

3 Cut out a 20cm/8in square from graph paper. Draw a 10cm/4in square centrally within it and cut out. Glue the paper to mounting board and cut out with a craft knife.

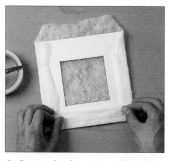

4 Centre the frame on a 25cm/10in square of wadding. Trim off the corners of the wadding, then fold and stick the surplus down with adhesive tape. Cut an "x" across the central square of wadding, trim to 2cm/¾in, turn back over the frame edges and tape down.

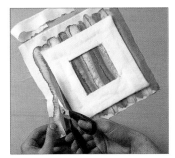

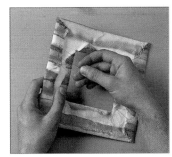

5 Pin the silk with the wrong side against the wadding. Trim the excess silk to 3cm/1¼in. Cut an "x" in the silk inside the frame. Trim to 3cm/1¼in. Fold the corners over the back, fold the flaps in and stitch the joins.

6 Wrap the inner edges over the frame and lace them to the outer edges with long stitches. Do not pull the silk too tightly or the shape will distort. Stitch a small ribbon rose to each inside corner of the frame.

7 Cut a 20cm/8in square of mounting board to make the backing. Cut a tall, right-angled triangle, score along the longest side 1cm/½in from the edge and bend it over to make a stand. Trim the bottom edge and check it will stand properly. Glue the stand to the backing, starting from the bottom edge. Attach the backing to the frame by gluing along three sides, leaving one side free so that a picture can be slipped inside. To make the picture permanent, add the picture before gluing all four sides and attaching the backing. Leave the glue to dry.

Transform a silk tie with coloured stripes and spots. The stripes are painted with a makeshift painting tool made from a peg (pin) and a cotton wool ball, and the spots are made by adding rock salt to the silk.

Salt-painted Tie

you will need

plain-weave silk tie, white or very pale, pre-washed

transparent gutta and applicator

cotton ball

clothes peg (pin)

iron-fix (set) silk paints, in 2 colours

rock salt

tweezers

medium artist's paintbrush

iron

1 Place the tie face down on the work surface. Draw a line with transparent gutta right round the reverse side, about 1cm/½in from the edge. This will prevent the paints from spreading round to the back.

2 Make a large painting tool by clipping a cotton ball into a clothes peg, as shown.

3 Using the first paint colour, apply a stripe of paint across the width of the tie front. While the paint is still damp, place evenly spaced salt crystals along the strip, using tweezers. Continue to apply paint and salt in this way down the length of the tie. When the tie is completely covered, leave it to dry for at least 20 minutes.

4 Using an artist's paintbrush, apply horizontal stripes in the second paint colour between the lines of salt. Leave to dry for 20 minutes.

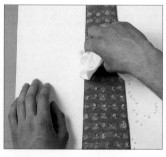

5 When the tie is dry, gently remove the salt crystals. Rock salt comes away quite easily, but smaller salt grains may stick. If this happens, gently rub the tie on itself and the grains will fall away. Iron the tie to fix (set) the paints, following the manufacturer's instructions, then wash it to remove the gutta and press again.

Simple flower stencils show up against a background of gently spotted colour, sprayed with a toothbrush. Practise the spraying technique first on paper to get the desired effect.

Patterned Seat Cover

you will need
chair with removable padded seat
paper and pencil
scissors
silk pins (push pins)
silk crêpe de chine, pre-washed
silk-painting frame
vanishing fabric marker
sponge brush
anti-spreading agent
tracing paper
thin cardboard
sticky-backed plastic (contact paper)
iron-fix (set) silk paint
small bowl
old toothbrush
white paper
iron
staple gun

1 Remove the padded seat from the chair, place it on a piece of paper and draw round it. Add a 5cm/2in seam allowance all round and cut out the shape. Pin the crêpe de chine to a silk-painting frame. Place the seat template on top and draw round it with a vanishing fabric marker.

2 Using a sponge brush, coat the fabric with anti-spreading agent. Trace the templates from the back of the book, transfer them to thin cardboard and cut out. Place each on sticky-backed plastic and draw around the shapes. Cut out approximately ten of each shape.

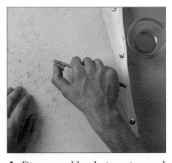

3 Peel away the paper backing and stick the shapes on to the fabric to form a pattern. Pour a little paint into a bowl.

4 Dip a toothbrush in paint, and lightly spray it over the fabric. Leave to dry, then peel off the plastic shapes. Sandwich the fabric between sheets of white paper and iron to fix (set) the colour. Hand wash and dry. Stretch it over the seat and attach it to the underside, using a staple gun.

Make good use of a spare scrap of silk by creating your own handmade card. Use a ready-made greeting card frame with a window cut in it, or mount the silk panels on handmade paper as in the main picture.

Salt-patterned Greetings Card

you will need

silk pins (push pins)

lightweight silk, pre-washed

small silk-painting frame

greetings card frame

soft pencil

iron-fix (set) silk paints

fine artist's paintbrushes

small bowls

rock salt and fine table salt

iron

scissors

spray adhesive (stencil mount)

scrap paper

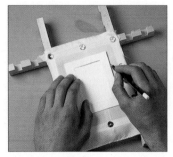

1 Pin the silk on to the silk-painting frame. Place the greetings card frame centrally on the silk and draw round it, using a soft pencil.

2 Begin to paint an abstract design on the silk within the drawn square. When first learning this technique, it is a good idea to confine your designs to simple spots, stripes, geometric shapes and patterns.

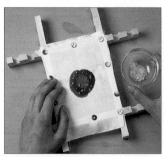

3 While the fabric is still damp with paint but not wet, drop on some rock salt. Build up the design by alternating painting and sprinkling salt. Use different-sized salt crystals, such as rock salt and fine table salt, to create an interesting pattern. Leave to dry completely – this should take about 20 minutes.

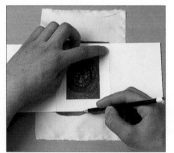

4 Remove the silk from the frame and brush the salt from the surface. Fix (set) the paint by pressing with an iron. Open the card and place the frame over the painted silk. Use a soft pencil to draw on the silk along the top and bottom edge of the card, indicating where the folds of the card fall. Close the card and draw the fold lines on the silk.

5 Cut the silk along the lines. Open the card and cover the section to the left of the frame with spray adhesive, protecting the rest of the card with scrap paper. Mount the fabric on the adhesive and trim any excess silk. Lightly spray the back of the frame with adhesive, then fold the card so that the silk is sandwiched in the frame.

This beautiful painted and embroidered shawl was inspired by the Indian custom in which a bride's palms are hennaed with intricate designs the night before her wedding.

Indian Motif Shawl

you will need
large heatproof bowl
tablespoon and teaspoon
salt
2 teabags
1m/1yd square of habotai silk, pre-washed
iron
tracing paper and pencil
masking tape
vanishing fabric marker
silk-painting frame
small hammer
dressmaker's pins
gutta applicator
gutta
iron-fix (set) silk paints
palette
medium artist's paintbrush
white paper
embroidery hoop
sewing-machine, with a darning foot
machine embroidery threads, in various colours
scissors
needle

1 Fill a bowl with boiling water. Dissolve 60ml/4 tbsp of salt and immerse two teabags in the water. Remove the teabags, then immerse the silk for 10 minutes. Rinse and press the silk using a cool iron.

3 Stretch the fabric over the wooden frame, using a hammer and pins. Ensure that the fabric is taut and that it has no wrinkles. Fill the dispenser with gutta and apply it along the lines of the design. Allow to dry.

5 Leave the paint to dry, then brush away the salt grains. Remove the silk from the frame and place it between two sheets of white paper. Fix (set) the paints, by pressing the silk with an iron following the manufacturer's instructions. Wash the fabric to remove the gutta. Draw star motifs freehand on the background fabric with the fabric marker.

2 Trace the hand template, enlarging as required. Stretch the silk over the template and tape it down. Trace with a vanishing fabric marker. Repeat the design by drawing a grid and rotating the design 90° each time.

4 Pour the silk paints into the palette compartments. Dot a little paint into the centre of each area to be coloured. Apply a wash of colour to the palm then, while the paint is still wet, drop 5ml/1 tsp of salt into the centre.

6 Place the fabric in an embroidery hoop and machine embroider the stars in coloured threads.

7 Using the fabric marker, draw additional circles to overlap the painted ones. Fill in the circles with matching embroidery, working a spiral from the centre to the outline. Stitch two or three lines around the palm area, working small bobbles at intervals. Cut away the excess fabric to within 5cm/2in of the design edge.

◄ **8** Using a needle, carefully pull away the threads around the raw edges to make a fringe.

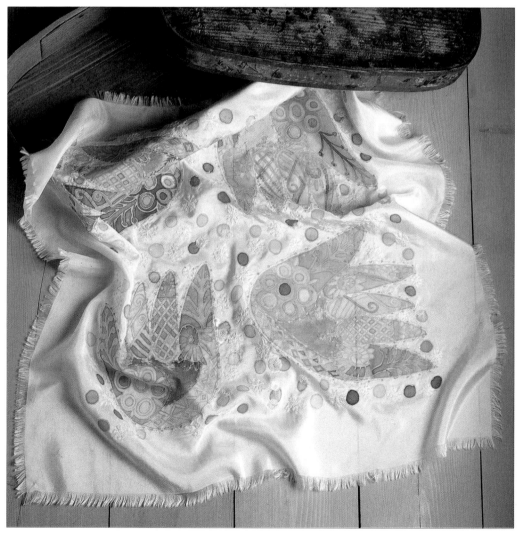

This vibrant picture uses transparent gutta to control the paints. Build up the design by overpainting, using the darkest colours last. Experiment with overpainting your choice of colours before you start.

Poppy Painting

you will need

tracing paper and pencil

paper

silk pins (push pins)

lightweight plain-weave silk, pre-washed

silk-painting frame

transparent gutta

gutta applicator

iron-fix (set) silk paints

small bowls

medium and fine artist's paintbrushes

iron

hand saw

heavy acid-free board or plywood backing

double-sided tape

picture frame (optional)

1 Enlarge the template from the back of the book to the size of the finished painting. Place the covered frame upside down on the design and trace the pattern onto the back of the fabric, using a soft pencil. Pin the silk to the right side of the frame.

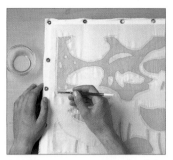

2 Apply transparent gutta around the areas where the palest colours will be. Fill in the palest colour, in this case a yellow which will be over-painted to create shades of green and orange-red. Fix (set) the paint, using an iron. Remove the painting from the frame and rinse away the gutta lines.

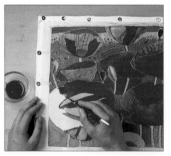

3 Continue to build up the design, keeping the darkest colours until last. Try not to apply the paint too quickly as the paints will bleed into each other.

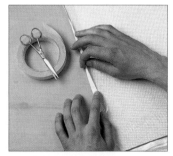

4 Cut a piece of backing to the size of the picture. Put a tiny piece of double-sided tape in each corner of the backing and position the silk on top. Turn the backing over and run double-sided tape along each edge, then pull the fabric round the edge and stick it down. Frame your work.

This decorative design is based on a Gothic cathedral window, so rich paint colours are appropriate. Black gutta is used to simulate the effect of the thick leaded lines separating the stained glass.

Stained-glass Silk Panel

you will need
tracing paper and pencil
picture frame
medium-weight silk, pre-washed
masking tape
silk pins (push pins)
silk-painting frame
flat artist's paintbrushes
black gutta
small bowls
iron
iron-fix (set) silk paints, in various deep colours
thickener
screw-top jar with lid
staple gun

1 Enlarge the template at the back of the book to fit inside the picture frame. Trace it on to the silk, then cover the areas between the lines with masking tape. Using silk pins, pin the silk to a silk-painting frame, pulling the fabric taut.

2 Using a flat artist's paintbrush, fill in the lines between the masking tape with black gutta. Leave the gutta to dry, then apply further coats to make solid lines. Leave to dry. Remove the tape, then take the silk off the frame. Fix (set) the gutta by ironing on the reverse side of the silk.

3 Pin the silk to the painting frame again. Fill in the spaces between the black gutta lines, using coloured silk paints. Leave to dry.

4 In order to paint in more detail, mix thickener into one of the darker colours by placing both in a jar and shaking vigorously. The thickened paint will give a textured brush effect.

5 Allow the paints to dry, then fix them with an iron, following the manufacturer's instructions. Remove the back from the picture frame. Mount the silk by stretching it over the backless frame, and then secure it at the back using a staple gun.

Batik

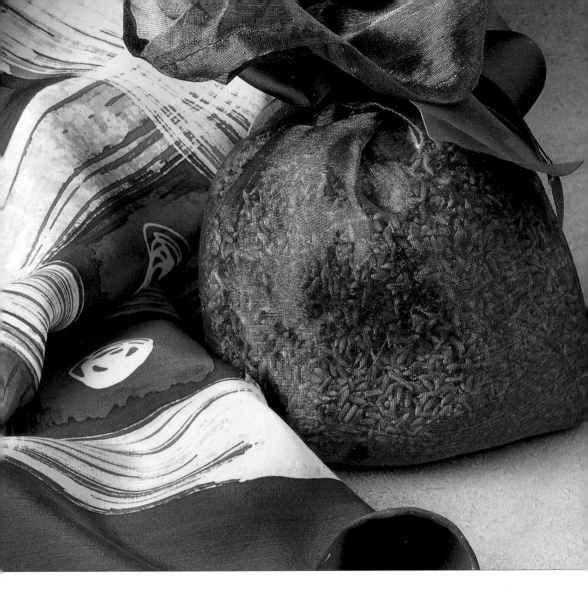

Traditional batik is known for its delicate patterns of vein-like lines, which are created by applying hot wax to the surface of the fabric and then cracking the wax when it is cold so that coloured dyes can seep in. This wax-resist method can be used to create a wide range of designs for large and small items, including table mats, napkins and runners, cushion covers, scarves, sarongs and decorative panels.

The most important materials used in batik are the wax for the resist, the double boiler to heat the wax, and the dyes or paints to colour the fabric, depending on which technique you are using.

Materials

wax and dyes to penetrate the fibres. Cotton can be boiled, but silk should be dry-cleaned to remove the wax.

General-purpose batik wax

Available ready-mixed in granular form from craft suppliers, this is the simplest wax for a beginner to use. Different waxes are available to create special effects. Heat and apply the wax following the manufacturer's instructions. Work in a well ventilated area.

Kitchen paper

Use to blot up excess paint.

Leather

Batik works well on leather, using a clear, water-soluble household glue or gum instead of wax as a resist. Don't use wax on leather as it will stain it. Special dyes and finishing treatments such as leather lacquer spray are available for leather – always follow the manufacturer's instructions.

Newspaper, brown craft or lining paper

Insert waxed fabric between sheets of paper and iron to remove the wax. Replace with new paper until all the wax is removed.

Sponge

Use to make a stamp.

Bleach

Colour can be removed from a pre-dyed fabric by placing it in a bowl of diluted bleach. Always wear rubber gloves and work in a well-ventilated area. Rinse fabric with water and vinegar to neutralize the bleach.

Cotton wool (Cotton balls)

Clip a wad of cotton wool into a clothes peg (pin) to make a homemade painting tool for covering large areas.

Dyes and silk paints

Use cold-water dyes, in powder or liquid form. Dyes or silk paints can also be applied to fabric in concentrated form. Special dyes are available for working with leather.

Fabrics

Use natural fabrics such as cotton and silk – those without texture are the most suitable. Pre-wash the fabric to remove any dressing, and to allow the

Heating wax for batik requires a wax pot or double boiler, and a thermometer. You will probably also use a dye bath or painting frame, and a traditional tjanting.

Equipment

Masking tape
Use to attach fabric to a board or work surface to hold it in place.

Paintbrushes
Artist's and decorator's paintbrushes of various sizes can be used. Use a separate brush to apply wax. Use sponge brushes to apply paint over large areas of fabric. Alternatively, use a large kitchen sponge.

Painting frame
Stretch fabric taut over a wooden painting frame before tracing a design on to the fabric surface.

Rubber gloves
Wear rubber gloves when dyeing fabric to avoid staining your hands.

Thermometer
Some wax pots are thermostatically controlled, but, if not, a kitchen thermometer is essential to keep the batik wax at a constant temperature while you are applying it to the fabric.

Chalk
Can be used to lightly trace a design on to dark-coloured fabric.

Craft (utility) knife
Use to cut thick paper and cardboard. Work on a cutting mat to protect the work surface.

Dye bath, buckets and bowls
Special shallow dye baths are ideal for batik dyeing. Alternatively, use a metal or plastic catering tray, or a large saucepan, bucket or bowl in which the fabric can move freely. If you are using a hot-water dye, the dye bath must be heatproof. Keep the fabric immersed so that the dye penetrates evenly.

Hairdryer and iron
Use a hairdryer to fix (set) silk dyes that are awkward shapes. Be careful not to melt the wax. Use an iron to remove wax from fabric and to set dye.

Tjanting
This traditional pen-like tool is used to draw wax designs on the fabric. Available with many size nibs (tips).

Wool dauber
A tool used to apply leather dyes.

Batik Techniques

Traditional batik Traditional batik is best used when large areas of colour are required. When using a dye bath, use a cold-water dye so the consistency of the wax is not affected, and keep the cloth flat while submerged in dye.

1 Place the batik wax in a wax pot or double boiler and gently heat it to a steady 80°C (170°F). Apply melted wax along the outline of the design, using a tjanting or other instrument such as a paintbrush or cotton wool. The wax should leave a transparent line on the fabric. If the wax is not hot enough, it will sit on the surface of the fabric without penetrating the fibres sufficiently. Leave the wax to dry.

2 Mix up a dye bath with a cold water dye, following the dye manufacturer's instructions. Remove the cloth from the frame. Dampen it and place it in the dye bath, keeping the waxed area as flat as possible. When the desired colour has been achieved, remove the fabric from the bath and rinse it in cold water. Unless cracking is required, be careful not to crease the fabric while rinsing. Hang it up to dry.

3 When the cloth is dry, re-pin it on to the frame, pulling it taut, and fill in any areas with wax that you want to remain the colour of the first dye. Check the back to make sure that the wax has penetrated sufficiently. Prepare a second dye bath. Add the fabric to it, being careful not to fold the waxed areas. After dyeing, rinse it thoroughly in cold water. Hang up to dry through.

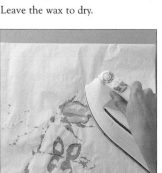

4 Remove the wax by ironing the cloth between pieces of newspaper, brown paper or lining paper.

5 Wax and dye can be added to build up more layers of colour and detail. However, most dyes can only be overlaid about three times.

False method or direct dyeing

This principle uses wax as a boundary, where one colour is separated from another by a line of wax. It is imperative that the lines of wax have no breaks, or the colours will bleed into each other.

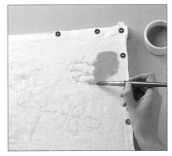

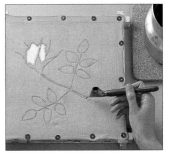

1 Pin the fabric to the frame, transfer the design and heat the wax as for the traditional batik method. Using a tjanting, draw in any outlines with wax. When the wax is applied, the fabric should become semi-transparent. If the wax has not penetrated the fibres sufficiently, the fabric will remain opaque. Check for breaks in the wax outline and fill them in by waxing on the back.

2 Using fabric dye (transparent dyes not containing binders, such as silk paints, are ideal), fill in the required areas with a paintbrush. Work quickly to ensure an even colour. If you choose to use a thick fabric paint, be sure to dilute it to the consistency of ink.

3 Draw in more of the outline with molten wax and tjanting. Check the back of the fabric again to make sure that the wax has penetrated the fibres of the fabric sufficiently.

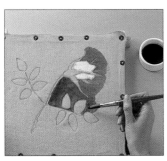

4 Using a different colour, fill in the background with a paintbrush. Further applications of dye can be made on the remaining non-waxed areas.

5 Apply a third colour. Waxing and dyeing can continue indefinitely or until the whole cloth is covered. To remove the wax, see Finishing.

Special treatments   Although the tjanting is the traditional tool used for applying wax, other tools such as paintbrushes and cotton wool pads can be used to achieve different effects. Once complete, take time to finish the work methodically.

Tjanting

The tjanting allows delicate designs to be drawn on to fabric with wax. Keep movements light and do not press on the fabric too hard as this may block the flow of wax.

Cracking

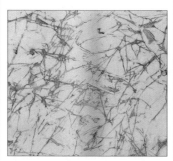

Here the fabric was coated in a layer of wax. It was crumpled, to crack the wax surface. Dye the fabric in a dye bath for best results and use a brittle crackle wax.

Decorator's paintbrush

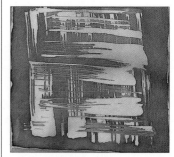

This cross-hatching effect was made using a medium-sized decorator's paintbrush. Lightly draw the waxed brush across the undyed fabric horizontally and then vertically.

Finishing   Wax must be removed from the finished batik to restore the fabric's drape. Ironing will remove most of the wax, but it will be necessary to boil or dry-clean the fabric to remove final marks and wax residue.

1 Break away as much of the hardened wax as you can. Do not scrub the fabric as this may damage the surface.

2 Place the batik between sheets of newspaper, brown or lining paper, and iron until the wax is absorbed. Repeat until wax is no longer being absorbed.

3 To use the boiling method, break off as much wax as possible then place the fabric in boiling water for about 10 minutes, stirring continuously.

A cheerful cup design decorates this simple cotton table mat. It is hand quilted with a layer of wadding (batting) inside, to absorb heat and protect your tabletop.

Quilted Table Mat

you will need

silk pins (push pins)

lightweight white cotton, pre-washed

painting frame

vanishing fabric marker

general-purpose wax

wax pot or double boiler

tjanting

medium artist's paintbrush

colourfast fabric dyes

iron

newspaper, brown or lining paper

scissors

medium-thickness wadding (batting)

needle

tacking (basting) thread

bias binding

dressmaker's pins

sewing-machine

matching sewing thread

embroidery thread (floss)

embroidery needle

1 Pin the cotton on to the painting frame. Enlarge the template from the back of the book. Turn the frame upside down over the design and trace with a vanishing fabric marker. Heat the wax in a wax pot or double boiler. Using a tjanting, wax the outlines of the cups.

2 Paint the background with sky blue dye. Fill in the cups with yellow. Draw the pattern on the cups using a vanishing fabric marker. Wax in the details using a tjanting and paint. Remove the batik from the frame and iron out as much wax as possible between sheets of paper.

3 Trim the batik to the finished size. Cut pieces of wadding and cotton for the back the same size. Tack (baste) the layers together. Cut a length of bias binding and open out. Align the raw edge of the backing with one edge of the binding. Pin then stitch to the edge of the mat, in the crease. Repeat on the other three sides. Stitch around the outlines of the design with embroidery thread.

Decorate a ready made cotton napkin (or set of matching napkins) with this stylish design. Use colourfast dyes that will withstand repeated machine washing.

Geometric Napkin

you will need
ruler
pencil and tracing paper
white cotton napkin, pre-washed
silk pins (push pins)
painting frame
vanishing fabric marker (optional)
general-purpose wax
wax pot or double boiler
tjanting
colourfast fabric dyes, in pale blue, lilac and cobalt blue
medium artist's spongebrush
iron
newspaper, brown or lining paper

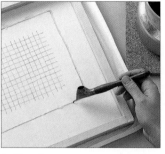

1 Draw a 10cm/4in cross in the centre of the napkin. Pin the napkin to the frame so that it is stretched taut. Draw a grid on tracing paper to fit the 10cm/4in cross. Turn the frame upside down over the design, lining up the central crosses. Trace the design on to the fabric, using a marker that will show through the fabric.

2 Heat the wax in a wax pot or double boiler (see Techniques). Draw in the main square with wax, using a tjanting. There should be no breaks in the wax outline and the cloth should appear semi-transparent. Check the back for areas of the cloth that remain opaque, and reapply the molten wax to the back.

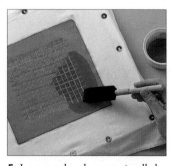

3 Using an artist's spongebrush, fill in the central square with pale blue dye. Do not overload the cloth or the colour may bleed into the white border. Allow the dye to bleed out from the brush, especially when working near the wax outline. Leave to dry.

4 When the napkin is completely dry, wax in all the horizontal lines using the tjanting. Paint the central square with lilac dye. Once again, do not overload the fabric with dye.

5 Leave to dry, then wax in all the vertical lines. Fill in the central square with cobalt blue. Remove the napkin from the frame. Place the napkin between sheets of newspaper, brown or lining paper and iron to remove the wax. Dry-clean the fabric.

This simple design of squares within squares is drawn freehand on a measured grid to give a spontaneous look. The two-tone background fabric adds extra interest.

Vibrant Silk Cushion Cover

you will need

pencil, ruler and set square (t-square)

two-tone dupion silk, pre-washed

vanishing fabric marker

silk pins (push pins)

painting frame

general-purpose wax

wax pot or double boiler

tjanting

iron-fix (set) silk paints

paintbrushes

iron

newspaper, brown or lining paper

scissors

dressmaker's pins

sewing-machine

matching sewing thread

40cm/16in-square cushion pad

1 Mark a 42cm/17in square on the silk with a pencil. Mark out a grid in the centre using a vanishing fabric marker. The grid should be three squares across and three squares down, each square measuring 10cm/4in.

2 Pin the silk taut to a painting frame. It should be springy to the touch. Heat the wax in a wax pot or double boiler (see Techniques). Wax in the grid using a tjanting. It is important that there are no breaks in the outline so check the back for areas of fabric that remain opaque once the wax has been applied. Fill in any breaks with wax on the back.

3 Fill in the grid with diluted silk paints. Allow the paints to blend out from the brush to the wax outline rather than overloading the fabric with dye, as this may cause the colour to bleed underneath the wax.

4 Leave to dry, then draw in the remainder of the design, squares within squares. Do not use a ruler for this – it will add to the effect if the squares are slightly irregular. Wax over the design lines.

5 Check the back for breaks in the outline and fill them with wax. Fill in the remaining colours using deep reds, purples, olive and brown. Use a different brush for each colour.

6 Remove the silk from the frame and iron out the wax between sheets of newspaper, brown or lining paper. To remove any remaining grease marks, have the finished cover dry-cleaned. Trim the fabric down to the marked 42cm/17in square.

7 Cut two pieces of silk 42 x 28cm/17 x 11in for the back. Stitch a double 1cm/½in hem along one long edge of each. Place the batik square right side up. Pin the two rectangles on top, face down, with the hemmed edges in the centre.

8 Stitch all the way round the cover, leaving a 1cm/½in seam allowance. Stitch a line of zigzag stitches between the sewn seam and the raw edge to prevent fraying. Turn the cover right side out and insert the cushion pad.

Use simple sponge shapes to create an alternating design of evenly spaced circles and stars on this lovely sarong. Areas of plain colour make an effective contrast to the batik.

Cotton Sarong

you will need
tracing paper and pencil
scissors
masking tape
sponge
felt-tipped pen
craft (utility) knife
150cm/60in of 90cm/36in-wide
thin cotton, pre-washed
plastic board or surface
general-purpose wax
wax pot or double boiler
large decorator's brush
large bowls
rubber gloves
dyes, in yellow and dark green
iron
newspaper, brown or lining paper
sewing-machine
matching sewing thread

1 Trace the templates at the back of the book. Cut them out and attach to a sponge, using masking tape. Draw around each template. With a craft knife, cut out the sponge shapes.

2 Pin one end of the cotton fabric on to a plastic board. Heat the wax in a wax pot or double boiler (see Techniques) and apply with a large brush around the edge of the sarong.

3 Using the circular sponge, apply the wax, leaving approximately 8cm/3in between each circle. Repeat the pattern around the edge of the border.

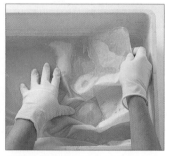

4 Wet the fabric thoroughly. Dye the wet fabric yellow, following the manufacturer's instructions. Hang it up to dry. Pin the fabric back on to the plastic board. Using the same brush, re-wax the border to keep the yellow crackle effect. Wax over the circles again, using the same sponge stencil. Using the cross stencil, apply the wax between the circles.

5 Put the fabric in a bowl of water, then dye the wet fabric dark green, following the manufacturer's instructions. Hang it up to dry.

6 Iron the fabric between sheets of paper, until no more wax appears through the paper. Dry-clean the fabric to remove the excess wax. Turn in the raw edges and stitch in place.

A wax grid forms the base of this simple design, painted in muted lilac and blue colours. Crêpe de chine is used here but any lightweight silk would be equally suitable.

Square Silk Scarf

1 Trace and enlarge the template provided. Pin the silk scarf to the frame. Turn frame side up. Place the design right side up under the corner of the silk, 7cm/3in from each side. Using a pencil, trace the design on to the back of the silk. To make the whole design, reverse the template so that the wider corner is at the outer edge. Repeat so that the wide border is around the edge of the scarf.

2 Heat the wax in a wax pot or double boiler (see Techniques). Apply the wax in spirals on the fabric using a tjanting. Keep your movements light. Make sure that the exterior of the tjanting is free of molten wax as this may smudge on to the scarf.

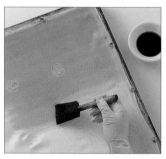

3 Using a sponge brush, apply light blue silk paint over the whole scarf. Allow the paint to bleed from the brush rather than overloading the fabric. Leave to dry.

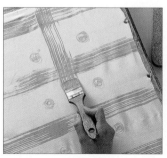

4 Using a brush, apply the wax in a grid design.

5 Paint the royal blue, lilac and purple paint in the squares. Leave to dry.

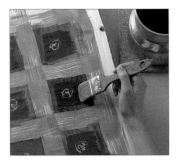

6 Cover the coloured areas of the design with wax brushstrokes.

◀ **7** Apply dark blue paint over the whole scarf. Blot any excess paint with kitchen paper. Leave to dry. Iron the scarf between sheets of newspaper, brown or lining paper. The heat will also fix (set) the silk paints. Keep changing the paper until no more wax appears. Have the scarf dry-cleaned to remove the excess wax. Roll the edges of the scarf and hand stitch.

This rich autumnal table runner is coloured with both paints and dyes in rich dark tones. Position the leaves at different angles to give the design a natural look.

Maple Leaf Table Runner

you will need

scissors and tape measure

dupion silk, pre-washed

tracing paper and pencil

Mylar film

craft (utility) knife and cutting mat

silk pins (push pins)

silk-painting frame

vanishing fabric marker

crackle or general-purpose wax

wax pot or double boiler

tjanting

brush (for wax)

fine artist's paintbrushes

direct-application dyes, in rusty brown

and olive green

brown dye

dye bath

iron

newspaper, brown or lining paper

needle

matching sewing thread

scissors

1 Cut a piece of dupion silk to the required size, adding a 2cm/¾in seam allowance all round and 2–4cm/¾–1½in wastage. Trace the maple leaf from the back of the book, and cut out of Mylar film using a craft knife.

2 Pin the silk to the painting frame. Using the template and a vanishing fabric marker, draw maple leaves randomly over the cloth. Place the leaves at different angles so that they look scattered rather than neatly placed.

3 Heat the wax in a wax pot or double boiler (see Techniques). Using a tjanting, apply wax around the outline of some of the leaves. Block in the remaining leaves with a brush. Check the back of the fabric for breaks in the wax outline, and fill in any gaps by waxing on the back.

4 Using a small artist's paintbrush, paint in the leaves that have a wax outline with dyes. Use rusty brown and olive green colours. Leave to dry.

5 Block in the painted leaves with wax. All the leaves should now be solidly waxed. Remove the fabric from the frame and crumple it in your hands to crack the surface of the wax.

6 Wet the batik and place it in a dark brown dye bath following the manufacturer's instructions. When the cloth is the desired colour, rinse it thoroughly. Leave to dry.

7 Iron the fabric between two sheets of paper until wax is no longer being absorbed. Have the fabric dry-cleaned to remove any wax residue.

8 Using a needle, remove individual threads from opposite ends of the runner to make a fringe. Press a 1cm/½in double hem on the two remaining sides. Hem stitch each hem in place by hand. Divide the fringe at the top and bottom into equal sections and knot threads together. Trim the ends of the tassels evenly.

For a sophisticated look, decorate either end of a plain Habotai silk scarf with stripes of colour. Seal off the end of each stripe with the wax so that the colours cannot bleed into each other.

Striped Bordered Scarf

you will need

tracing paper, soft pencil, felt-tipped pen, ruler or set square (t-square)

silk pins (push pins)

lightweight habotai silk, pre-washed

silk-painting frame

general-purpose wax

wax pot or double boiler

tjanting

iron-fix (set) silk paints

paint palette

fine artist's paintbrush

hairdryer

iron

newspaper, brown or lining paper

scissors and needle

matching sewing thread

1 Enlarge the design provided at the back of the book. Trace off the horizontal lines. Pin one end of the silk to the frame. Choose a frame that is slightly deeper than the height of the border design, remembering to allow for wastage all round.

2 Turn the frame upside down on to the design and trace off all the horizontal lines, using a soft pencil. Heat the wax (see Techniques). Wax the horizontal stripes using a tjanting. Close in the ends of each stripe to prevent the paints from bleeding. The waxed lines should be semi-transparent. Wax any that aren't on the back.

3 Fill in the stripes with pale colours, such as smoky blue, terracotta or pale pink. Leave to dry. Fix (set) the silk paints using a hairdryer; be careful not to melt the wax.

4 Replace the frame upside down on the design and trace off the detail and patterning. Wax in these details with the tjanting.

5 Paint over the stripes and details with darker colours, such as purple, blue, deep red and brown. Remove some of the hardened wax with your fingers. Repeat the process for the opposite end of the scarf.

◀ **6** Iron the batik between sheets of paper to remove the wax. The fabric will still be stiff at this stage. Trim off the wastage. If possible, tear the silk to ensure a straight edge. Roll the edges of the scarf and hand stitch. Dry-clean the finished scarf to restore the drape and sheen of the silk.

Leather may seem an unusual material for batik, but you can crumple it in the same way as fabric to create the distinctive "cracked" effect. Use gum instead of wax, and special leather dyes.

Leather Book Cover

you will need

tracing paper, pencil and ballpoint pen

leather

cotton wool (cotton balls)

craft (utility) knife and cutting mat

brush

gum

rubber gloves

wool dauber (optional)

leather dyes, in yellow, red, green and black

soft cloth

board

spray adhesive (stencil mount)

mount board

leather lacquer spray

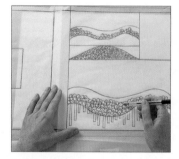

1 Trace the template at the back of the book. Dampen the leather with cotton wool, then transfer the design from the paper on to the leather. Cut out the leather for the book cover, using a craft knife and cutting mat. Leave the leather to dry. Brush the gum over the leather on the areas that will remain neutral.

2 Wearing rubber gloves, dip a cotton wool pad or a wool dauber, into the green dye. Press the pad on to a scrap of leather to remove any excess dye. Beginning in one corner, gently move the pad over the leather surface. Leave to dry naturally. Apply gum to those areas that will remain green. Repeat with the yellow dye.

3 Leave the green dye to dry naturally, and coat with gum in the same way. In turn, apply red dye to the leather with a cotton wool pad. When completely dry, block out with gum those areas that are to remain red or green.

4 Add the black in the same way. Crumple the leather to achieve a good "cracked" effect on the surface. Place the leather on a board and remove the gum with a large piece of damp cotton wool. Wash thoroughly with plenty of cold water.

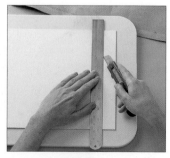

5 Bend and fold the leather into the desired shape while it is still damp. Mitre the corners. Leave to dry. Spray adhesive on to the reverse side. Place a piece of mount board over the top and press the pieces together. Spray with lacquer.

This colourful abstract on black cotton was inspired by the artworks of Joan Miró. Test the cotton first to check that it is bleachable. Some of the wax remains in the fabric to keep it slightly stiff.

Modern Painting

1 Trace the template to the required size on to thin paper using a black pen. Pin the fabric to the frame, then tape the design on the back of the fabric. Hold the frame up to a light source and lightly trace the design on the front of the fabric, using chalk.

2 Heat the wax in a wax pot or double boiler (see Techniques). Apply it with a medium decorator's paintbrush to the areas that will remain black. Check that the wax has penetrated to the back of the fabric. If necessary, wax the same area from the back.

3 Remove the fabric from the frame. Wearing rubber gloves and working in a ventilated area, place the fabric in a bowl of thin bleach. Leave the fabric until it has turned cream, agitating it to allow even bleaching. Rinse in water, then rinse in water with a splash of vinegar to neutralize the bleach. Rinse in water again.

4 Pin the fabric back on the frame and leave it to dry. Check that the waxed lines are solid and re-wax any lines that are cracked. Using a dye brush, paint the dyes in the non-waxed areas, following the manufacturer's instructions. Leave to dry.

7 Hem both sides of the picture. Stitch a 2cm/¾in hem at the top and bottom. Insert a piece of dowelling at both ends. Attach a piece of fishing wire or string to both ends of the top piece of dowelling for hanging.

5 Apply wax to the coloured areas so that all the fabric is covered in wax. This is to avoid a wax shadow on the final picture. Remove the fabric from the frame.

6 Iron the fabric between sheets of newspaper, brown or lining paper. Continue ironing, replacing the paper until no more wax appears through. The cloth will remain slightly stiff.

This intricate batik design uses four different dye baths to build up the layers of colour. Chrome yellow, turquoise, peacock blue and navy make a stunning combination.

Abstract Cushion Cover

1 Cut one 47cm/18½in square and two 47 x 30cm/18½ x 12in rectangles of fabric. Enlarge the template from the back of the book on to a 41cm/16in square of paper and go over the lines with a felt-tipped pen. Trace the design on to the centre of the square.

3 For larger areas of the design, carefully outline them with the tjanting first, then fill them in using an old artist's paintbrush. Once all the white areas have been waxed, turn the frame over and, if necessary, re-wax any areas the wax has not penetrated completely. Leave to dry thoroughly.

2 Heat the wax in a wax pot or double boiler. Stretch the fabric square on to the tapestry frame and secure with drawing pins. Use a tjanting to wax the areas you want to remain white. Use a pad of paper towels to prevent drips.

4 Prepare a yellow dye bath. Half fill a bucket with cold water, dissolve 30ml/2 tbsp of urea in 600ml/1 pint of lukewarm water. In a separate container mix 5ml/1 tsp of chrome yellow dye to a paste. Stir the urea solution into the dye paste and pour into the bucket. Dissolve 60ml/4 tbsp salt in 600ml/1 pint of lukewarm water and add to the bucket. Add the batik square and the rectangles, and stir for 6 minutes. Dissolve 15ml/1 tbsp of soda/sodium carbonate in a little warm water and add to the bucket. Leave the fabric to soak for 45 minutes, stirring occasionally. Remove and rinse in cold water until the water runs clear. Hang the fabric out to dry.

5 Apply wax to the areas that are to stay yellow. Prepare a turquoise dye bath in the same way and immerse the fabric for 45 minutes. Rinse and dry it, then apply wax to the areas that are to remain green.

6 Prepare a blue dye bath with 10ml/ 2 tsp of dye, and leave the fabric in it for 1 hour. Rinse and dry the fabric, then wax the areas that are to remain blue. Plunge the fabric into cold water to crack the large areas of wax. Prepare another dye bath using 15ml/1 tbsp of navy dye. Leave the fabric to soak for several hours, then rinse and leave to dry.

7 Protect your ironing board with an old sheet. Place the batik between several layers of paper and iron over it to melt the wax. Keep replacing the newspaper until most of the wax has been removed. The last traces of wax can be removed by dry-cleaning or by immersing the fabric in boiling water. Press all the pieces while they are still damp.

8 Stitch a small hem along the long edge of each rectangle of fabric. Overlap the hems to make a 47cm/ 18½in square, right sides facing up, then pin and tack (baste) together.

9 With right sides together, pin the front and back of the cover together. Stitch around the outside edge of the batik. Trim the seams, clip the corners and turn right side out.

10 Remove the tacking threads. Ease out the corners and press the seams. Pin and stitch close to the inside edge of the border, and trim the threads. Sew a small piece of Velcro to the inside of the opening edges of the cover. Insert the cushion pad and close the Velcro.

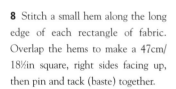

Fabric Dyeing

Dyeing is one of the simplest ways to infuse colour into fabric, and it need not be messy. Compared to stamping, printing and fabric painting, the craftsperson has much less control over the look of the finished piece, but this unpredictability is a major part of its appeal. Each of these popular dyeing techniques – tie-dying, tea-dyeing, spray-dyeing, dip-dyeing and marbling – produces quite different effects.

The most important materials used in this chapter are the dyes. Household dyes, suitable for most fabrics, are widely available. Special dye kits, including a thickening medium, are available for marbling.

Materials

dry. Remember to take the colour of the original fabric into account if you are dyeing a coloured fabric. Pre-wash fabrics to remove any dressing.

Marbling thickening medium
This solution is added to the water in the dye bath before adding marbling dyes. Carefully follow the manufacturer's instructions.

Paper
Use stiff white paper to make patchwork templates, remembering that you need to hand stitch through the paper as well as the fabric. You can also clean the marbling dyes from the dye bath with newspaper layers.

Resist medium
Painted on to areas of fabric to prevent them taking up the dye.

Absorbent cloth or paper
Use for resting dyed fabrics on to dry.

Dyes
Available in powder or liquid form. Hot-water dyes provide better colour penetration into the fibres, but may shrink the fabric, so cold-water dyes are preferable for some fabrics, such as wool and silk. Always follow the dye manufacturer's instructions. Special water-based dyes are available for marbling effects.

Fabric etching medium
Use to remove the pile from fabrics such as velvet. Available in a bottle with a nozzle for drawing designs.

Fabrics
Tie-dyeing works well on luxury fabrics such as velvet and silk, as well as on cotton fabrics. Lightweight fabrics without texture, such as fine silk or cotton, are most suitable for marbling. Unwieldy fabrics such as fake fur can be dip-dyed, then hang outdoors to

Rubber bands
Use to bind circular tie-dyed objects, to form a barrier to the dye.

Salt
Often added to a dye bath to fix (set) the dyes. Follow the dye manufacturer's instructions.

String and cord
Use to tightly bind tie-dyed objects. Experiment with various thicknesses to create different effects.

The essential piece of equipment is a dye bath. Use a bath large enough and deep enough to immerse the fabric completely so that it is evenly dyed. Work outdoors if possible.

Equipment

Masking tape
Use to attach fabric or a design temporarily to the work surface.

Measuring jug (cup)
Use to mix dyes and marbling thickening medium before adding them to a dye bath.

Measuring spoon
Used to measure powder dyes.

Needle
Use an ordinary sewing needle for hand stitching, and an embroidery needle for embroidery thread (floss).

Paintbrush
Use a fine artist's paintbrush to drop marbling dyes on to the surface of the dye bath solution.

Pipette (eye dropper)
Use to drop marbling dyes on to the surface of the dye bath solution.

Rubber gloves
Wear rubber gloves to avoid staining your hands.

Set square (t-square)
Useful for checking accurate squares.

Vanishing fabric marker
Use to draw temporary designs on to fabric, or use tailor's chalk.

Cocktail stick (toothpick)
Use to pull or drag circles of marbling dye into patterns. A wooden cocktail stick (toothpick) is most suitable.

Comb
Use to create feathery marbling patterns. Make a marbling comb by taping pins to a piece of dowel.

Dye baths
Use plastic bowls or a cat litter tray for cold-water dyeing, and a heatproof metal bowl or an old saucepan for hot-water dyeing. The bath must be large enough for the fabric to be immersed completely and as flat as possible. A large, shallow dye bath is used for marbling.

Iron
Use to press pleats into fabric before tie-dyeing. Also use an iron to press the finished dyed fabric and to fix (set) the dyes, following the dye manufacturer's instructions.

The dyeing techniques used in this chapter are all very simple to do. If you are dyeing a coloured fabric, consider how the colours will blend to create the final result.

Fabric-dyeing Techniques

Making up a dye solution Household dyes are sold in tablet form. These dyes penetrate the fibres of natural fabrics such as cotton, silk, wool and linen easily.

1 Dissolve the tablet or powder dye in the specified amount of water. Stir, then add to the dye bath.

2 Add the fabric. The dye bath should be large enough for the fabric to move freely.

3 Tea dyeing dyes fabric so that it has an antique cream colour. Place a tea bag in water until the required shade has been achieved.

Dip-dyeing This technique is very useful if you want to dye an object such as a fabric lampshade that cannot be immersed in a dye bath. You can also use it to dye areas of fabric with more than one colour.

1 If you want to keep the dye colours separate, leave the fabric to dry after dipping it in the first colour and leave a small space between each colour so that the dyes cannot run together.

2 Alternatively, an attractive feathery effect can be created by dipping dip-dyed fabric into another colour while it is still slightly damp so that the two colours bleed into each other.

3 For a very simple but dramatic effect, dip just the edges of tassels or folded fabric briefly into the dye.

Tie-dyeing   The charm of this technique is its unpredictability. A great variety of designs can be achieved by folding, pleating or tying objects into the fabric so that these areas resist the colour when it is immersed in a dye bath. Experiment with scraps of fabric before embarking on a project.

To make a circular design, tie round objects such as coins, buttons or lentils into the fabric before dyeing. Bind them tightly with cord, string or rubber bands so that none of the dye can leak underneath.

To create horizontal lines, fold or pleat the fabric evenly or unevenly accordion-fashion, then bind it tightly at regular intervals.

For a lacy, speckled effect, roll the fabric round a piece of string. Pull the ends of the string round to form a loop, then slide the fabric away from the ends to make a tightly gathered circle. Tie the string ends securely.

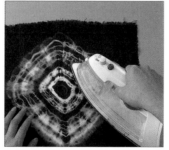

Spray-dyeing

For a spider's web effect, bind a flat circular object in the fabric, then wrap string tightly around the fabric bundle. Wearing rubber gloves, prepare the dye bath using a hand dye and following the manufacturer's instructions. Use a container big enough for the fabric to be kept moving in order to achieve an even colour. Immerse the prepared fabric and move it around to ensure the dye can penetrate all areas.

When the desired colour has been achieved (it will become more intense the longer the fabric is in the dye), remove the fabric and rinse in cold water until the water runs clear. Remove the bindings, then wash the fabric in warm water with a mild detergent. Iron flat while still damp, following the dye manufacturer's instructions, to fix (set) the dye.

Measure 2.5ml/½ tsp dye into a glass. Stir to a paste with cold water. Make up to 300ml/½ pint with chemical water and stir well. Measure 20ml/4 tsp of this solution into a spray bottle. Add an equal amount of soda solution. Spray the fabric, leaving a few minutes' between colours. Spray evenly over the whole piece, or concentrate colours in various areas. Areas may be masked by pinning paper shapes to the fabric after one colour has been sprayed and then spraying another colour. Remove the masks and allow the fabric to dry. Press with a hot iron. Wash the fabric in hot soapy water, allow to dry then iron again.

Marbling

Marbling fabric is similar to marbling on paper. Lightweight and untextured fabrics such as fine silk or lightweight cotton are most suitable as they quickly and evenly absorb the dye. Special marbling dyes and dye kits are available.

1 Use a dye bath deep enough for the dye solution to be at least 4–5cm/1½–2in deep, and large enough to arrange the fabric flat. Using a measuring jug (cup), mix the marbling thickening medium then pour it into the dye bath.

2 Using a fine artist's paintbrush or pipette (eye dropper), drop the marbling dyes on to the surface of the water. The colours will spread and float on the surface. If too much dye is used, it will sink to the bottom of the dye bath and "muddy" the solution.

3 When the surface of the dye bath is covered with colour, gently tease the surface with a fine tool such as a wooden cocktail stick (toothpick) or skewer. For a feathery texture, drag a comb lightly over the surface. Make patterns by dropping dyes of different colours on top of each other, creating large ringed circles.

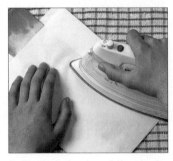

4 When a pleasing pattern has been arrived at, carefully place the fabric on to the inked surface. Place either the top edge or the centre of the fabric on the surface first to prevent air bubbles from forming. When the fabric has soaked up the dye, peel it away and rinse under cool water. Leave to dry before ironing.

5 Fix (set) the dyes, following the manufacturer's instructions. This usually involves ironing the fabric on the reverse side.

In this lovely design, the mermaids' bodies are painted with a resist medium to stop them taking up the dye, and then outlined in gold. Use cold hand dyes to give a random "watery" effect.

Mermaid Shower Curtain

you will need

scissors

8m/8yd muslin (cheesecloth)

fabric marker pen

medium artist's paintbrush

resist medium

cloth or towel

iron

sea-green cold-water dye and dye bath

gold contour-lining fabric paint

dressmaker's pins

shower curtain liner

sewing-machine

matching thread

2m/2yd net curtain heading tape

2m/2yd Velcro tape

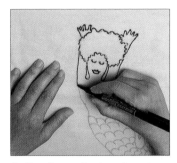

1 Cut the muslin into four pieces each 2m/2yd long and mark the position of the mermaids. Enlarge the mermaid template at the back of the book. Place each piece of muslin over the photocopy and use the fabric marker pen to draw the outline of the mermaids on to the fabric.

2 Paint the whole area of the upper body of each mermaid with resist medium. Leave to dry. Press under a cloth or towel with a hot iron for 2 minutes, to fix (set) the medium. Fold the fabric and hand dye it sea green, following the manufacturer's instructions. Iron the fabric when dry.

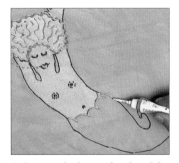

3 Paint in the hair and scales of the mermaid in gold contour paint, and add bubbles. Leave to dry flat. Pin the muslin panels together and make up to the same size as the shower curtain liner. Gather the fabric tightly on to net curtain heading tape. Attach the curtain to the liner with Velcro tape.

Dye a plain fabric lampshade in two rich colours, terracotta and cherry red, to create a lovely feathered effect. The beaded trim around the bottom is a perfect finishing touch.

Dip-dyed Lampshade

you will need
deep dye bath
cold water dyes, in cherry red
and terracotta
rubber gloves
white linen lampshade
absorbent cloths
paper and pencil
protractor
ruler
cherry red stranded embroidery
thread (floss)
large-eyed embroidery needle
12 large red glass beads
12 small beads (optional)
scissors

1 Using a deep dye bath, mix up the cherry red dye. Wearing rubber gloves, hold the lampshade by the base and dip it in the dye so that two-thirds of it is submerged. After a few seconds remove the lampshade. Repeat the process to intensify the colour. Stand the lampshade on an absorbent cloth.

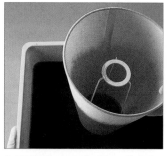

2 While the lampshade is still slightly damp, dip the top 5cm/2in in a dye bath containing terracotta dye. Stand the lampshade on an absorbent cloth to dry, allowing the second colour to bleed through the first.

3 Stand the dry lampshade upright on a piece of paper and draw around its base with a pencil. Using a protractor and ruler, divide the circle into 30° sections.

4 Stand the lampshade back on the circle, and very lightly mark the 30° sections on the bottom of the shade with the pencil.

5 Double a piece of embroidery thread and thread the loop through a needle. Push this through one of the marks on the lampshade. Take the needle through the thread loop and pull tight. Thread on a large bead and tie a knot 3cm/1¼in from the base of the shade. If the knot is too small and the bead slips, thread on a small bead before knotting.

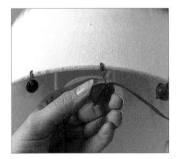

6 Take the needle back up through the large bead to hide any untidy ends, then neatly cut the thread. Following the pencil marks, repeat steps 5 and 6 until you have decorated the bottom edge of the lampshade.

Quilt a piece of marbled silk fabric so that it will hold a pair of spectacles safely. Decorate the diagonal quilting pattern with small rocaille beads, and finish with ribbon roses around the top.

Marbled Spectacle Case

you will need

shallow dye bath 30cm/12in square
marbling thickening medium
fine artist's paintbrush
marbling dyes
wooden cocktail stick (toothpick)
ruler
scissors
silk, pre-washed
iron
wadding (batting)
cotton lining
needle
tacking (basting) thread
vanishing fabric marker
sewing-machine
matching sewing thread
dressmaker's pins
narrow ribbon
5mm/¼in rocaille beads
6 ribbon roses

1 Prepare a shallow dye bath and add the marbling thickening medium. Scatter drops of dye on to the surface. Drag a cocktail stick through the dyes at intervals, first horizontally then vertically, to create a feathery pattern.

2 Cut a piece of silk 30cm/12 square to fit the dye bath. Gently place it over the marbled surface, positioning the top end or centre of the fabric on first to prevent air bubbles from becoming trapped underneath.

3 When the silk has soaked up the dye, carefully peel it away and rinse under cool water to remove the thickening medium. Leave the silk to dry, then press with a warm, dry iron to fix (set) the dyes, following the manufacturer's instructions.

4 Cut the wadding 30cm/12in square, and the lining slightly larger. Place the lining on the work surface, centre the wadding on top, then the silk. Tack (baste) the layers together, in rows 3cm/1¼in apart. Using a vanishing fabric marker, draw a diagonal grid across the surface with the lines 2.5cm/1in apart.

5 Machine stitch along the marked lines to quilt the fabric. Cut a 20cm/8in square from the finished piece and fold in half, right sides together. Pin along the bottom and side edges, then machine stitch 1cm/½in from the edge. Neaten with zigzag stitch then turn right side out.

6 Cut a 20cm/8in length of ribbon, press in half and stitch over the raw edges. Hand sew a rocaille bead at every point where two quilting lines cross. Hand sew ribbon roses below the opening.

Soak pieces of blanket in tea bags and brown dye, then use them to make a soft, appealing cover for a child's hot water bottle. A drawstring cord holds the cover in place.

Tea-dyed Hot Water Bottle Cover

you will need

2–3 tea bags

dye baths

rubber gloves

old blanket or wool fabric, pre-washed

iron

cloth

brown hand dye

hot water bottle

pencil and paper

scissors

tailor's chalk

sewing-machine

matching sewing thread

1.5cm/⅝in-wide brown ribbon

satin bias binding (optional)

1m/1yd fine brown cord

safety pin

vanishing fabric marker

stranded embroidery thread (floss)

embroidery needle

tiny buttons

needle

1 Soak two or three tea bags in hot water in a small dye bath until the tea is quite strong. Immerse a small piece of the old blanket or wool fabric. Agitate until you are happy with the colour, re-dyeing if necessary. Allow to dry and press under a damp cloth.

2 Dye a larger piece of fabric for the hot water bottle cover using brown hand dye and following the manufacturer's instructions. Dry and press under a damp cloth.

3 Using a hot water bottle, make a paper template for the cover. Fold the brown fabric in half. Place the template on top, then draw around it with tailor's chalk. Cut out a rectangular back and front large enough to fit the hot water bottle.

4 On the wrong side of each front and back, stitch a length of ribbon about 5cm/2in below the top short raw edge. Using a 1cm/½in seam allowance, stitch the back and front together, leaving a gap just below the ribbon. Bind the long raw edges. Fold in the bag top so that the ribbon is at the top edge of the bag, and stitch.

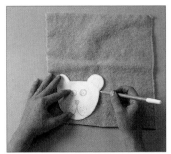

5 Cut the cord in half. Using a safety pin, thread one piece through a side opening, around the casing and out through the same opening. Knot the ends. Repeat with the second piece of cord through the second side opening.

6 Enlarge the teddy motif at the back of the book to fit the tea-dyed fabric. Draw around the template using a vanishing fabric marker. Cut out a face. Draw in the features on the teddy's face.

7 Hand embroider the features using stranded embroidery thread. Add small buttons for the eyes. Slip stitch the face to the bag front, taking care not to catch the back of the cover in the stitching.

Dip-dyeing lengthways and then widthways creates subtle blends of colour, but choose your colours carefully to avoid a "muddy" effect. Finish these simple mats with contrast ribbon borders.

Double-dyed Place Mats

you will need

scissors

white cotton fabric

cold water hand dyes, in 3 colours

large dye bath

rubber gloves

clothes pegs (pins)

iron

ribbon, in contrast colours

dressmaker's pins

needle

tacking (basting) thread

embroidery thread (floss)

needle

1 Cut the fabric to the desired size for each mat, cutting along the grain of the fabric to ensure a square edge. The fabric may fray during dyeing, so allow 1–2cm/½–¾in wastage. Prepare the first dye bath following the manufacturer's instructions. Dampen the fabric with water.

2 Holding the fabric lengthways, dip each rectangle no more than two-thirds into the bath. When the fabric is the desired colour (it will become more intense the longer it is in the dye), remove it and rinse in cold water until the water runs clear.

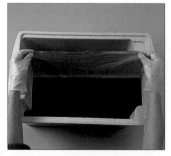

3 Prepare the second dye bath. While the fabric is still damp, dip each rectangle in the dye bath lengthways so that the undyed area is submerged. Prepare the third dye bath.

4 Dip each mat widthways so that half of it is submerged. Peg the fabric to the edge of the dye bath. This colour will cover both of the previously dyed colours, creating subtle colour blends. Wash the mats using a mild detergent, and rinse until the water runs clear. Iron while damp.

5 Trim the edges of each mat. Press the ribbon in half lengthways and pin around the outside of the mat so that the crease lies on the edge. Tack (baste) in place. Using embroidery thread, work blanket stitch through the edge of the ribbon to hold it in place. Remove the tacking.

If you have a store of warm, wool blankets you no longer use on the bed, colour one softly using dye to create a beautiful throw with a luxurious velvet ribbon trim.

Velvet-edged Throw

1 Trim the fabric to a square or rectangular shape and wash to remove any dressing. Make up the dye in a large dye bath and check the colour on a sample piece (which you can take with you when choosing ribbons for the edging). After dyeing, rinse the fabric very thoroughly and press under a damp cloth when dry.

2 To bind the edges, machine stitch satin bias binding to the right side all round the edge. Fold the binding over to the wrong side, and baste in place. Either machine or hand stitch in place on the wrong side to finish, folding in the excess neatly at the corners.

3 On the right side, stitch a length of ruffled ribbon close to the edge of the binding to cover it. Stitch along both long edges of the ribbon using matching thread.

4 Cut four lengths of velvet ribbon to fit the edges of the throw. Join the lengths by stitching diagonally across each corner, with right sides together, to create mitres.

5 Pin the ribbon carefully to the throw and stitch down on each side by hand or machine. Take care when pinning velvet as it can mark easily.

Neatly pressed pleats create this simple design, which is then bound with fine cord or string to create the tie-dye effect. Only one shade of dye is used on coloured fabric.

Pleated Table Runner

you will need

iron

lilac silk dupion, pre-washed

ruler

scissors

fine cord or string

rubber gloves

dye bath

blue hand dye

needle

matching sewing thread

1 Iron the washed silk while still damp. Cut to the size required for your table (the length should include the fringe), allowing 4.5cm/1¾in wastage on all sides.

2 Using an iron, pleat the fabric accordion fashion, making each pleat about 3cm/1¼in wide. If your runner is very long, horizontal pleats may become unmanageable, so you may prefer to make the pleats vertically.

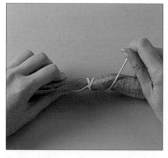

3 Using fine cord or string, bind the fabric tightly along the pleats, spacing each binding about 7.5cm/3in apart. Start in the centre and work out towards the edges.

4 Wearing rubber gloves, prepare a dye bath big enough to allow the fabric to move freely. Dampen the tied cloth before placing it in the bath. Dye the fabric according to the manufacturer's instructions. When it is the desired colour, remove it and rinse under cold water until the water runs clear. Remove the bindings and wash to remove any dye.

5 Iron flat while still damp. Using a needle, make a fringe at each short end by pulling out the weft threads to about 4cm/1½in deep. Fold the cloth in half to ensure that it is square, then trim 2.5cm/1in from each long side. Press under a 1cm/½in double hem on each long side, then slip stitch it neatly in place. Trim the ends of the fringe level at each end.

Children will love this strong fake fur and cotton cushion, perfect for when they are sitting on the floor. Two contrast dye colours have been used to dip-dye the fabric.

Doughnut Floor Cushion

you will need

80cm/32in square of paper
ruler or tape measure
50cm/20in length of string
soft pencil
scissors
dressmaker's pins
1m/1yd white acrylic fake fur fabric
1m/1yd heavy white cotton fabric
rubber gloves
cold water dyes, in turquoise and red
dye bath
sewing-machine
matching sewing threads
bag polystyrene (Styrofoam) pellets
large cup or beaker

1 Fold the paper into quarters. Loop the string around a pencil 7.5cm/3in from one end. Hold the end of the string in the corner of the paper and draw an arc from fold to fold. Lengthen the loop to 35cm/14in and draw another arc. Open out the pattern and pin it to the fake fur. Cut one shape. Cut another from cotton.

2 Measure the two circumferences and add 10cm/4in to each measurement. Cut three lengths of cotton, each 20cm/8in wide, two for the outside edge and one for the inside edge of the doughnut. On the wrong side of each piece of fabric, mark the halfway line with a soft pencil.

3 Wearing rubber gloves, mix each dye in a bath, following the manufacturer's instructions. Dampen each fabric piece to within 2cm/¾in of the halfway line. Dip one edge of damp fabric into the turquoise dye bath, leaving the other half outside. Remove the fabric, allowing the dye to drip back into the bath. Allow to drip dry.

4 Dip the undyed half of each piece of fabric into the red dye in the same way. Leave a 2–3cm/¾–1¼in gap between the two colours so that they do not bleed into each other.

5 With right sides together, fold one inside edge side panel in half and stitch the 20cm/8in ends together for the inner circle. Pin one edge of the inside circle to the inside edge of the fur circle. Stitch in place. Zigzag stitch the raw edges. Pin and stitch the two outer sides together into a loop. Pin and stitch the outer side to the fur circle. Turn inside out, pin and stitch the outer edge of the base to the cotton circle. Finish the edges with zigzag stitch. Carefully turn the cushion right side out.

6 Turn in the inside raw edges. Whip stitch the inside circle to the hole in the bottom of the cushion, leaving a 15cm/6in opening. Pour in the polystyrene pellets to fill the cushion. Stitch the opening shut.

Cover a selection of notebooks, a shoebox and a cardboard tube with marbled fabric to make a co-ordinating desk set. The metal fittings add a traditional finish to the whole effect.

Marbled Fabric Desk Set

you will need
large shallow dye bath
marbling thickening medium
rubber gloves
marbling dyes, in black and white
small pointed instrument such as
a skewer
scissors
cotton sateen fabric
double-sided tape
2 short lengths of square
wooden dowel
notebooks, shoebox and large
cardboard tube
strong fabric glue
metal label frames
bradawl or awl
pop rivet tool and metal rivets

1 Fill the dye bath with cold water to a depth of about 5cm/2in. Add the marbling thickening medium. Wearing rubber gloves, drop a small amount of black marbling paint on to the surface.

2 Drop a small amount of white marbling paint on to the surface of the black paint.

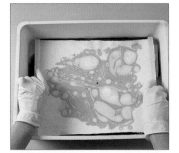

4 Cut the fabric into rectangles that will fit into the dye bath. Using double-sided tape, attach each end of the first piece of fabric to a length of wooden dowel; this will hold the fabric flat and make it easier to handle. Holding the dowels, gently arrange the fabric, right side down, on to the surface of the water.

5 Lift the fabric carefully, then untape the dowels and hang up to dry. Repeat with the remaining fabric until you have enough to cover the desk set.

3 Using a small pointed instrument, gently mix the two colours into a swirly marbled pattern.

6 To cover the large notebook, apply strips of double-sided tape to the book cover. Take a piece of fabric about 5cm/2in larger all round than the notebook and wrap it around it, pressing firmly. Snip across each corner. Apply fabric glue to the exposed edges, then stick them to the inside. Place a metal label frame on the front. Pierce a hole through each fixing (attachment) point, using a bradawl or awl. Use a pop rivet tool and rivets to hold the metal frame in place.

7 For the pen pot, cut a piece of fabric 5cm/2in deeper than the cardboard tube and 1cm/½in longer than its circumference. Fold and glue a small hem along the lower edge. Apply fabric glue to the tube, then wrap the fabric round it. Glue down the overlap. Snip tabs into the excess fabric at the top. Apply glue to the inside of the tube, then fold the tabs into the inside.

Tie-dyeing works well on rich fabrics such as velvet and silk-satin. Bind patches of different fabrics round circular objects such as buttons and beads, then assemble the patchwork by hand.

Tie-dyed Patchwork Cushion

you will need
small piece of cardboard
ruler
scissors
selection of light-coloured fabrics (e.g. velvet, silk dupion, silk-satin)
vanishing marker pen
coins, lentils, buttons and beads
rubber bands
rubber gloves
cold water hand dyes, in 4 colours
dye bath
iron
stiff paper
dressmaker's pins
needle
tacking (basting) thread
matching sewing thread
cushion pad

1 Divide the dimensions of the cushion front and back by the required number of patches. Add on 2cm/¾in all round and cut out a cardboard template to that size. Cut the required number of squares using the template as a guide. In the centre of each, place a circular object such as a button or coin and bind securely with a rubber band. Divide the bundles into four, putting a mix of fabrics in each pile.

2 Wearing rubber gloves, prepare each dye bath following the dye manufacturer's instructions, then immerse the bundles for the specified length of time. Rinse in cold water until the water runs clear. Remove the bindings and wash the squares in warm water using mild detergent.

3 Iron the fabric flat while still damp. Trim the fabric squares by 1cm/½in all around.

4 Cut away 2cm/¾in all around the cardboard template. Use it to make paper templates. Centre a template on the wrong side of each square. Fold in the excess fabric and pin.

5 Mitre the corners and tack (baste) around the edge, stitching through the fabric and the paper. Arrange the squares into a rectangle four squares wide by eight squares long, which, when folded in half, will make up the front and back of the cushion cover. Ensure that you are happy with the arrangement of colours.

◀ **6** Oversew all the squares right sides together. Sew the mitred corners in place, except on those that appear around the outside edge of the rectangle. Remove the tacking threads and the templates, then press the seams flat under a damp cloth. Fold the patchwork in half, right sides together, and stitch along two sides.

7 Fold over the seam allowance on the open side and tack. Turn the cover through to the right side and insert the cushion pad. Pin, then sew the open side closed.

These pretty little pyramid-shaped bags are made out of triangles of spray-dyed fabric, decorated with small beads and a ribbon loop for hanging over a coat-hanger.

Spray-dyed Lavender Bags

you will need

reactive dye solutions, in red, blue and violet, made up in chemical water

spray-dyeing equipment, including rubber gloves, spray bottles, measuring beakers and syringes

scraps of loosely-woven white cotton fabrics (e.g. cheesecloth or voile), pre-washed

paper and pencil

scissors

sewing-machine

matching sewing thread

narrow ribbon

dried lavender

needle

small pearl beads

1 With your choice of colours spray-dye the fabric (see Techniques at the beginning of this chapter). Enlarge the template at the back of the book and cut out, marking the positions a, b, c, d, e and f. Using the template, cut out the fabric for the bags, matching the direction of the grain. One triangle makes one bag.

2 Leaving 5mm/¼in seam allowances throughout, fold point a to point b. Machine stitch down to d. Fold point c to meet point ab then stitch down to e. The fabric should now resemble a pyramid shape.

3 Fold a 10cm/4in length of ribbon into a loop. Pin the ends to align with the raw edges of the fabric at point abc, at the top of the pyramid. Pin and stitch down to point f. Turn the bag right side out.

4 Fill the bag loosely with lavender. Neatly slip stitch the opening closed.

5 Stitch small pearl beads around the base of the pyramid shape, securing the thread every three or four beads with a back stitch.

Ribbonwork

For centuries, ribbons were used as practical fastenings for garments, and also as purely decorative additions, often transforming a simple item into something utterly luxurious. Although now much less frequently used for clothing, ribbons have retained their appeal. Today they can be seen fashioned into bows and roses embellishing all kinds of gifts and millinery. They also add a tactile and often luminous finish to soft furnishings and fashionable outfits.

Ribbons come in myriad textures, colours and widths, and there is a ribbon for every possible style, from baby pastels and frothy sheers to designer prints and brocades.

Ribbons

1 Cut-edge craft

Made from a wide fabric and cut into strips. It is available wired or unwired. The special finish stops the ribbon from fraying.

2 Grosgrain

These ribbons have a distinctive crosswise rib and are a stronger, denser weave than most other ribbon types.

3 Jacquards

An intricate pattern is incorporated in the weave.

4 Lace-edged satins and jacquards

Ribbons with a lace edge.

5 Merrow-edge

This describes the fine satin-stitched edge, usually incorporating a wire, that

is added to elaborate cut-edge ribbons for stability and decoration.

6 Metallics

Made from or incorporate metallic or pearlized fibres.

7 Moiré

Describes the result of a water-mark finish applied during manufacture.

8 Ombré taffeta

A finely woven taffeta with colour shading across the width.

9 Plaids and checks

Popular classics, plaids and checks are usually taffeta weaves.

10 Satins

Satin ribbons are either shiny on both sides or shiny on one side and matt on the other.

11 Sheers

Fine, almost transparent ribbons.

12 Shot-effect taffeta

The use of different, often contrasting colours for the warp and weft results in a really lustrous, colour-shaded finish.

13 Velvets

The deep, plush pile of velvet is unmistakable and the depth of colour is exceptional. Imitations are available.

14 Wire-edged taffeta

A fine weave with a matt finish. This ribbon looks the same on both sides.

15 Woven-edge ribbon

Woven in narrow strips, with a non-fraying selvedge along both edges. They are ideal for items that need to be laundered or will have heavy wear.

A simple sewing kit of needles, thread and scissors is all that you need for basic ribbonwork, but a few of the projects that follow require more specialized items, which are readily available from craft suppliers.

Equipment

Dressmaker's chalk

This makes an easily removed line to mark templates or specific intervals on to fabric or ribbon.

Dressmaker's pins

Long, straight pins have many uses in ribbonwork. Glass- or pearl-headed versions are easier to handle and are used for weaving.

Florist's tape (stem wrap)

Flexible and stretchy, this green self-sticking tape is used to conceal wire stems and bind the stems of fresh flowers together.

Above: Special equipment such as a glue gun, florist's tape and stub wire is required for some of the projects in the book. For many of them a good range of sewing equipment is all that is needed.

Glue

Although not essential, a glue gun will quickly become indispensable once purchased. They apply glue with speed and accuracy, even in tricky areas, and are available in various sizes. A small gun is ideal for beginners. As with any adhesive product, it is important to

keep glue guns out of the reach of children. PVA or white craft glue is ideal for larger-scale sticking and dries clear. Double-sided tape is good for paper projects and gives a neat finish.

Sewing thread

Polyester thread comes in a wide range of colours, so you should always be able to find a reel to match the ribbon you are using.

Scissors

Use small, sharp-bladed scissors for trimming thread and cutting ribbons, and larger dressmaking shears for fabric. Keep a third pair especially for cutting paper only.

Stub (floral) wire

Florists use this thick, straight wire for supporting flower stems. It is used to make the stalks of ribbon roses.

Tape measure

This is useful for checking the length of ribbons and fabric before cutting and also for measuring the progress of ribbon weaving.

Weaving board

A heat-resistant, fabric-covered soft board that will take pins easily is needed for weaving, although an ironing board is a good substitute.

Wire cutters

An essential tool for cutting florist's and stub wire. Some pliers, such as those illustrated here, can be used to cut wire, as well as to shape it.

Weaving ribbons can produces some dazzling effects. It can be used for many different soft furnishings or on a smaller scale in panels on accessories. The methods described here are all fused on to iron-on interfacing. When working with velvet, place the ribbon face down to protect the pile and iron the interfacing on to the back of the finished piece.

Ribbon Weaving

Basic steps for weaving

Any type of ribbon can be used for weaving, but if the item is to be laundered you should work with washable, woven-edge ribbons.

you will need

felt-tipped pen
ruler
tape measure
iron-on interfacing
weaving board
ribbon
glass-headed pins
scissors
iron with damp cloth

1 Cut the interfacing to the size of the weaving area, marking in a 2.5cm/1in seam allowance all around. Pin to the board, glue upwards.

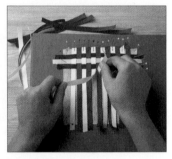

2 Pin the top ends of the warp, or vertical, ribbons along the top edge. Weave in the weft, or horizontal, ribbons and pin down both ends, angling the pins outwards.

3 Pin down the bottom of the warp ribbons, then fuse the completed weave to the interfacing using a medium dry iron. Press the outer edges with the tip of the iron.

4 When the ribbons are secure, remove all the pins. Turn over and press again with a steam iron or with a damp cloth, then leave to cool.

RIBBON QUANTITIES FOR
WOVEN SQUARES
Quantities given are for the whole square. If using two or more colours, divide the quantity by that number. All measurements include a seam allowance.

RIBBON WIDTH	RIBBON LENGTH
	20cm (8in) square
5mm (⅛in)	20m (22yd)
7mm (¼in)	14.6m (16yd)
9mm (⅜in)	11m (12yd)
15mm (⅝in)	6.6m (7¼yd)
23mm (⅞in)	4.6m (5yd)

Plain weave	Patchwork weave	Zigzag weave

you will need

For a 30cm/12in square:
lightweight iron-on interfacing,
35cm/14in square
red ribbon, 15.1m x 6mm/16½yd x ¼in
blue ribbon, 15.1m x 6mm/
16½yd x ¼in

1 Prepare the interfacing as in the steps shown opposite. Cut both ribbons into 15cm/4in lengths. Pin the top ends of the red warp ribbons, edge to edge to the top of the interfacing.

2 Weave the first blue weft ribbon over the first warp, under the second, then under and over to the end. Push it up to the top line and pin tautly at each end. Weave the next weft under the first warp and over the second, and so on to the end.

3 Alternate the weft ribbons in this way until the whole of the weaving area is covered. Check the ribbons are all neatly lined up before pressing as shown opposite. If the last weft ribbon overlaps the bottom seam line by more than 9mm/⅜in, push the weft ribbons closer or remove the last ribbon.

you will need

for a 30cm/12in square:
lightweight iron-on interfacing,
35cm/14in square
blue ribbon (A), 8.5m x 10mm/
13¼yd x ⅜in
yellow ribbon (B), 12m x 10mm/
13¼yd x ⅜in
red ribbon (C), 5.5m x 10mm/6yd x ⅜in

1 Prepare the interfacing as in the instructions on the opposite page and cut all the ribbons into 35cm/14in lengths. Pin the warp ribbons along the top edge in the sequence: blue, yellow, red, yellow (ABCB).

2 Starting at the top-left corner, pin the ends of the weft ribbons down the side in the same order.
Weave them in the following sequence of four rows:
row 1: over AB, under C, then over BAB, under C to the end.
row 2: under A, over BCB to the end.
row 3: over A, under B, over C, under B to the end.
row 4: as row 2.

3 When complete, bond the ribbons to the interfacing as shown opposite.

you will need

for a 30cm/12in square:
lightweight iron-on interfacing,
35cm/14in square
yellow ribbon, 15.4 x 6mm/
16¾yd x ¼in
blue ribbon 14.6m x 6mm/16yd x ¼in

This weave is most effective in two colours. Subtle or bold colours will give totally different looks, as will choosing contrasting or complementary ribbons. You can also vary the ribbon widths.

1 Prepare the interfacing as before and cut the ribbons into 35cm/14in lengths. Pin alternate yellow and blue ribbons along the top and left edges.

2 Weave the weft in the following four-row sequence:
row 1: under two, over two to the end.
row 2: under one, over two, under two, over two to the end.
row 3: over two, under two to the end.
row 4: over one, under two, over two under two to the end.

3 Bond the ribbons to the interfacing as detailed opposite.

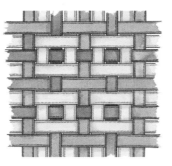

Glamorize plain bedlinen by edging a pile of pillows with ribbon bands and bows. Bright ginghams work well in a child's bedroom, but you could adapt the idea using cooler colours for a more sophisticated look.

Pillowcase Edgings

you will need

plain white cotton pillowcases

plain and gingham ribbons of
various widths

tape measure

scissors

fusible bonding web

iron

needle and matching thread

dressmaker's pins

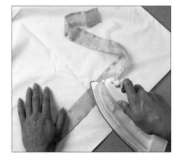

1 For the banded pillowcase, cut lengths of three different ribbons about 5cm/2in longer than the width of the pillowcase. Cut three lengths of fusible bonding web to size and use to attach each of the ribbons.

2 Turn in the raw edges and stitch the ribbons to the pillowcase at each end. Hand sew with tiny stitches along each long edge of the pillowcase.

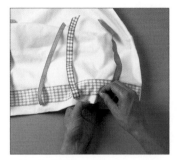

3 For the pillowcase with ties, cut two 30cm/12in lengths from each of five different narrow ribbons and pin one of each pair at regular intervals along the folded edge of the pillowcase opening. Stitch in place at the ends.

4 Use fusible bonding web to attach a length of wide ribbon to conceal the stitched ends of the ties. Hand or machine stitch around all four edges.

5 Attach the matching ribbon lengths to the other side of the pillowcase opening, folding in the raw edges and stitching neatly to secure.

6 To decorate the pillowcase with ties, cut lengths of ribbon of differing widths and pin them across the corners. Slip stitch to secure.

7 Fold the loose ends to the back of the pillowcase. Cut a second length of each ribbon, tuck under the ends to conceal the raw edges and slip stitch in place.

8 Finish the corner with a small ribbon bow, stitched through the knot to prevent it from coming undone.

The pleasure given by your gifts will be doubled when they are presented in these gorgeous wrappings. Plain boxes – new or recycled – can be painted brightly and adorned with ribbons to suit any occasion.

Gift Boxes

you will need

wire-edged shot-taffeta ribbons
in various widths

gift boxes

scissors

tape measure

PVA (white) glue

needle and matching threads

Red gift box

1 Cut a 105cm/41in length of 4cm/ 1½in ribbon and fold into seven 15cm/6in concertina pleats. Trim the ribbons into chevrons. Carefully cut a small nick in the centre of each long side and tie a small piece of ribbon around the middle to secure the loops.

2 Open out each fold to make a rounded loop. Hold the bow in place on the gift box lid. Tuck the ends of the ribbon under the box lid and glue in place. Cut off the excess ribbon.

Large purple gift box

Green gift box

Cut four lengths of green ribbon. Wrap each length around one side of the box and tie in a single loop bow at one corner. Slip each new ribbon under the previous bow. Cut the end of each ribbon into a chevron.

1 Wrap a length of purple wire-edged shot-taffeta ribbon around the gift box and cut off, leaving a little extra for tying a knot. Fold the ribbon into small pleats widthways at regular intervals. Secure the pleats with neat stitches in matching thread.

2 Wrap the ribbon around the box, gluing in place at the points where the ribbon is tied. Tie the ribbon in a knot close to one corner of the box and cut the ribbon ends in chevrons.

Small purple gift box

Dark blue gift box

1 Glue a length of pink ribbon around the edge of the lid. Cut two equal lengths of ribbon and glue one end of each to the inside of the lid on opposite sides. Cut three 38cm/15in lengths of ribbon and twist together in the middle. Place the twist in the centre of the lid and tie the two glued ribbons together over the twisted ribbons.

2 Making sure that the ends are all level, tie all eight ribbons together with an overhand knot. Cut the ends at a diagonal angle and ease the ribbons apart to give depth to the trim.

Cut two lengths of pink ribbon. Tie one length around the box in one direction and the other ribbon in the opposite direction. Holding the ribbons together in pairs, fasten in a single-loop bow. Pull the loops and tails apart. Cut the extending ribbon ends into chevrons.

Trimming is the main function of ribbon, and here a plain place mat is transformed to brighten up a table setting. As with any other item that will be laundered, check the ribbon and mat are both washable.

Ribbon Table Mats

you will need
woven table mats
ruler
contrasting grosgrain ribbon,
1cm/½in wide
contrasting checked ribbon,
2.5cm/1in wide
toning grosgrain ribbon,
15mm/⅝in wide
scissors
dressmaker's pins
needle and contrasting
and matching threads
iron and damp cloth

1 Calculate the ribbon requirements by measuring all around the edges of the table mats, adding 20cm/8in for turnings. Cut each colour of ribbon into four lengths, one for each edge of the mat plus a 2.5cm/1in turning allowance at each end.

2 Starting from the outside edge, lay the ribbons in place around the mat. Use the ruler to ensure the ribbons are parallel to the edge. Pin each one in place, leaving the ends free.

3 Interlace the ribbons to produce a woven effect where they meet and overlap at the corners and pin in place. Tack (baste) them down with contrasting thread and remove the pins.

4 Sew the ribbons down with matching thread using an invisible slip stitch along each edge, working the stitches closely together. Turn under the raw ends and sew to the back of the table mat. Press the piece under a damp cloth with the right side down.

Lantern frames are available in many different shapes and sizes, so this idea is very versatile. Measure the four sides of the frame and select a width of ribbon that can be multiplied to fit into this length exactly.

Ribbon Lantern

you will need
basic lantern frame
tape measure
ribbon, length and width depending
on size of frame
scissors
iron
needle and matching threads
beads (one small, one large and
one rocaille per ribbon)
PVA (white) glue

1 Cut pieces of ribbon to twice the finished frame length. To mitre one end of each ribbon, turn in 1cm/½in along the raw edge and press lightly with a dry iron to hold in place.

2 Fold in one corner to the centre of the ribbon, then fold in the other corner to make a triangular, mitred point. Iron to hold in position.

3 Thread a needle and tie a knot in one end. Pass the needle through the point of the mitre, then thread a small bead followed by a large bead and a rocaille. Pass the needle back through the large and small bead so the rocaille forms a stopper. Secure with a small stitch on the inside of the point.

4 Starting close to the final stitch, slip stitch along the central join of the mitre, keeping a neat point at the end of the triangle.

5 Turn the other end of the ribbon over, and loop the ribbon over one side of the frame. Fold under and slip stitch the other end of the ribbon to the top of the mitre, making sure that the wrong sides of the ribbon will be inside the frame. Make all the other ribbons in this way.

Give your prettiest clothes the care they deserve with these luxurious padded hangers, decorated with roses and bows made from exquisite silk and brocade ribbons in beautiful muted shades.

Ribbon-rose Coat Hangers

●●●

you will need

wadding (batting)

scissors

wooden coat hangers

needle and matching thread

satin ribbon, 8cm/3in wide

selection of organza, silk,

Petersham or grosgrain

and brocade ribbons

1 Cut a 5cm/2in wide strip of wadding and wind it around the wooden part of a hanger. Secure it with a few stitches at each end.

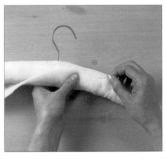

2 Cut a long, narrow rectangle of wadding to cover the hanger. Fold it over the bound wadding and sew in place along the top edge, folding over and neatening the ends as you go.

3 Cut two lengths of wide satin ribbon to make the cover for the hanger and, with right sides together, stitch each end in a gentle curve.

4 Stitch the two ribbons together along one long edge of the satin cover and turn to the right side.

5 Fit the cover over the hanger and slip stitch the top edges neatly, gathering the ends gently and easing in the fullness as you sew.

▶

6 To make a rose to decorate the hanger, fold a tiny piece of wadding into the end of a length of organza ribbon and secure with a stitch.

7 Fold and wind the rest of the ribbon around this central bud, stitching through the layers to secure. Tuck in the raw edge and stitch down. Make two roses for each hanger.

8 To make a rosette, cut a length of silk ribbon about five times its width and join the raw edges.

9 Gather the ribbon with a running stitch slightly above the centre. Pull up and secure. Flatten the ribbon out with your fingers to complete the rosette. Make two for each hanger.

10 To make a leaf, take a small piece of green petersham or grosgrain ribbon and fold both ends down to the side. Work a running stitch along this side and pull up the gathers tightly, securing with a stitch. Make four for each hanger.

11 Tie a length of brocade ribbon around the centre of each hanger to finish in a bow around the hook. Use this as a foundation to attach the roses, leaves and rosettes. Decorate with loops of ribbon to make a pleasing arrangement.

Ruched organza ribbons, sewn on to translucent voile in a fine tracery of delicate spirals, give an interesting, three-dimensional effect to this light and airy curtain.

Appliquéd Ribbon Café Curtain

you will need
tape measure
voile
dressmaking scissors
dressmaker's pins
sewing-machine
matching thread
iron
thin cardboard
pencil
fabric marker
needle
organza ribbons in green and pink

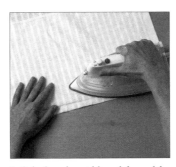

1 Calculate the width and drop of the curtain (drape) and cut out the voile, adding 5cm/2in to the width and 15cm/6in to the length. To make the facing, cut a second piece of voile to the same width by 30cm/12in. Turn under and machine stitch a 6mm/¼in hem along the lower edge of the facing. Press. With right sides together, pin the facing to the curtain, matching the top edges.

2 Enlarge the scallop template at the back of the book, and cut out of thin cardboard. Add the width of the template to the proposed width of each fabric loop (4–7cm/1½–2¾in) and divide the finished curtain width by this figure to calculate the number of scallops required. Allow for a strip at each end of the curtain. Draw around the template along the top of the curtain, using a fabric marker.

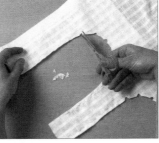

3 Machine stitch the facing to the curtain along the marked lines. Cut out the scallops, leaving a 1cm/½in seam allowance. Clip the corners and snip into the curves.

4 Turn the curtain through to the right side and press. Topstitch around the seams, 4mm/⅛in from the edge.

▶

5 Turn under and press a double hem 1cm/½in wide down each side edge of the curtain. Turn under and press a 5cm/2in double hem along the bottom edge.

6 Mitre the corners and slip stitch them neatly in place. Turn under and press a 1cm/½in single hem down both side edges of the facing. Slip stitch the facing and all the hems in place.

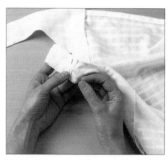

7 To make the fabric hanging loops, turn 5cm/2in of each strip to the wrong side of the curtain. Pin and slip stitch them to the facing, taking care not to let the needle pass through to the right side.

8 Cut the green ribbon into 1m/1yd lengths. Set the machine to a long straight stitch and sew down the centre of each length. Pull up the bobbin thread from each end to gather the ribbon, then adjust the ruffles so that they lie evenly.

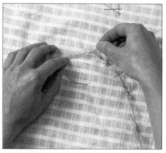

9 Draw a series of freehand spirals randomly across the curtain, using a fabric marker. Pin the ruched ribbons along the lines. Machine stitch along the gathering threads, being careful not to trap the ribbon under the stitches.

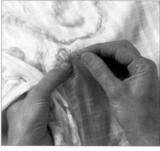

10 Gather the pink ribbon as before and cut a strip 15cm/6in long for each flower. Fold each one into three small loops and pin the flowers to the curtain in the spaces between the spirals. Machine stitch, securing the loops in place. Insert a narrow pole through the hanging loops and fix it in place at the window.

The cover for this striped lampshade consists entirely of ribbons, allowing you to introduce a rich variety of colour and texture. They are simply stuck side by side on to a piece of lampshade backing material.

Satin and Velvet Ribbon Shade

●●●

you will need
graph paper
pencil
drum-shaped lampshade frame
with reversible gimbal,
top diameter 18cm/7in,
bottom diameter 20cm/8in,
height 20cm/8in
scissors
self-adhesive lampshade
backing material
satin bias binding
selection of coloured velvet and
satin ribbons
PVA (white) glue
clothes pegs (pins)
needle
matching thread
ceramic lamp base
spray enamel paint and face mask

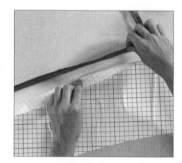

1 Make a paper pattern to fit the frame. Cut a piece of self-adhesive backing material to the size of the pattern. Remove the backing paper from the lower edge of the backing material to expose the adhesive. Cut a piece of satin bias binding to the length of the lower edge plus 2cm/¾in. Press one edge of the bias binding to the lower edge of the backing material.

2 Cut lengths of satin and velvet ribbon to fit the circumference of the shade, leaving a 1cm/½in overlap at one end. Lay a length of ribbon alongside the bias binding, following the curve of the pattern. Lay more lengths of ribbon across the backing until the last one is 6mm/¼in from the top edge. Alternate velvet with different coloured satin, and remove the paper.

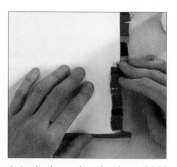

3 Cut a piece of binding to fit the top edge, with a 2cm/¾in allowance. Lay one edge of the bias binding along the top edge. Apply glue to the wrong side of the backing at top and bottom. Fold over to the wrong side.

4 Apply glue to the side edge and fold the raw ribbon ends to the wrong side. Leave to dry. If the ribbons begin to curl away from the backing, place under a heavy object. Neaten untidy edges or hanging threads with scissors.

5 Apply a thin line of glue to the underside of the same edge. Take care to wipe away any glue that squeezes on to the ribbons. Roll into a drum shape and lap the glued edge over the opposite edge, matching up the stripes of colours perfectly. Use two clothes pegs to hold the edges together firmly at the top and bottom until the glue is completely dry.

6 Where the raw edges of the bias binding meet, turn under 1cm/½in of one raw edge and stick it down so that it overlaps the other raw edge. Use the clothes pegs to hold the bindings together until the glue is dry. Slip stitch the folded edge in place. Apply a line of glue to the outside edge of the frame and insert it into the cover.

7 Working in a well-ventilated space, and wearing a face mask, spray the lamp base with a thin coat of pink enamel paint. Leave to dry before applying a second coat. Spray the shade with flame retarder if necessary, before attaching to the base. Use a medium-wattage bulb.

Shocking pink ribbon in a variety of styles – embroidery, satin, velvet and wire-edged – makes up this pretty tie-back. A satin band holds the curtain in place, while the tassel hangs decoratively to one side.

Tasselled Tie-back

you will need

large-eyed tapestry needle

narrow embroidery ribbon

wooden beads in two sizes

scissors

selection of satin, velvet and

wire-edged ribbons

needle and strong thread

2 brass rings

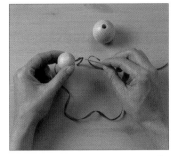

1 Using a large-eyed tapestry needle, thread narrow embroidery ribbon around two large wooden beads to make the tassel head.

2 When the beads are completely covered, tie off the ends securely. Create a hanging loop at the top of the smaller bead.

3 To make a rosette, cut a length of satin ribbon and join the ends neatly together, turning in the raw edges. Work a running stitch along both edges of the ribbon.

4 Gather up the edges tightly to make a puff shape and secure the threads. Make a second rosette, using ribbon of a different width and colour.

▶

5 To make a loop rosette, cut two pieces of narrow velvet ribbon: 30cm/ 12in lengths will make a rosette that is 15cm/6in across – cut longer lengths for a larger rosette. Fold the raw ends of the first to the centre and secure with a few stitches.

6 Fold and stitch the second length in the same way. Place this loop at right angles across the centre of the first to form a cross, then stitch through all the layers to form the rosette.

7 Select satin and wire-edged ribbons for the skirt of the tassel, cutting them to twice the finished length: this will depend on the size of the tassel head, so experiment until the tassel looks right. Arrange the ribbons in a star shape and secure by stitching through all the layers in the centre.

8 To assemble the tassel, thread the large needle with several lengths of strong thread and stitch through the centre of each element, starting with the skirt. Fasten off securely when you reach the top of the smaller bead.

9 To make the tie-back, cut a suitable length of wide satin ribbon. Neaten the raw edges and stitch a brass ring securely to each end. Cut a second piece of the same ribbon twice the length of the tie-back and gather by working a line of running stitches along the centre.

10 Draw up the fullness to fit the foundation ribbon and stitch down the centre. Sew the tassel's hanging loop to one end of the tie-back, so that it will hang at the side of the curtain.

This luxurious little evening bag exudes style and elegance. The velvet is painted with luxurious gold stripes, then woven through with complementary coloured ribbons.

Classic Evening Purse

you will need

black velvet, 40cm/16in square

black lining fabric, 20cm/8in square

scissors

large sheet of paper

masking tape, 2.5cm/1in wide

gold fabric paint

paintbrush

thin cardboard

fabric marker

small sharp-pointed scissors

silver ribbon, 1.6m x 6mm/1¾yd x ¼in

green ribbon, 1.75m x 6mm/2yd x ¼in

maroon ribbon, 1.75m x 6mm/
2yd x ¼in

tape measure

tapestry needle

dressmaker's pins

needle and matching threads

iron

1 Enlarge the three pattern pieces at the back of the book to size. A seam allowance of 1cm/½in is included. Cut two of the larger rectangles from black velvet, two of the smaller rectangles from the black lining fabric and one circle from each fabric.

2 Place one rectangle of velvet fabric face up on a sheet of paper (to protect the work surface). Lay vertical strips of masking tape over the velvet, leaving a gap of 2.5cm/1in between them. Lay a double strip of masking tape across the centre of the fabric.

3 Apply gold paint lightly and evenly to the exposed areas of fabric with a dry brush. Leave to dry completely, then peel off the tape carefully. Follow the manufacturer's instructions for fixing the paint.

4 Make a template for the ribbon insertion, cutting points from a strip of card cut to the length of the painted stripes. Mark six evenly spaced points along one edge of the strip. Transfer these points to the velvet with a fabric marker along both sides of each painted strip. Mark only the bottom half of the whole piece of velvet. ▶

5 Use sharp scissors to cut 6mm/¼in slits in the fabric at the marked points. Cut the ribbons into 20cm/8in lengths. Use a tapestry needle to thread one through each row of slits, alternating the colour with each row. Thread the ribbon loosely, allowing it to fall naturally.

6 Secure the ends of each ribbon on the back of the velvet with a few stitches. Repeat steps two to six with the second rectangle of black fabric to make the other half of the bag.

7 With right sides facing, pin, tack (baste) and sew the long sides of the two rectangles together, leaving a space in each seam where indicated on the pattern. Sew both lining rectangles together along the short edges, leaving a gap in one seam for turning.

8 With right sides facing, pin, tack and sew the long sides of the lining to the upper edge of the bag, matching up the seam lines. Press lightly and stitch the seam.

9 Turn the bag inside out and, with right sides facing, pin, tack and sew the circle of velvet to the bottom edge of the bag. Join the circle of lining fabric to the bottom edges of the lining. Turn the bag through the opening to the right side. Fold along the fold line and press gently.

10 Tack along the stitching lines indicated on the pattern to form the drawstring channel, then stitch. Close the side opening with slip stitch. Thread the remaining ribbon through the channel and tie the ends together to form a drawstring.

This handy case brings together two types of needlework: patchwork and embroidery. The crazy design will be unique for every case made and requires only a little planning to create a stunning look.

Roll-up Needlework Case

●●●●
you will need
lightweight canvas, 60 x 30cm/
24 x 12in
pencil
ruler
dressmaking scissors
five different toning ribbons,
1m/1yd of each
needle and matching threads
toning embroidery threads (floss)
dressmaker's pins
ribbon for binding, 1.5m x 2.5cm/
1²⁄₃yd x 1in
ribbon for ties, 50cm x 6mm/
20 x ¼in

1 Cut the canvas into four rectangles, two measuring 30 x 20cm/12 x 8in and two 30 x 10cm/12 x 4in. Cut the toning ribbons into various lengths between 2.5 and 7.5cm/1 and 3in.

2 Use running stitch or back stitch to sew the ribbon pieces on to one of the 30 x 20cm/12 x 8in canvas rectangles. Turn under the raw edges of the ribbon before applying. Continue until the entire panel is covered. Don't worry about any small gaps: these add to the crazy patchwork look and can be filled with embroidery stitches.

3 Oversew the edges of the ribbon pieces using three or four different embroidery threads and a range of stitches. Cross stitch, running stitch and chain stitch all work well.

4 Work blanket stitch around three edges of one of the 30 x 10cm/12 x 4in rectangles, leaving one of the long edges unsewn. On the second 30 x 10cm/12 x 4in rectangle work blanket stitch along one long edge.

5 Draw the pocket lines on this rectangle. Place the wrong side of this rectangle on top of the right side of the second large rectangle, long raw edges aligned. Stitch together along the pocket lines.

6 To assemble the case, place the patchwork panel face downwards. Place the pocket piece on top, right side up. Tack together and bind the side and bottom edges with the 2.5cm/ 1in ribbon. Use a small running stitch to secure the ribbon, stitching through all the layers.

7 Place the remaining rectangle above the pocket piece to form a flap, with the unsewn edge at the top. Pin in place and bind the top edge with ribbon as described in step 6.

8 Fold the length of 6mm/¼in ribbon in half and at the centre point stitch it inside one side edge of the case. Use this ribbon to secure the needlework case, when rolled up.

Create an heirloom gift for a new baby by combining the freshness of pure white cotton and broderie anglaise with the silky soft appeal of floral ribbon embroidery in delicate pastels.

Ribbon-embroidered Baby Pillow

●●●●

you will need

white cotton piqué,
90 x 30cm/36 x 12in

dressmaking scissors

tape measure

lightweight iron-on interfacing,
23cm/9in square

iron

fabric marker

embroidery hoop

chenille needle

satin ribbon in pale pink, dusky pink,
pale mint green, pale lime green
and pale aqua, 1.75m x 3mm/
2yd x ⅛in of each

narrow broderie anglaise insertion,
1.4m/1½yd

broderie anglaise edging,
1.4m x 7.5cm/1½yd x 3in

dressmaker's pins

needle and matching and
contrasting threads

ribbon, 1.4m x 6mm/1½yd x ¼in

tapestry needle

cushion pad, 30cm/12in square

1 Cut a 23cm/9in square of cotton piqué and iron the interfacing to one side. Trace the template at the back of the book and mount in a hoop. For the rose centre, sew a star of four pale pink straight stitches. In dusky pink work a ring of stitches around the star.

2 Work the leaves in straight stitch with the green ribbons and the rosebuds in pink. Complete the rest of the design using a range of random stitches, and add a bow to the space at the bottom edge. Trim the fabric down a 15cm/6in square.

3 Cut four 9cm/3½in squares and four 15 x 9cm/6 x 3½in pieces of piqué. From the broderie anglaise insertion, cut four 9cm/3½in, two 15cm/6in and two 33cm/13in lengths. Position the pieces and the lace around the embroidered square.

4 Make the front panel by joining the pieces together in three rows with the short lengths of lace insertion, leaving a 1cm/½in seam allowance. Use the two long strips to join the three rows together. Press the seams away from the insertion. Join the two ends of the broderie anglaise edging and run a gathering thread along the raw edge.

5 Fold the edging into four equal sections, marking each quarter division with a small scissor cut. Pin each of these cuts to one corner of the front panel on the right side. Draw up the gathering thread to fit the front panel. Distribute the gathers evenly, allowing a little more fullness at the corners. Pin the broderie anglaise around the outside edge so that it lies on top of the cushion.

7 Tack (baste) and sew in place. Thread the 6mm/¼in ribbon through the insertion using the tapestry needle. Secure each end with a few tacking stitches.

8 Cut a 30cm/12in square of cotton piqué for the panel back. Pin to the right side of the front panel, ensuring that the lace is free of the seam line. Sew around three sides then turn to the right side. Insert the cushion pad and slip stitch the fourth side closed.

The beautiful blooms that make up this romantic coronet will require special care to keep them pristine: give them a long drink before use and mist the finished headdress lightly with a water spray.

Flower and Ribbon Headdress

● ● ● ●

you will need

12 small clusters of *Aronia melanocarpa* berries

scissors

stub (floral) wire, 0.38mm/28g

12 small clusters of *Hydrangea* florets

12 *Leycesteria formosa* flower heads

small garden roses

12 *Lizianthus* flower heads

12 single *Antirrhinum* florets

florist's tape (stem wrap)

burgundy sheer ribbon, 8m x 23mm/ 8¾yd x ⅞in

tape measure

stub wire, 0.71mm/22g

1 Trim the berry stems. Cut short lengths of fine stub wire to double leg mount them. Hold the stem of the cluster between index finger and thumb. Place a wire behind and at a right angle to the stem, one third of the way up. Bend it into a "U" so that one leg is twice as long as the other.

2 Holding the short leg against the stem, wrap the long leg twice around both the stem and the other wire. Straighten both legs, which should now be about equal and in line with the stem. Mount the roses, hydrangeas and leycesteria in the same way.

3 Wire each lizianthus flower head by piercing the seedbox with a length of stub wire. Push it about one third of the way through, then bend the wire legs down and wrap the legs around the stem as described for double leg mounting (as step 1).

4 Remove the flower heads of the antirrhinum from the main stem and cut two short stub wires for each one. Fold one wire in half and twist into a loop at the bend. Push the legs down through the throat of the flower and out at the base to create a stem.

▶

5 The loop will sit in the narrowest part of the flower, preventing the wire from pulling all the way through. Use the second piece of wire to double leg mount the protruding wires and any natural stem that remains, as shown in steps 1 and 2.

6 Cover all the stems and wires with florist's tape. Hold the end against the top of the stem. With the other hand, hold the rest of the tape at an angle to the stem. Slowly rotate the stem and, keeping the tape taut so that it stretches slightly, wrap it in a downwards spiral, overlapping and pressing it in place.

7 Make 14 three-loop ribbon bows, each with two tails. For each bow, cut a 55cm/22in length of ribbon and divide it into six equal sections. Fold the ribbon accordion-style, pinching the folds together at the base. Double leg mount each bow using stub wire.

8 Cut several equal lengths of heavy stub wire to make the headdress foundation. Group four wires together so each overlaps the next by 3cm/1¼in. Starting at one end, bind them together with florist's tape. As the tape reaches the end of the first wire, add in another length.

9 Continue in this way until the wire measures 3cm/1¼in more than the circumference of the wearer's head. Tape the wired flowers and ribbons to the foundation in your chosen arrangement. Continue to within 3cm/1¼in of the end, curving the wire as you work.

10 Overlap the undecorated end of the stay wire with the decorated beginning. Tape the wires together under the flowers.

A project for a dressmaker, this lined waistcoat will fit a medium adult: adjust the ribbon requirements accordingly for another size. Choose a paper pattern without any darts in the front panels.

Woven Ribbon Waistcoat

you will need

iron-on interfacing

commercial waistcoat pattern

scissors

pencil or fabric marker

ruler

masking tape

gold ribbon, approximately 20m x 2.5cm/22¼yd x 1in

iron and damp cloth

needle and matching threads

small gold beads

blue lining fabric, 1.5m x 115cm/ 1⅔yd x 45in

dressmaker's pins

sewing-machine, with zip foot

3 buttons

1 Place the iron-on interfacing, glue side down, on top of the waistcoat front pattern piece. Cut the interfacing around the pattern. Transfer the markings to the interfacing. Turn the pattern piece over and repeat to cut out the second waistcoat front. Draw two crossing diagonal lines as a guide for weaving.

2 Tape the interfacing, glue side up, on a board. Following the pencil lines, lay and cut ribbons side by side in one diagonal direction, overlapping the edges. Tape one long ribbon on the opposite diagonal at both ends and weave in further lengths of ribbon (see page 123). Adjust the ribbons to keep the weave neat as you work.

3 Continue weaving until the interfacing is covered. Press with a dry iron. Remove the tape, turn over and press again with a steam iron or under a damp cloth.

4 Trim the ribbons to the edge of the interfacing. Iron an extra strip of interfacing to the front edge of each piece to provide a firm base for the buttonholes and buttons. Overlap the seamline slightly.

▶

5 Using a double thread with a knot at the end, sew a small gold bead to each point where the ribbons cross. Work along the diagonal and keep the seam allowances free of beads. Secure each bead with a double stitch before going on to the next bead.

6 Cut an outer back, a back lining, and two front pieces from the blue lining fabric. Mark the position of the back ties and buttonholes. Pin and machine stitch the front lining and woven fronts together, right sides facing. Fit a zip foot, and machine stitch around the front edge, along the bottom and around the armholes, leaving the shoulder and side seams open. Trim the seams and corners, clipping the curves. Turn right-side out.

7 Cut two 60cm/24in lengths of ribbon for the back ties. Fold in half and sew down both sides, stitching in the same direction to avoid puckering. Hand sew in place on the waistcoat back, trimming the raw ends to 6mm/ ¼in and folding them neatly under.

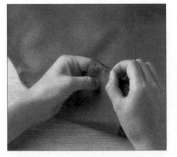

8 Join the waistcoat back to the back lining with right sides facing. Stitch around the neck and armholes. Trim and clip the seam allowances and turn to the right side. With right sides facing, sew the front and back together along the shoulder seams.

9 Stitch through one layer, leaving the linings free. Trim and press the seam open. Fold the lining seam allowance inside and slip stitch closed. Sew the side seams in the same way. Slip stitch the bottom edge of the waistcoat back closed.

10 Make three buttonholes, using gold thread on top of the machine and blue in the spool case, so that the thread matches the fabric on both sides. Snip the buttonholes and sew the buttons in position.

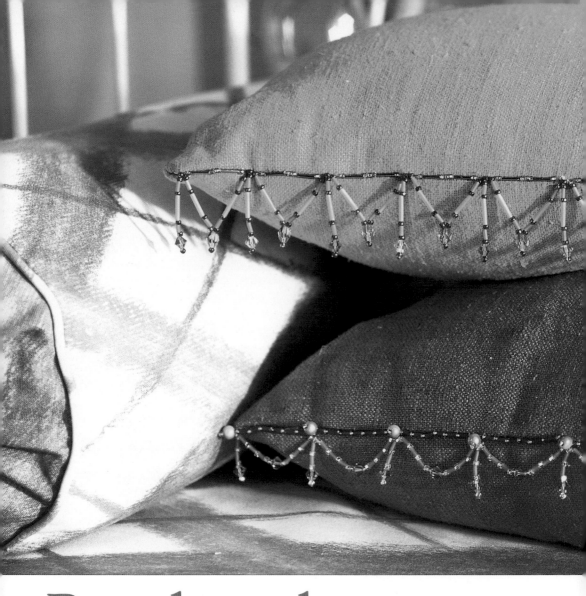

Beadwork

Some of the most desirable home accessories are adorned with, or made from, a glittering array of beads. Window decorations, candle-holders and fringed lampshades all make the most of their light-enhancing quality, while traditional beadwork techniques, including wiring and off-loom weaving, can be used to create a wide range of stunning jewellery.

An enormous range of beads can be found at specialist suppliers, in a variety of styles and shapes, in materials ranging from enamel and glass to wood or semi-precious stones.

Beads

1 Rocailles

These small, slightly flattened glass beads are very popular. Many varieties, such as opaque, transparent, metallic and iridescent, are available.

2 Small glass beads

Also known as seeds, small glass beads are used in many beading projects. They are spherical.

3 Venetian glass beads

These highly decorative beads are from one of the world's most famous beadmaking centres.

4 Millefiori (thousand flowers)

Long rods of coloured glass are fused together then sliced into mosaic-like cross-sections.

5 Bugle beads

These narrow glass tubes, widely available in many sizes, are effective when used in contrast with small glass beads.

6 Sequins

Flat plastic shapes with one or two holes, are available in different colours and finishes.

7 Drop beads

Shaped like teardrops, these are used to finish a strand.

8 Lampwork beads

Made in India, these glass beads are decorated with molten glass trailed in intricate patterns such as leaves or flowers. Some lampwork beads have a central core of silver foil, which is visible through the coloured glass.

9 Wound beads

Molten glass is wound around a metal rod to create swirling patterns.

10 Crystals

Usually cut glass, these beads have a faceted surface and are available in different shapes such as hearts and diamonds. Use beeswax to protect the beading thread from their sharp edges.

11 Semi-precious stones

Stones such as amber, turquoise, coral and jade are expensive, but artificial imitations are also available.

12 Metal beads

These beads often have sophisticated shapes may be silver- or gold-plated. They are used in jewellery to separate larger beads or at the end of a string.

Cloisonné

These intricate enamel beads are made from a basic metal bead covered with wire outlines. Coloured enamels fill in the areas.

Natural materials

Beads made from nuts, seeds, shells, mother-of-pearl and bone are regarded as potent talismans in some countries.

Pearl beads

Artificial pearl beads with a pearlized finish come in colours, white and ivory.

Beadwork is an ideal small-scale hobby as it requires very few specialist tools. Basic equipment such as scissors and needles will probably already be close to hand in the sewing basket or around the home.

Equipment

Bead loom

This small loom is specially designed for beadwork. The warp threads are fitted between metal springs and wound around wooden rollers.

Beading needles

These fine, long needles are available in various sizes and can be used to thread several beads at a time.

Beeswax

This is used to run along the beading thread to prevent it from snagging. It is useful when using faceted beads.

Craft (utility) knife

A strong knife is needed to cut out

card. Use with a cutting mat for safety.

Drawing pins (thumb tacks)

These are used to pin strands of beads on to a pin board.

Dressmaker's pins

These are used to pin fabric before tacking (basting) or slip stitching.

Embroidery hoop

Two tightly fitting rings hold fabric taut. Plastic hoops are recommended for use under a sewing-machine.

Embroidery scissors

These small, sharp scissors are used to cut and trim thread and fabric.

Fabric marker

The marks made with this specialized pen fade on contact with air or water.

Graph paper

This is used to measure and check the length of fringes and tassels.

Metal scissors

Use metal scissors to crack damaged beads and remove them from a string.

Needles

Some sewing needles, called "sharps", may be small enough to pass through beads. Leather needles, with triangular points, are used to stitch beads to tough material such as leather.

Paintbrush

Used to apply fabric paint.

Palettes

When working on a project that involves a number of beads, it is useful to decant the beads into palettes.

Pin board

Fringing should be pinned on a board to for accuracy. Small pieces can be pinned to an ironing board.

Ruler

A metal-edged ruler is the most suitable for these projects.

Tape measure

Use instead of a ruler for measuring fabric and curved surfaces.

Tweezers

Useful for picking up individual beads.

Wire cutters and round-nosed (snub-nosed) pliers

Essential for bending and cutting wire.

Apart from the beads themselves, only a few other materials are needed for beadwork, depending on the project. Some are widely available, but for others you will need to find a specialist supplier.

Materials

Beading thread

Use a strong, smooth polyester or one of the many threads designed especially for beadwork.

Beading wire

This is available in gold, copper and silver, and in many diameter sizes: 0.4mm and 0.6mm are the most useful.

Bookbinding fabric

This closely woven cotton fabric has a paper backing that can be glued. It is available from bookbinding suppliers.

Brass screw binders

These are used to hold sheets of paper together to make a book.

Buttons

Mix buttons with beads for extra decorative effect.

Cord

Beads can be wrapped around a core of three-ply cord, available from furnishing suppliers and haberdashers.

Cotton spheres

These are made of compressed cotton fibres and come in various shapes and sizes. They are usually available from specialist trimmings and beading suppliers.

Cover buttons

Sold in kit form in haberdashery departments, cover buttons consist of two pieces: a top, over which the fabric is pulled, and an underside with shank attached.

Embroidery threads (floss)

These include perlé cotton (a high-sheen 2-ply thread), stranded embroidery thread (separate the 5-ply strands for fine work) and machine embroidery threads. They are available in a full range of colours, including metallics.

Fabric paints

Water-based, non-toxic paints that are fixed by ironing are recommended.

Felt-tipped pen

This is useful for marking outlines and is also used for drawing decorative patterns for beadwork.

Fishing twine

For heavy beads, such as glass, fishing twine is recommended. It is stronger than polyester thread but more difficult to work with.

Floss thread

This fibrous thread has a silk-like sheen. Use it to cover wire stems.

Fusible bonding web

Ironed on to the back of appliqué fabric, this bonds it to the background fabric before stitching.

Interfacing

Normally used as a fabric stiffener, this also makes a good background fabric.

Jewellery findings

Gold- or silver-plated hatpins, earring wires, clasps, brooch backs, chains, jump rings and other findings are available from beadwork suppliers.

Lil pins

Shorter than dressmaker's pins, these are ideal for pin-beading.

Ribbon

Silk, satin and velvet ribbons can all be used to embellish beadwork.

Tape

Fringes are stitched to fabric tape before being inserted into seams or rolled into tassels.

Tapestry canvas and wool (yarn)

This stiff, grid-like canvas is available in various weave sizes. Stitch over it with colourful, matt tapestry wools.

1 Tapestry wool; 2 Cord; 3 Beading thread; 4 Tape; 5 Ribbon; 6 Fabric paint; 7 Fabric paint; 8 Cotton spheres; 9 Fishing twine; 10 Floss thread; 11 Beading wire; 12 Jewellery findings; 13 Lil pins; 14 Brass screw bindings; 15 Bookbinding fabric; 16 Buttons; 17 Cover buttons.

When learning any new skill, it is worth taking time to master the basics before progressing to more complex techniques. Start with a straightforward project like stringing beads or making a short fringe.

Beading Techniques

Bead picot

Use a tape measure and fabric marker to mark even points. Thread a needle, insert it into the fabric at one end of the picot and secure with a knot. Pass the needle through a large bead, followed by a small bead – the small bead will prevent the large one slipping off. Push both beads as far as possible up the needle then pass the needle back through the large bead. Make a stitch in the fabric to the next marked point.

Long fringe

1 Cut a piece of thread four times the length of the strand desired. Thread both ends through a needle. Insert into the fabric and knot. Pass the needle through the thread loop and pull taut.

3 Pass the needle through the second to last bead. Check that no thread is visible. Make a fastening-off stitch between the third and fourth beads from the end then continue up the string of beads, making fastening-off stitches every four beads.

2 Mark the length of the fringe on graph paper and place next to the thread. Thread on the required number of beads, pushing them up as far as possible.

4 Pull the strand gently to remove kinks in the thread, then trim the thread close to the beads.

Short fringe

This is worked with a continuous length of thread. Mark the length desired on graph paper. Insert the needle in the fabric and secure the thread with a knot. Thread on the required number of beads, pushing them up as far as possible. Pass the needle through the second to last bead, then back up the full length of the string. Insert the needle back into the fabric and bring it out at the next point on the fringe.

Pointed fringe

Thread a needle, insert in the fabric and secure with a knot. Thread on a bugle bead, a small glass bead and another bugle. Push the beads up as far as possible to form points, then insert the needle at the next point along.

Drop fringe

Thread a needle, insert in the fabric and secure with a knot. Thread on a small glass bead, a drop bead and another small glass bead. Push the beads up as far as possible, then insert the needle at the next point along.

Lattice fringe

1 This pretty open diamond fringe uses long bugle beads, and can be made to any depth. It is worked on to a length of narrow petersham ribbon so that it can then be sewn on to a lampshade, bag or other accessory. Make a series of pencil marks along one edge of the ribbon, 1cm/½in apart.

2 Thread a beading needle with a long, strong thread and fasten it on at the first mark. Thread one small, one large and one small rocaille, then a bugle, a large rocaille, a second bugle, a large rocaille, a third bugle, a large rocaille and three small rocailles. Take the needle back through the last large rocaille and add a bugle, a large rocaille and another bugle.

3 Go back through the first single large rocaille of the first strand and add another bugle, a small rocaille, a large rocaille and another small rocaille. Take the needle through the edge of the ribbon at the next pencil mark, then come back through the first two beads. Add a small rocaille, a bugle, a large rocaille and another bugle, then go through the second single large rocaille of the last strand. Continue in this way to the end.

Looped fringe

Mark points at even intervals with a fabric marker. Thread a needle, insert into the fabric at the first point and secure with a knot. Thread on enough beads to give the desired size of loop, pushing them up as far as possible. Insert the needle back at the same point to form a loop, then insert the needle at the next point along.

Looped fringe with stems

Before making a loop, thread on the required number of beads for the stem, then add the beads for the loop. Pass the needle back through the stem, then insert at the next point along.

Needle-woven beading

In this technique, a continuous thread runs through rounds of beads, with the second round of beads fitting between pairs of the first. The second round is joined to the first by interweaving. The following instructions are for a three-dimensional object. For a two-dimensional design, work rows instead of rounds.

1 For round 1, thread on the required number of beads, tie around the neck of the bottle and knot the ends.

2 For round 2, pass the needle through the first bead of round 1, then thread the first bead of round 2 between the first and second beads. Pass the needle through the third bead of round 1. Continue until the design is complete.

Couching

Pre-strung beads are laid down on fabric to create or embellish the lines of the design, then stitched over (couched down) with thread to secure. Add a second thread of beads on top for extra texture.

Scallops

Mark points at even intervals. Thread a needle, insert it into the fabric at the first point and secure with a knot. Thread on enough beads to give the desired length of scallop, pushing them up as far as possible, then insert the needle back in at the next point.

Bead weaving

Weaving with beads is a fascinating and easy-to-learn technique, with roots that go back to traditional Native American craftwork. It is used to make long strips of bead-work with complicated patterns, by following charted designs in which each coloured square represents a bead. The weaving is worked on a simple loom: a wire frame that holds the vertical warp threads and keeps them under tension. The horizontal threads, or weft, that carry the beads are worked across the warp. Use long, specially manufactured bead-ing needles for weaving – they are fine enough to pass through the smallest beads but tend to snap and distort easily, so keep a spare packet to hand.

1 The warp threads run along the length of the design. They should all be the same length: the length of the finished piece of weaving, plus 25cm/10in. You will require one more warp thread than the number of beads across the design, i.e. for a 15-bead design you need 16 threads. Measure and cut the threads and tie them together at one end with an over hand knot. Knot the other end.

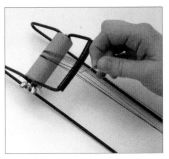

2 Divide the threads in half to form two bundles. There is a pin in the centre of each spool: slip one knot over the first of these. Slip the second knot over the other pin. Loosen the wing nut and turn the spool towards you until the threads are taut. Spread the first threads out over the wire separator so that each one lies in the groove between two coils. You may find it helpful to pick up and separate each thread with a needle.

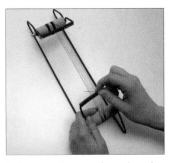

3 Separate the threads at the other end, ensuring that they all lie parallel. Tighten the wing nuts to maintain the tension.

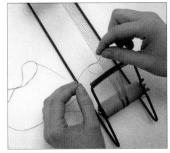

4 Position the loom so that the shorter end of the warp is facing towards you. Cut a 60cm/24in length of Nymo and thread it through a beading needle. Knot the long end to the bottom of the first thread on the left, leaving a loose tail of 5cm/2in.

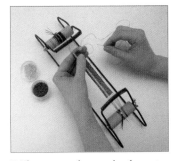

5 The patterns for most bead weaving projects are given as coloured squares on a grid. Each of these squares represents a single bead in a different colour. For the first row of the pattern, use the point of the needle to pick up a bead to match each square, working from left to right.

Wire beading

Wire brings a third dimension to beadwork, enabling you to make more sculptural forms. It is made from many different metals, from pure silver and brass to flexible alloys, which are often plated in bright colours. The diameter of all wire is given as the gauge (g): the smaller the 'g' number the thicker it is, from 10g up to fine 40g. Use 20g for making jewellery and 24g for wrapped techniques and flowers.

Bead Chains

Individually wired beads can be linked together to make attractive necklaces or set between lengths of chain – a good way to show off just a few expensive beads. Use 20g wire and round-nosed (snub-nosed) pliers to make the loops and flat-nosed pliers to join them together. Make a loop at the end of a short length of wire, as shown on page 167. Thread on the beads, then clip the wire to 6mm/¼in. Bend this end into a second loop, ensuring that it curls in the opposite direction to the first.

1 Wire up the next beads, leaving the second loop partly open. Join the loop on to the first bead, then close it with flat-nosed pliers. Repeat until you have the required length, then add a fastener to each end.

2 Joining the beads with lengths of chain gives a pretty, flexible look to the finished piece. Cut the chain into equal-sized lengths, each with an odd number of links, then use the wired beads to join the chains together.

Wrapping

Use this technique to embellish plain bangles and headbands. Thread small beads on to fine wire and secure the end by twisting around the foundation. Slide the beads down and wrap the wire so that the rows of beads lie close together. Finish off by twisting the loose end with flat-nosed pliers.

Memory wire

This industrial-strength coiled wire retains its shape even when stretched. It comes in three diameters for chokers, bracelets and rings. Cut it with heavy-duty wire cutters and use round-nosed pliers to make a loop at one end. Thread on the beads, then secure the end with another loop.

Tiger tail

This strong wire is coated with a layer of plastic in a range of bright colours. It works well with crimp beads, which can be used to secure feature beads at intervals along its length to make floating necklaces and bracelets. Use flat-nosed pliers to squeeze the crimp beads into place.

Bead flowers These exquisite flowers have been made for centuries and were particularly popular on the Venetian glass-making island of Murano. Long-lasting and naturalistic, they were used to create garlands, posies and tiaras. Use small rocailles or short bugles threaded on fine wire. The same basic method, which is surprisingly easy to master, can be used to make leaves and petals of any size.

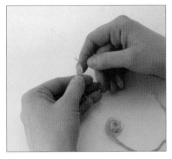

1 Thread the beads on to a reel of fine, flexible wire. Bend the last 15cm/6in into a loop and, leaving about 7cm/2¾in free at the end, twist the remaining wire loosely to make the stem. Slide the first five beads down the wire so they lie above the twist.

2 Wrap the working wire behind and in front of the loose end. Count off seven beads and hold them to the left of the centre beads. Take the wire once around the top of the stem below the beads, count off another seven, and bring it up to the right.

3 Wrap the wire once around the loose wire, just above the top bead. Make another round in the same way with nine beads on the left and eleven on the right. Continue adding more rounds until the petal is the required size, adding another two beads on each side as you work.

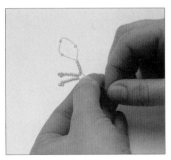

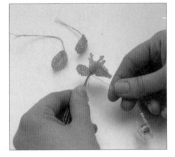

4 Finish off by bending both wires back down behind the beads. Twist all four strands together to complete the stem, and clip with wire cutters. Make another four petals in the same way and curve them gently between finger and thumb to give a natural shape.

5 To make the bead stamen centre, thread ten gold beads 30cm/12in along the wire. Pass the loose end back through the first seven beads, then repeat this seven times. Twist the loose ends together and clip them.

6 Hold the first petal up against the stamens and keep it in place by wrapping wire tightly around the top of the stem. Add the other petals, arranging them evenly around the centre core. Conceal the wires by binding the stalk with florist's tape (stem wrap).

Using findings

Findings are the metal pins, clasps and loops that will transform your beads into items of jewellery. They come in a range of finishes to suit all styles from classically elegant to ruggedly ethnic.

Jump rings

1 These wire circles are used to join fasteners to necklaces and earrings to stud posts, to link chains and droppers and to make earrings. Open sideways with a gentle twisting action, using pliers if necessary: forcing them from the centre will distort the shape.

2 For an earring, thread on dropper beads and an ear hook. Close the ring by twisting it in the opposite direction so the two ends touch again. Thicker rings may require pliers to open and close them but softer, small jump rings can be carefully opened by hand.

Triangles

Teardrop beads have a hole at the narrow point, rather than through the centre, and are fixed to other findings with triangular links. Use pliers to open the space, slip over the top of the bead and gently squeeze the triangle shut with flat-nosed pliers.

Head pins

 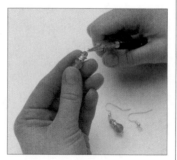

1 Head pins are for making bead drops or simple earrings. If the holes in the beads are too wide, thread on a small, matching bead first. Add more beads until there is 6mm/¼in of wire left.

2 Bend into a loop with round-nosed (snub-nosed) pliers. Just before the loop is complete, bend the wire back to centre the loop above the pin. Thread on a dropper and ear hook and complete the loop.

Eye pins

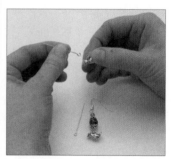

These pins have a small loop at the end for small charms and droppers. Open and close the loop with pliers. Make the top loop at a right angle so the charm will face forward.

Shell calotte

Make a knot (two or three if the thread is fine) close to the end of the thread. Seal with glue and, when dry, trim the end to 2mm/¹⁄₁₂in. Hold the calotte (see box) over the knot and squeeze it shut with pliers. At the other end, knot the thread close to the last bead, clip the end and fix a calotte over the knot.

Crab claw

These functional, spring-loaded fasteners are joined on to a calotte with a jump ring. They come in several sizes: the smaller the beads, the smaller the crab claw should be. Fix a second jump ring to the other calotte to complete the fastening.

Hook and eye fastener

This fastener, which has a hollow tube at each end, is designed for use with leather thong or thick cord. Trim the cord to the required length and put a spot of superglue on the end. Insert the end into one part of the fastener and gently squeeze with pliers. Repeat at the other end.

Spacers and bars

For multi-stranded bracelets or necklaces, the rows of beads are kept apart with these special findings, which accommodate anything from two to seven threads.

1 Tie the end of each strand securely to one of the loops on the spacer and pass the thread through the holes in a bar as you add the beads.

2 Space the bars at regular intervals – a bracelet will require two – and fasten the thread to a second spacer. For a necklace, you will need to increase the number of beads in each row so that it lies flat on the chest when worn.

Making necklaces and bracelets

Depending on its length, a string of threaded beads can be made into a bracelet, choker or necklace. Very long necklaces of 100cm/40in can be slipped over the head, but anything shorter will need a fastening of some kind. Each end of the thread is finished with a metal knot cover called a calotte: a small, hinged metal ball with an opening at one end and a loop at the other. The fastening is joined to the small loops. You can obtain jewellery findings from specialist companies selling them to the trade; most of these operate mail order schemes.

The bead droppers that hang from this pretty charm bracelet are made from an eclectic selection of pearl, iridescent glass and faceted crystal beads, in shades of amethyst and silver.

Beaded Charm Bracelet

you will need

silver chain link bracelet

selection of pearl, crystal
and glass beads

silver rondelles

2.5cm/1in silver head pins

a few rocailles in matching colours

round-nosed (snub-nosed) pliers

silver jump rings

silver charms

flat-nosed pliers

1 Make a dropper for every other chain link of the bracelet by threading a large bead, a rondelle and a small bead on to a head pin. Use a rocaille first, as a stopper, if the first bead has a narrow hole.

2 Bend the end of the wire into a loop using the round-nosed pliers. Gently ease the wire between the jaws to make a smooth curve, then just before you complete the ring, bend the wire at a right angle to make a question mark shape. Close the loop.

3 Add a jump ring to the top of the first dropper. Open up the ring by gently twisting the two halves apart with a sideways movement, using the flat-nosed pliers. Slip one end through the wire loop.

4 Slot the open jump ring on to the second chain link and squeeze it closed with flat-nosed pliers. Add the other droppers on to every other link along the bracelet.

5 Use a jump ring to attach a silver charm to the first empty link. To complete the bracelet, fix the remaining charms to the other links.

No Victorian tea tray was complete without a dainty beaded cover to protect the milk. Here is an updated version of this traditional idea, which is now making a come-back.

Bead-trimmed Voile Jug Covers

Checked cover

1 Cut out a 20cm/8in diameter circle of checked fabric. Turn under and tack (baste) a narrow double hem around the curved edge. Machine or hand stitch the hem, close to the inner fold, with matching thread.

2 Fold the hemmed circle into quarters, then eighths, then six-teenths. Press the folds lightly with an iron to divide the circle into 16 equal sections. Mark each of the creases with a pin.

3 Secure a length of matching thread to the hem at a pin marker, then thread on one large orange plastic bead, one medium pink frosted, one red frosted and one orange rocaille. Pass the thread back through the first three beads and make a double stitch at the hem to secure.

4 Feed the thread along the hem halfway to the next pin marker and thread on one medium pink frosted bead, one red frosted and one orange rocaille. Pass the thread back through the first two beads and make a double stitch at the hem. Repeat the pattern all around the hem to complete.

Plain cover

1 Prepare the plain voile as before and fasten on. Add a square bead, a small pink, a square, a small pink, a square, a large pink and a rocaille. Go back through the large pink and last square beads. Repeat for the other side.

2 Secure at the hem with a double stitch. Add one square, one red, one square, one small pink and a rocaille. Go back through the pink and repeat.

3 Double stitch at the hem to secure. Continue round the hem to complete.

Perfect for a small window, multicoloured beads will dress your window without blocking the light. Nylon line supports the beads, and large crystal drops at the end of each strand define the shape.

Glittering Window Decoration

you will need
pencil and ruler
length of 4 x 4cm/1½ x 1½in wooden
batten (furring strip) to fit outside
window frame
drill
scissors
nylon fishing line
selection of plastic beads, including
large drops and long or bugle
beads, in various colours and sizes
large pendant beads
4cm/1½in wide ribbon
staple gun
2 screw-in hooks

1 Using a pencil and ruler, mark points 2.5cm/1in apart all along the wooden batten, 2.5cm/1in from one edge. Allow enough space between the first and second holes at each end for the window frame. Drill a hole at each point.

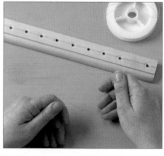

2 Cut a length of fishing line twice the length of the window plus 50cm/20in. Thread both ends through the second hole, then through the loop formed by the doubled thread.

3 Pull the fishing line taut. Thread on the beads in a random manner, using bugle or long beads to space out the round beads.

4 When you reach the desired length, thread on a large pendant bead, pass the fishing line back through the last few beads and make a knot. Thread the fishing line back up the length of the strand, knotting the ends twice more, and trim the ends.

5 Repeat the process for the other strands, making them shorter towards the centre of the window. Cut a length of ribbon to the length of the batten plus 2cm/¾in. Staple it in position at either end. Attach a screw-in hook at either end of the batten from which to hang the curtain.

Inspired by ethnic beadwork, this bag is made of traditional ikat fabric from Indonesia, lined with a plain fabric that acts as a binding and casing for the ties. An ideal first project for a newcomer to beadwork.

Little Fringed Bag

you will need

30 x 15cm/12 x 6in ikat fabric

dressmaking scissors

tape measure

set square or ruler

fabric marker

pencil

sheet of paper

dressmaker's pins

35cm/14in square plain-coloured fabric, in contrasting colour

iron

sewing-machine

matching thread

sewing needle and thread to match lining

beading needle

black beading thread

small black glass beads

small multicoloured glass beads

2 black shoelaces, each 50cm/20in long

12 large beads with large holes

1 Cut the ikat fabric into two 15cm/6in squares. On the right side of each piece, mark a line diagonally from corner to corner in both directions, then mark parallel lines 2cm/¾in apart. Draw a bag shape similar to the bag in the finished picture on paper.

2 Pin the template to both pieces of ikat fabric and cut out. Cut two pieces of plain fabric 16 x 20cm/6¼ x 8in for the lining. With the marked lines right side up, tack (baste) one bag piece to each lining piece. Using running stitch, stitch along the lines. Trim the excess lining fabric.

3 To make the casing, cut two pieces of lining fabric 7 x 12cm/2¾ x 4½in. Press in half lengthways then press under a narrow turning all round. Pin one long edge to the top of a bag piece and machine stitch. Repeat with the second casing.

4 Place the two bag pieces right sides together. Pin, then machine stitch 1cm/½in from the raw, curved edges. Leave the top open.

5 Turn the bag right side out. Fold the casings over the raw edges and slip stitch in place. Thread a beading needle with beading thread and fasten just below the casing.

6 Thread on seven black beads and a coloured bead, then go back through the last black bead. Thread on six black beads and make a small stitch 1cm/½in along the seam. Repeat all around the bag.

7 Thread one shoelace through each casing for the drawstring. Thread three large beads on to the end of each shoelace and knot. Tie the two shoelaces together at either end.

Add a touch of contemporary boho chic to your favourite outfit with this avant-garde, low-slung hipster chain belt – you can also use the same method to make a matching necklace.

Silver Chain Belt

you will need

60cm/24in medium-gauge silver wire

round-nosed (snub-nosed) pliers

25 flat glass beads,
15mm/⅝in diameter

6 silver beads, 6mm/¼in diameter

wire cutters

75cm/30in silver chain with large links

60 silver jump rings

3 silver head pins

40cm/16in silver chain with small links

fastening chain

silver crab-claw fastener

1 Mount each of the beads on silver wire by making a small loop at one end of the wire with round-nosed pliers and threading on the bead. Trim the end to 6mm/¼in and bend in another loop in the opposite direction.

2 Cut the large-link chain into 4cm/1½in sections. Use jump rings to link alternate wired beads and chains, until the belt is the right length.

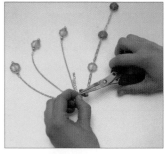

3 For each dropper, thread a silver, a glass and a silver bead on to a head pin. Clip the end and bend it into a loop. Cut the fine chain into three and fix a dropper to each one with a jump ring. Join the three chains and the fastening chain together using a jump ring and fix this to the belt. Fix the fastener to the other end with a jump ring to complete the belt.

Ornate hatpins were once an indispensable accessory, used to secure the wide-brimmed headgear worn by fashionable Edwardian ladies. These contemporary versions can be pinned, brooch-style, to the lapel.

Beaded Hatpins

you will need
decorative and diamanté beads
hatpin bases with safety ends
glue gun or impact adhesive
lengths of 6mm/¼in-wide ribbon
in several colours
matching sewing thread

1 Choose a selection of beads in matching or complementary colours and in various shapes and sizes. Pick out a small bead to put on to the pin first to prevent the others slipping off. Smear the shaft of the pin with a very thin coat of glue, then add on the other beads.

2 Streamers can be added by threading a length of narrow ribbon between the beads. Tie into a bow and secure with a few stitches.

3 Make tiny roses from the ribbons, as described on page 134 for the coat hangers. Sew the ends firmly and trim, before glueing the roses between the beads for a flowered effect.

Rocailles in restrained shades of grey, white and gold are used to make this sophisticated container, and the colours come to life in the flickering light. For safety, always use a candle in a metal holder.

Bead Candle-holder

you will need

wire cutters

tape measure

0.6mm/$\frac{1}{40}$in gold wire

glass tumbler

adhesive tape

large rubber band

0.2mm/$\frac{1}{120}$in gold wire

round-nosed (snub-nosed) pliers

grey glass beads, 4mm/$\frac{1}{6}$in

white glass beads, 4mm/$\frac{1}{6}$in

gold glass beads, 4mm/$\frac{1}{6}$in

1 Cut two pieces of thick gold wire twice the height and diameter of the glass plus 10cm/4in. Twist the wires together at their halfway points, then tape the knot to the centre of the glass base. Slip a rubber band over the glass to hold the wire in place. Fold the wire ends over the lip of the glass.

2 Cut two pieces of fine gold wire approximately 1m/40in long. Find their halfway points, then twist both pieces around the knot on the base of the glass. Wrap each wire around your hand first to stop it becoming tangled.

3 Thread the grey beads on to the thick wire. To begin the winding wire, bend one end of the thick wire into a 2cm/$\frac{3}{4}$in flat spiral with pliers. Secure at the centre of the base by weaving the thin wire over and under the frame of thick wire and the spiralled wire.

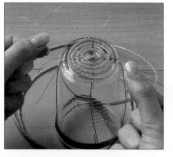

4 Thread more grey beads on to the winding wire and continue to wind it into a spiral, weaving the thinner wire under and over the frame. Continue up the sides of the glass to within 1cm/$\frac{1}{2}$in of the top. Remove the rubber band.

5 To make a lip, ease the top of the frame outwards and thread on some white beads. Continue to weave the thinner wire under and over the winding wire and the frame. Thread on small gold beads. Open out ends of frame, remove glass, trim ends and fold over. Secure the ends to the frame.

These sinuous bracelets are made using a simple off-loom weave known as peyote stitch. Once you have mastered the technique, you can create all kinds of designs.

Spiral Bracelets

●●●

you will need

Nymo or quilting thread to match beads

scissors

beading needle or size 10 sewing needle

rocailles in metallic green and red and green stripes

2 bell caps

2 silver beads, 2.5mm/¹⁄₈in

small jump ring

crab-claw fastener

1 Thread a 2m/2yd length of thread through the needle. Thread on nine green beads and tie them into a loop with a reef knot, 25cm/10in from the end. Hold the end of the thread between finger and thumb.

2 To make the first round, add a striped bead, then skip one bead and take the needle through the next bead. Thread on a green bead, skip one bead and pass the needle through the next bead.

3 To complete the round, add a striped bead and pass the needle through the next but one bead, then thread on a green bead, skip one green bead and go through the next bead. You will now have a flat, four-pointed star shape.

4 Start the next round by threading on a striped bead and taking the needle through the next striped bead to the right. Add a green bead and take the needle through the next green bead. Repeat this twice more and pull the thread up tightly so that the beads begin to form a cylinder.

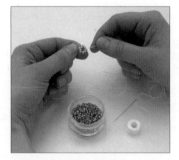

5 When the thread runs out, join on another length with a reef knot. Use the point of the needle to position the knot so that it sits close to the last bead, then continue weaving, leaving the ends trailing on the outside of the cylinder. Taper the end with three beads between the next two beads. Repeat until you reach the required length, with space for the fastening.

6 Thread the needle once again through the last four beads. Bring it out through the centre of the cylinder and add a bell cap, a large silver bead and the jump ring. Go back through the findings five times, then fasten off.

7 Re-thread the needle at the other end, then complete in the same way, adding the fastener after the silver bead. Darn in the loose threads by taking them back through the weave for 2.5cm/1in and trim the ends.

8 To make striped patterns, work rounds of beads in a single contrasting colour or use three colours in one round to vary the width of the stripes. A bracelet made in a single colour is also very effective.

Use large glass beads in strong colours to make tie-backs that will become the focal points of your window. Before you begin, gather up the curtain (drape) in a tape measure to calculate the length.

Chunky Bead Tie-backs

for each tie-back you will need

2 split rings

2 decorative dividers with attachments for three strings

glue gun and glue sticks

2 flat-backed blue glass nuggets

scissors

pencil

paper for template

tape measure

strong non-stretch beading thread

clear nail polish

cylindrical orange handmade glass and ceramic beads

round blue glass beads

large blue glass beads

1 Attach one of the split rings to the loop at the top of each triangular divider. These will be slipped over the wall hooks. Using a glue gun, attach a flat-backed blue glass nugget to the centre of each divider.

2 Cut a curved, symmetrical paper template to the required shape of the finished tie-back. Make sure it is wide enough to hold all the folds of the curtain (drape) and deep enough to accommodate all three rows of beads.

3 Cut a length of strong thread, 30cm/ 12in longer than the width of the template. Knot one end securely to the top loop of the first divider. Dab the knot with clear nail polish to keep it in place.

4 Thread on the large and small beads in a symmetrical pattern, using the main picture as a guide to the sequence. Pass both the main length of thread and the spare end through the first few beads to secure them.

5 Thread on enough beads for the first row to fit across the top of the template and knot the loose end of thread firmly to the second divider. Trim the end and secure the knot with a blob of nail polish as before.

6 Pass the spare tail of beading thread back through the last few beads on the strand and snip off the remainder.

7 Thread up the second and third rows following the same sequence, adding extra beads to make each row a little longer than the previous one. Repeat for the other tie-back.

Hang these pretty tassels from keys in the bedroom or bathroom. Worked in colours that co-ordinate with the rest of the room's decor, they make charming decorative details.

Silken Key Tassels

you will need

2 skeins stranded embroidery thread (floss) for each tassel, plus extra for loops and ties

stiff cardboard

scissors

tape measure

sewing needle and matching thread

2 large ceramic beads

beading needle

small glass rocailles in red, orange and turquoise

large glass rocailles in red and turquoise

medium red glass crystals

small red opaque rocailles

1 To make a plaited tassel, wind two skeins of stranded embroidery thread around a piece of stiff cardboard. Cut a 20cm/8in length of thread and tie it into a hanging loop, then tie the ends tightly around the top loop of the wound thread. Carefully slip the tied bundle of thread from the card.

2 Holding the knot in one hand, cut through the other end of the loop to form the tassel. Separate six threads into three pairs and make a tight plait. Use a needle and matching thread to secure the end. Make another three plaits in the same way around the tassel.

3 Trim the ends so they are level. Thread the hanging loop through the two ceramic beads, then tie the loop in a small knot to secure.

4 To make a beaded tassel, repeat steps 1–3, then tie a length of thread around the bundle about 2cm/¾in down from the top. Stitch a length of thread to the top of the tassel and thread on eight small red rocailles. Tie off with a double knot to make a ring around the hanging loop.

5 Passing the thread through alternate rocailles in the previous round, make three loops of two orange, two turquoise, two red and one large red rocailles, reversing the sequence to complete the loop. Make three more similar loops, passing the thread through the large red rocailles.

6 Link the large red beads from step 5 with a round of six red rocailles between each, then add a round of six orange rocailles. Link the large beads again with six turquoise rocailles. Suspend a pendant loop from each large red bead: thread three red, three turquoise, thee orange and one red rocaille, then one medium red glass crystal and one small red opaque. Go back through the last two beads and reverse for the other side.

7 Again passing the thread through the large red rocailles to link them, make three loops of three red, three turquoise and three orange rocailles, one red rocaille, then one large turquoise rocaille and one small red opaque. Go back through the last two beads and reverse for the other side. Finish off with a knot.

A delicate butterfly made entirely of wired beads, to perch on a favourite hat, a hair clip or a bag – just make sure that there are no projecting wire ends before you wear it.

Crystal Butterfly

you will need

30cm/12in medium-gauge silver wire

3mm/⅛in faceted pale lilac oval beads

6mm/¼in faceted oval beads in blue and lilac

flat-nosed pliers

reel of floristry wire

wire cutters

silver rocailles

2 heart-shaped blue beads, 15mm/⅝in

2 heart-shaped blue beads 8mm/⅓in

4 round green beads, 4mm/⅙in

round green bead, 8mm/⅓in

4 bicone green beads, 8mm/⅓in

round-nosed (snub-nosed) pliers

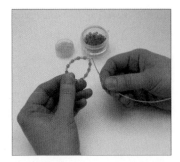

1 Make a small loop at one end of the silver wire, then thread on 12 small pale lilac beads interspersed with 11 large blue faceted beads. Pass the loose end of the wire through the loop, pull it up tightly to make the butterfly's upper wing shape and then bend it outwards.

2 Thread on eight more small beads interspersed with seven large lilac beads. Bend the wire into a loop for the lower wing and pass the end through the loop. Wrap the wire tightly once more through the loop, clip the end and bend it over with the flat-nosed pliers.

3 Fix a 30cm/6in length of floristry wire to the wire frame of the upper wing, just above the fifth large blue bead. Thread on a large lilac, a silver rocaille, a large heart, another rocaille, a large lilac bead and another rocaille. Finish off the wire at the bottom edge, just above the first large blue bead.

4 Thread on another rocaille, a large lilac bead and a rocaille, then twist the wire around the opposite side of the wire frame, just above the top of the final large blue bead. Add a rocaille, a large lilac bead and another rocaille, then pass the wire back up through the heart bead.

5 Add a rocaille, a large lilac bead and a rocaille, then fasten off three beads along from the start. Re-fasten it one bead along, add a rocaille and a small lilac bead, then twist the wire around the top of the heart. Add another small lilac and a rocaille, then fasten off two beads before the start point.

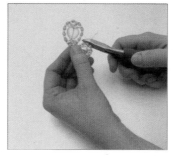

6 Fasten another 30cm/6in length of wire close to the original loop. Thread on a small lilac bead, a large lilac bead, a rocaille, a small heart, a rocaille and a small lilac bead. Secure the other end of the wire to the opposite side of the lower wing just below the seventh bead of the original round.

7 Fix the wire to the frame one bead to the right, and add a small lilac and a rocaille. Twist the wire around the bottom of the heart and add a rocaille and a small lilac. Twist the wire twice around the frame, two beads to the left, add a rocaille, a lilac bead and a rocaille. Twist around the frame, three beads along, then fill the remaining space in the same way. Make the second wing as a mirror image.

8 Bind the wings together along the centre with floristry wire. Make a loop in the end of the remaining silver wire and thread on the green beads to make the head and body. Clip the wire to 6mm/¼ in to complete the body. Twist the rest of the wire to make the antennae and slip them through the top loop. Wire the body over the join. Wire a brooch backing to the wrong side if you wish.

This stylish and contemporary choker is woven in shades of peacock green and silver beads. Once finished, it is mounted on a strip of soft suede and can be tied loosely around the neck.

Loom-woven Choker

you will need
bead loom
black Nymo thread
beading needle
2mm/¹/₁₂in rocailles in three
shades of green
2mm/¹/₁₂in silver rocailles
2 beads, 6mm/¹/₄in, in a
contrasting colour
soft dark blue suede
tape measure
dressmaking scissors
PVA (white) glue
sewing needle
matching sewing thread

1 Following the instructions on page 165, thread up a 50cm/20in warp of 11 threads. Knot a 1m/40in length of Nymo to the first thread on the left and, using the chart at the back of the book as a guide, thread on the first row of beads. Take the needle from left to right under the warp.

2 Gently lift the beads upwards with the tip of a finger and push them so that one sits in each gap between the warp threads. Slide the needle back through the beads, keeping it above the threads without piercing them. Continue to follow the chart.

3 To make a fringe strand, add on extra beads. Go back through the last but one bead to form a stopper, then pass the needle through the remaining beads and complete the row as usual. Do the same for each strand, adding large beads as indicated.

4 When finished, remove the weaving from the loom. Cut off the knots and knot the remaining threads together securely in pairs.

5 Cut a strip of suede the same width and 50cm/20in longer than the choker. Glue the weaving to the centre, tucking under the threads. When dry, slip stitch the edges neatly to the suede.

The plainest cushion cover can be dramatically transformed with a fringe of beads: these three designs show how beads of different sizes and colours produce different effects.

Bead-fringed Cushions

you will need

tape measure

dressmaking scissors

iron

sewing-machine

sewing thread

dressmaker's pins

beading needle

beading thread

for the yellow cushion:

yellow velvet

square cushion pad

6mm/¼in white glass beads

7mm/⅜in opaque yellow beads

small copper glass beads

7mm/⅜in opaque white beads

7mm/⅜in opaque blue beads

for the striped cushion:

rectangular cushion pad

striped fabric

fabric marker

graph paper

pencil

small glass beads in pink and yellow

7mm/⅜in yellow disc-shaped beads

for the pink cushion

rectangular cushion pad

pink velvet

small glass beads yellow and pink

6mm/¼in white glass beads

6mm/¼in turquoise glass beads

Yellow cushion

1 Cut a piece of velvet 2.5cm/1in larger all around than the cushion pad. Cut two back panels to the same depth and two-thirds of the length. Turn a hem on one long side of each back panel. With right sides down, overlap the two hems until they are the same size as the cushion front.

3 Thread a beading needle with double beading thread and fasten to one corner. Thread on two white, a yellow and a copper bead. Go back through the yellow bead and thread on two white glass beads. Insert the needle into the seam 2cm/¾in along.

2 Place the two back panels right side down on top of the right side of the cushion front. Pin and baste around the edges. Machine stitch around the outside edge allowing a 1cm/½in seam. Clip the corners and turn through, pushing out the corners. To iron velvet, always place a towel on the ironing surface so that the pile isn't flattened by the heat of the iron. Always use a warm, not hot, iron setting and press carefully. The pile may melt if the iron is too hot.

4 Make a tiny stitch, then thread on a blue or white opaque bead and a copper bead. Pass the needle back through the blue or white bead, then insert the needle 2cm/¾in farther on. Repeat this sequence along each side of the cover.

Striped cushion

1 Cut a piece of striped fabric 5cm/2in wider and 20cm/8in longer than the rectangular pad. Cut two back panels to the same width and two-thirds the length as the pad.

2 Turn a hem on one short side of each back panel. With right sides facing down, overlap the hemmed edges until the back is the same dimensions as the cushion front. Place on top of the cushion front with right sides together. Stitch 1cm/½in from each long edge. Turn through. Stitch a line 10cm/4in from each raw edge and fringe the fabric to this line.

3 Mark the 10cm/4in length of fringe on graph paper. Cut thread at least four times this measurement and double through the needle. Insert the needle at the inner edge of the first stripe of the fabric and secure with a knot, pass the needle through the loop and pull taut.

4 Mix a few pink and yellow beads. Thread on 9.5cm/3¾in of beads. Add a disc and a small yellow bead. Pass the needle back through the disc, make a finishing stitch, pass the needle up the strand and make another finishing stitch. Pull gently on the strand to remove any kinks. Trim the thread. Repeat with the other stripes.

Pink cushion

1 Make up the pink velvet cover for the yellow cushion, this time making a rectangular cushion rather than a square one. Mark points 15mm/⅝in apart along two opposite sides. Fasten a double length of beading thread on to one corner.

2 Mix a few yellow and pink beads together, and thread on 2cm/¾in of beads. Add a white bead, 2cm/¾in of pink or yellow and one turquoise and one copper bead. Go back through the turquoise bead, thread on 2cm/¾in pink or yellow, a large white, then more pink or yellow. Insert the needle at the third point.

3 Make a back stitch to bring the needle out at the second marked point. Thread on 2cm/¾in of pink or yellow beads, then pass the needle through the large white bead already in place, on the strand to the right. Thread on another 2cm/¾in of pink or yellow beads, one turquoise and one copper bead. Repeat this sequence along each side of the cushion.

These more intricate bead edgings, made from rocaille, bugle, pearl and crystal beads, have a delicate appearance, but they are stitched along the seams with strong thread and are unlikely to break.

Beaded Cushion Trims

●●●●

you will need

50cm/20in each purple and green linen

dressmaking scissors

tape measure

dressmaker's pins

sewing-machine

matching sewing thread

cushion pad 35cm/14in square

cushion pad 30cm/12in square

beading needle

strong non-stretch beading thread

iridescent beads in pink and green

rocailles in gold, silver and red

frosted bugle beads in pink, blue and green

green metallic bugle beads

small crystal beads in pink, blue and yellow

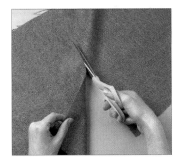

1 To make up the cushion covers, from purple cut a 38cm/15in square for the front of the large cushion, and two back panels each 38 x 28cm/15 x 11in. For the small cushion, from green cut a 33cm/13in square and two back panels each 33 x 23cm/13 x 9in.

2 Turn a hem on one long edge of each back panel. Place them on top of the front, with right sides facing and hems overlapping at the centre. Stitch around all four sides of each cushion cover with a 12mm/½in seam. Turn right-side out and insert the pads.

3 The trim for the purple cushion is made up of alternate swags and drops and is stitched along two opposite edges of the cushion. Measure one edge of the cushion and divide it at equidistant points approximately 5cm/2in apart. Mark each point vertically with a pin.

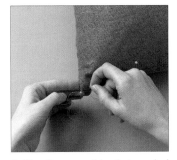

4 The first row of beads is worked along the seam line. Fasten on at the left corner and thread on an iridescent pink bead followed by a gold rocaille. Take the needle back through the pink bead, into the seam and back out along the stitching, beside the pink bead.

▶

5 Thread on 2.5cm/1in of alternate pink bugles and gold rocailles. Make a small stitch through the seam to secure, then repeat until the first marker pin. Secure the thread. Attach a green iridescent bead with a gold rocaille as for the pink bead. Repeat to the second corner.

6 Starting again at the corner, make the drop from a silver rocaille, a blue bugle, a silver rocaille, a blue bugle, a silver rocaille, a pink crystal and another silver rocaille. Take the needle back through the crystal and the rest of the strand. Secure with a small stitch in the seam and come out one bead to the right.

7 For the swag, thread a silver rocaille and a frosted bugle. Repeat twice, then add a silver rocaille, a gold rocaille and a pink crystal. Thread the beads on the other side of the crystal as a mirror image. Secure at the seam, just under the iridescent bead. Continue making drops and swags to the end of the row.

8 Pin at 3cm/1¼in intervals along the green cushion. For the drop, thread two red rocailles, a blue bugle, a red rocaille, a green bugle, a red rocaille, a blue bugle, a red rocaille, a blue crystal and a red rocaille. Go back through the crystal and the strand. Secure, then come out one bead along. Starting with a single red rocaille, thread the same sequence but using a yellow crystal and a rocaille. Go back through the crystal.

9 Thread the second side of the triangle as a mirror image of the first. Secure to the seam just to the left of the next pin and secure. Continue making alternate drops and triangles to the end. Starting again at the corner, conceal the seam as before with a line made up of a gold rocaille, a green metallic bugle, three gold rocailles, a green bugle and a gold rocaille.

Glass beads are at their most beautiful and magical when lit from behind, or in this case from within: even a plain paper lampshade can be transformed with the addition of a long bead fringe.

Fringed Lampshade

●●●●

you will need

yellow oil-based marker pen

tubular white paper lampshade

tape measure

sharp sewing needle

scissors

yellow and white beading thread

beading needle

pencil

graph paper

small yellow glass beads

small purple glass beads

4cm/1³⁄₄in purple bugle beads

purple teardrop beads

small transparent glass beads

1 Draw freehand stripes of varying widths down the length of the lampshade using the oil-based marker pen. Leave until dry.

2 Using a sharp needle, pierce a row of holes 6mm/¼in apart just above the bottom rim.

3 Cut a piece of yellow beading thread twice the desired length of the fringe plus 25cm/10in and double through the beading needle. Knot the ends together and pass the needle through a hole on a yellow stripe, then loop through and pull taut.

4 Mark the bead sequence on graph paper. Thread on small beads: 12cm/4½in of yellow, one purple, one yellow, one purple and one yellow. Add a bugle, then alternate five small yellow and four purple. (On alternate strands, add an extra two of each colour.) Add three yellow.

5 Add one purple teardrop and three yellow beads. Insert the needle just below the purple teardrop and make a fastening-off stitch, checking that no thread is showing. Pass the needle back up the strand.

6 Make a fastening-off stitch below the bugle then pass it up through the bugle and make another fastening-off stitch. Pull gently on the strand to remove kinks. Continue around the shade. For the white stripes, use white thread and substitute transparent beads for yellow ones.

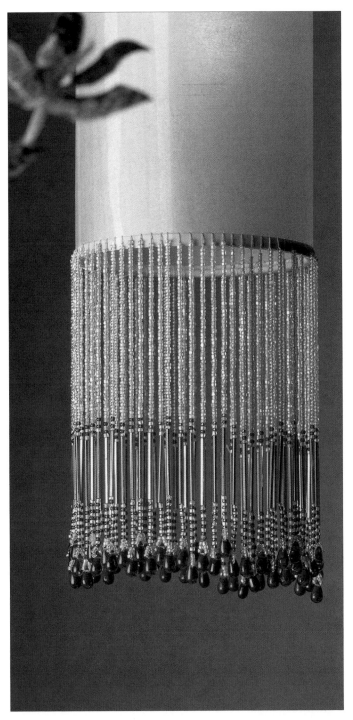

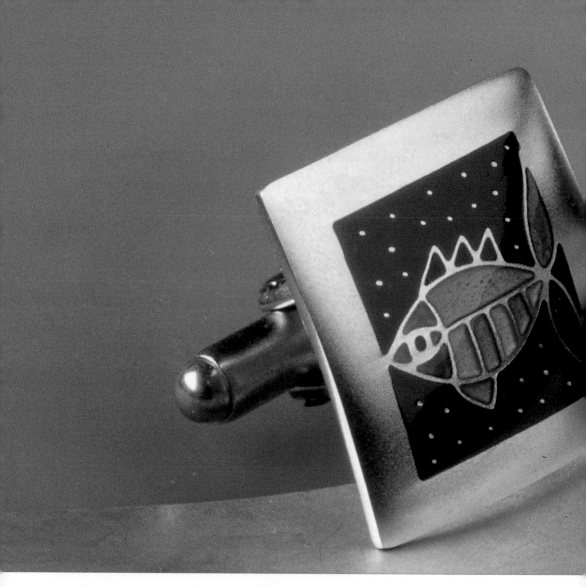

Enamelling

As soon as early people learnt how to work metal, they valued it as much for its beauty as its practical uses. Enamelling has a long history of decorative use and early craftspeople used it in jewellery to imitate precious stones. Specialized materials and equipment are required for this ancient art, and a careful hand is needed when following the designs shown here. However, the truly stunning results are well worth the effort involved.

Enamel is a form of glass and enamelling is the process of fusing it to metal using heat. Most materials need to be obtained from a specialist supplier: start by buying what you need for the simplest projects.

Materials

Acids and pickles
Dilute solutions of various acids are used to degrease and de-oxidize metal before or after firing.

Ceramic fibre
This can be moulded to support awkwardly shaped pieces during firing.

Enamels
Jewellery enamels are available in lump or powder form, with or without lead. Leaded and lead-free enamels cannot be used together. Use transparent, translucent or opaque enamels to create different effects.

Enamel gum solution
Various organic gum solutions are available, some as sprays. Dilute solution is used to position *cloisonné* wires; a weak solution is used to hold powder enamel before firing. Use sparingly.

Etchants
Solutions of nitric and other acids are painted on metal to produce etched designs for filling with enamel.

Foil
Fine gold (23.5 ct) and silver (.995 ct) foil are available in a variety of thicknesses. Gold leaf is usually too thin for enamelling purposes.

Kaolin (ballclay, batwash)
This helps prevent enamel adhering to the firing support or the kiln floor.

Mica
In the technique called *plique-à-jour*, "windows" of translucent enamel are created in a pierced metal form. A sheet of mica can be used to support the enamel when firing such items.

Pumice powder
A pumice and water paste is used to polish enamel and metal after firing.

Resists
Stopping-out varnish can be painted on to areas of metal to be protected during etching. PnP blue acetate film produces a photographic resist.

Sheet metal
Copper and silver sheets come in various thicknesses and sections. Silver should be at least .925 (Sterling) quality. Avoid beryllium-containing copper.

Solder
Hard (4N, "IT" grade) silver solder should be used prior to enamelling.

Washing soda crystals
Use a soda solution to neutralize acids.

Water
In hard-water areas use bottled water or rainwater, as limescale and additives can impair the clarity of enamels.

Wire
Copper, fine silver and fine gold wire are available in rectangular section, pre-annealed, for *cloisonné*.

The main piece of equipment needed for enamelling is a domestic-sized gas or electric kiln. This and other specialist items are available from enamellers' and jewellers' suppliers.

Equipment

Artist's brushes
Pure sable paintbrushes are the traditional tools for applying wet enamel.

Brass brush
Use a suede or other brass brush to clean metal after pickling.

Diamond-impregnated paper
This is a cleaner and faster abrasive than carborundum, the traditional abrasive for enamel, and is invaluable for concave surfaces.

Doming block, swage block, mandrel and punches
These blocks of steel, brass or hardwood are used to shape metal. Use a hammer with steel and brass blocks and a mallet with wood.

Felt polishing mop
Impregnated with pumice powder and water, a felt mop is used to polish fired enamel, either by hand or connected to an electric polishing motor.

Files
Use hand files to remove burrs after cutting metal. Diamond files can be used with water to abrade fired enamel.

Glass fibre brush
This will not scratch metal and can be used to clean enamel. Avoid contact with the hands.

Kiln
Electric kilns take longer to heat up to firing temperature than gas-fired kilns but are comparatively inexpensive. A regulator (thermostat) is needed to prevent overheating and a pyrometer gives an accurate temperature reading. Use ready-made firing supports or make them from stainless-steel mesh.

Pestle and mortar
Use only vitrified porcelain to grind and wash enamels.

Quills
Goose quills, from calligraphers' suppliers, are used to apply wet enamel.

Rolling mill
Use to impress textured designs on sheet silver for *champlevé* enamel.

Sieves (strainers)
Use to apply dry enamel. Match the size of the mesh to that of the ground enamel fragments.

Soldering equipment
You need solder, charcoal, a gas blowtorch and borax-based flux (auflux).

Tongs and tweezers
Brass or plastic tongs or tweezers must be used to move metal in and out of pickle or etchants.

Enamelling involves high temperatures and hazardous substances. Work in a well-ventilated place, wear protective clothing, follow all manufacturers' instructions and turn off the kiln when not needed.

Enamelling Techniques

Preparation of metal Metal must be degreased and de-oxidized (pickled) before enamelling. To make it more malleable, anneal it by heating with a blowtorch to cherry-red. Allow it to return to black then quench in cold water and pickle to remove oxidation.

1 To degrease, abrade metal with emery paper. Treat copper by placing in a general pickle solution (a 10% solution of sulphuric acid, safety pickle or alum).

2 Cover sterling or Britannia silver in neat nitric acid and swill gently until the metal appears white. (Fine silver does not need de-oxidizing.)

3 Brighten all metals with a brass brush and washing-up liquid (liquid soap) solution. Dry on a clean cotton cloth, taking care not to touch the area to be enamelled with your fingers.

Soldering When designing a piece, aim to have as little soldering as possible under enamelling, to avoid the enamel discolouring or bubbling. During soldering, support the work with binding wire or tweezers if necessary, so that the sections do not move while you work.

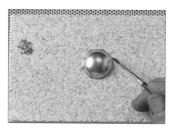

1 Apply borax-based flux (auflux) to the joint. Cut a length of solder into small pieces and apply them to the joint using a brush laden with flux.

2 Play a flame over the whole piece to dry the flux without letting it bubble. When it is crystalline, direct the flame on the joint to heat both sides evenly until the solder melts.

3 Cool the piece then immerse in general pickle solution to remove fire stain and flux. Rinse the metal under running water, dry and remove any excess solder using a file.

Acid etching

After metal has been pickled and brightened, the surface can be etched ready to take enamel. Wear protective gloves and goggles when working with etchants, and use only brass or plastic tweezers.

1 To protect the back and edges of the prepared metal from the etchant, paint on three coats of stopping-out varnish. Leave to dry.

2 Paint the design on the front in varnish. The acid will etch away any areas that are not covered by varnish. Alternatively, cover the whole surface then remove the varnish from areas to be etched using a fine steel point.

3 Place the piece in a solution of 1 part neat nitric acid to 3 parts cold water in an open plastic container. Stroke away bubbles using a feather. Remove the piece when the required depth of etching is achieved (not more than one-third of the thickness of the metal).

4 Rinse the metal under running water, using a glass fibre brush to clean off the etchant. Remove any remaining varnish with brush cleaner and brighten the surface by cleaning with a brass brush and washing-up (dishwasher) liquid solution.

Photo-etching

Instead of painting the design on the metal, you can create a resist photographically. Draw a high-contrast black and white design, twice final size, with all lines at least 0.7mm/0.03in thick. (The black areas represent the metal and the white the enamelled areas.) Reduce the design to actual size on a photocopier.

Photocopy the reduced image at high contrast on a sheet of PnP blue acetate film, emulsion side up. Iron the resist on to the prepared metal, using a cotton/dry iron setting, to fix the image. Paint the back and edges of the piece with stopping-out varnish and etch with nitric acid as above.

Preparing enamel

Intricate designs and curved surfaces usually require the enamel to be more finely ground than large, flat pieces. To start, break up enamel nuggets by wrapping them in a cotton cloth and hitting with a hammer.

1 In a clean mortar, cover a small piece of enamel with purified water and hit it with the pestle until it resembles granulated sugar. Add another piece and repeat until you have enough for your project, adding water to cover if necessary.

2 Hold the pestle upright and grind firmly with a circular action until the enamel feels soft and powdery. Allow to settle, then pour off the water. Rinse until the water runs clear and the enamel is uniform in colour.

Wet application of enamel Pour the rinsed enamel into a palette and keep covered with water. It should be applied in several thin layers rather than one thick one, using a fine artist's brush, goose quill or stainless-steel point.

1 Pour off excess water and tip the palette so the waterline lies across the enamel. Pick up the enamel from just above the water. Apply evenly to the metal, pushing it well into any corners as it will draw back during firing.

2 Draw off any excess water by touching the edge of the metal with a clean cotton cloth. Do not touch the enamel itself as this will impair the finish of the fired surface. Fire the piece as soon as possible.

Dry application of enamel Once the enamel is ground and cleaned, pour off as much water as possible then spread the paste on cooking foil, cover and leave to dry on top of the kiln or a radiator.

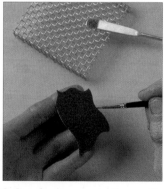

1 Having prepared the metal by degreasing and de-oxidizing it, cover the area to be enamelled with a layer of enamel gum, applying it thinly with a brush. Place it on a sheet of paper.

2 Place the enamel powder in a sieve (strainer), hold it about 5cm/2in above the metal and tap gently. Lift the metal and clean any excess enamel from the sides with a fine brush. Place the piece on a trivet ready for firing.

3 On subsequent layers, if you wish, you can paint a design in the enamel gum, or use a stencil, before sifting the enamel. Alternatively, you can scratch a design in the enamel before firing, using a paintbrush or steel point.

Kiln firing   The temperature of the kiln should be about 900°C/1,650°F for small items. Place the piece to be fired near the kiln to remove any moisture. Put it in the kiln when the surface looks crystalline and no more steam rises.

1 The enamel will lighten when it is first placed in the kiln and the metal will oxidize. Later the enamel will darken, still appearing matt (flat) and granular.

2 The enamel will then start to melt and look uneven but shiny.

3 Fully fired enamel looks smooth and shiny. If it pulls away from the edges and discolours, then it is overfired. It is best to underfire the first layers slightly and keep the highest firing for the last.

Finishing   In order to achieve a smooth finish, the enamel needs to be abraded and polished after it has been fired. Depending on the shape of the piece you can use carborundum stones, diamond-impregnated paper or silicon carbide (wet and dry) paper, all of which are readily available in a range of grades.

1 Abrade the enamel using plenty of water and working in all directions. The surface will appear matt, showing up any low spots that may need to be filled with enamel and re-fired. Remove the residue with a glass fibre brush and water. Dry with a cotton cloth and do not touch the surface.

2 Re-fire the piece. When it is cool, place in a general pickle solution. Polish the enamel and metal with a paste of pumice powder and water, using a felt polishing mop either by hand or using a polishing motor running at 900–1200 rpm.

Make a set of these wonderful buttons in any size, to suit a special garment. They are decorated with a delicate scattering of tiny gold or silver shapes and dabs of brightly coloured enamel.

Multicoloured Buttons

you will need

drill

20 gauge/0.8mm/0.03in copper discs, size as required

pumice powder

toothbrush

pestle and mortar

enamel gum

artist's brushes

sieve (strainer)

opaque enamels in various colours

kiln and firing equipment

stilts to fit buttons

scissors

flat gold or silver *cloisonné* wire

hole punch

34 gauge/0.16mm/0.006in silver sheet

1 Drill two large holes side by side in the centre of each copper disc.

2 Clean the copper with pumice powder and water, using a toothbrush.

3 Grind and clean the enamels. Lightly apply enamel gum to the back of each button. Using a sieve, apply enamel, using different colours. Leave to dry, then fire in the kiln. Clean the fronts and repeat, supporting the buttons on stilts. Apply a second layer of enamel if necessary.

4 Using scissors, cut tiny squares and triangles off the end of the gold or silver wire. Punch holes in the silver sheet to make tiny circles.

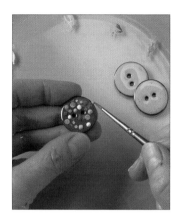

5 Decorate the buttons with the metal shapes, secured with enamel gum. Moisten a little enamel powder with enamel gum to make a paste, then apply to the buttons in small dots using a fine paintbrush.

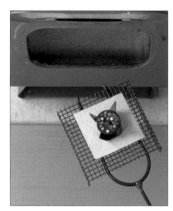

6 Support the buttons on stilts and fire in the kiln until the enamel dots have fused. When cool, remove oxidation by cleaning with pumice powder and water, using a toothbrush.

This stylized – and stylish – bird, who carries a heart in his beak, is enamelled on silver to make an attractive lapel pin. Try varying the colours, to go with different outfits.

Bird Lapel Pin

you will need

tracing paper and pencil

double-sided tape

16 gauge/1.3mm/0.05in silver sheet

piercing saw

drill

silver tube and wire (inner diameter of tube to match thickness of wire)

soldering equipment

hard solder

pliers

burnisher

pestle and mortar

opaque enamels: white, bright red and mid-blue

black transparent enamel

enamel gum

glass fibre brush

trivet

fine artist's brush or quill

kiln and firing equipment

diamond-impregnated paper

fine-grade silicon carbide (wet and dry) paper

nail buffer

epoxy resin glue

1 Trace the template at the back of the book. Stick the tracing on to the silver sheet using double-sided tape and cut out with a piercing saw. Drill a hole so that you can thread the saw blade through to reach the area between the heart and the bird.

2 Cut and file a piece of silver tube 5mm/¼in long. Solder it in an upright position on to the back, using hard solder. For the pin, cut a 6cm/2½in length of silver wire. Bend with pliers 5mm/¼in in from one end to make a right angle.

3 Burnish the edges of the bird to provide a "grip" for the enamel to adhere to. Grind and clean the enamels then add a drop of enamel gum to each and water to cover.

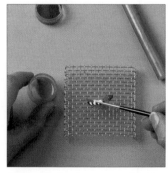

4 Degrease the silver using a glass fibre brush and water. Place the bird on a trivet and apply the enamel using a paintbrush or quill.

5 Place the bird on top of the kiln to dry, then fire it. Apply two more layers of enamel, firing each layer.

6 Abrade the enamel with diamond-impregnated paper and water. Smooth with damp silicon carbide paper and rinse. Leave the enamel surface matt (flat). Buff the plain silver side of the bird. Glue the pin into the tube using epoxy resin glue.

Create your own design for these earrings, using transparent enamels in pale, clear colours. The holes should be large enough to allow the light to shine through but small enough to hold the wet enamel.

Plique-à-jour Earrings

you will need

pencil and paper

16 gauge/1.2mm/0.05in silver sheet

piercing saw

drill

tweezers

brass brush

washing-up (dishwashing) liquid

pestle and mortar

transparent enamels in pale colours

fine artist's paintbrush

trivet

kiln and firing equipment

sheet of mica (optional)

diamond-impregnated paper

pumice powder

jeweller's rouge

earring wires

1 Draw your design on paper and attach it to the silver sheet. Using a piercing saw, cut out the shapes. Drill holes where the enamel will appear, then insert the saw into each hole and cut out. Use the saw to smooth the edges from front and back.

2 Shape the silver with a pair of tweezers. Clean the silver with a brass brush and washing-up liquid solution. Grind and wash the transparent enamels.

3 Using a fine paintbrush, apply the wet enamel into the spaces in the earrings. Practise getting the right consistency – if the enamel is too wet, it will fall through the holes.

4 Fire while the enamel is still damp. Beginners may find it easier to fire on a sheet of mica. Remove from the kiln as soon as the enamel begins to melt. Refill the holes if the enamel has pulled to the side, and re-fire.

5 When the holes are completely filled, abrade the earrings with diamond-impregnated paper. Rinse and fire again. Polish with pumice powder and water, then jeweller's rouge. Attach the earring wires.

A central band of enamel with a simple photo-etched design makes an elegant decoration for this silver ring. You can omit the final firing if you would prefer a matt (flat) finish to the enamel.

Banded Ring

1 Photocopy the template provided at the back of the book to produce a high contrast black-and-white design for photo-etching on to the ring blank (see Enamelling Techniques section). Place the ring blank in a clamp and shorten it to the required finger size by filing the ends. Smooth the sides with a file and then emery paper.

2 Using a pair of pliers, carefully bend in the ends to form a ring. The shape doesn't need to be perfectly round at this stage. Now file the ends of the ring so that they will meet exactly and make a good joint.

3 Twist binding wire around the ring. Solder the joint with hard solder, then quench in cold water and dry. Remove the wire, then pickle the ring.

4 File off the excess solder. Place the ring on a ring mandrel and tap with a mallet until it is perfectly round. Remove firestain by placing the ring in nitric acid, and then rinse. Now, using a brass brush, brush the silver with water and washing-up liquid solution until it is shiny.

5 Grind and clean the enamels, then add a drop of enamel gum and water to cover. Apply carefully to the etched band using either a fine paintbrush or a quill. Leave the enamel to dry, then fire in the kiln. Now leave to cool.

6 Using medium-grade diamond-impregnated paper and water, abrade the enamel until you expose the silver design. Rinse the ring and apply more enamel to any shiny areas of the design then repeat the firing and abrading. Polish with fine-grade diamond-impregnated paper, rinse then fire again to glaze the surface if you wish. Leave to cool then pickle, rinse and polish the ring.

Choose transparent enamels in watery colours for these fish, set against a deep blue sea. The photo-etched design needs to be reversed for the second blank so that the cufflinks make a symmetrical pair.

Fishy Cufflinks

you will need

silver cufflink blanks to fit the template or 17 gauge/1.1mm/0.045in silver sheet

PnP blue acetate film and iron

piercing saw

ring clamp

file

emery stick (board)

wooden doming block

wooden doming punch

mallet

nitric acid

brass brush

washing-up (dishwashing) liquid

pestle and mortar

transparent enamels

enamel gum

fine artist's paintbrush or quill

trivet

kiln and firing equipment

diamond-impregnated paper

emery paper

soldering equipment

easy solder

cufflink findings

general pickle solution

pumice powder or felt polishing mop

(optional)

1 Photocopy the template at the back of the book to produce a high contrast black-and-white design. This needs to be photo-etched on to the cufflink blanks or silver sheet (see Enamelling Techniques section). Cut out the cufflink shapes with a piercing saw, place each one in a clamp and file the edges straight. Polish the edges with a fine emery stick.

2 Place each cufflink in the doming block. Tap the silver with a doming punch and mallet to create the desired domed shape.

3 De-oxidize the silver by placing each piece in nitric acid for a few minutes and then rinsing in cold water. Using a brass brush, scrub with washing-up liquid solution until the metal is shiny.

4 Grind and clean the enamels and add a drop of enamel gum to each. Apply the wet enamels to the design, using a paintbrush. Do not mix the colours. Leave to dry, then fire in the kiln until molten. Leave to cool.

5 Using a medium-grade diamond-impregnated paper and some water, abrade the enamel to expose the silver design, and then rinse. Apply more enamel and repeat. Polish with fine-grade paper, then fire again. Leave to cool. Remove the oxidation with emery paper.

6 Melt easy solder on to the foot of each finding and solder to the back of the cufflink. Cool, then pickle and polish the cufflinks.

The design for these jolly earrings is transferred to a pair of silver blanks using the photo-etching technique. Remember to apply it to the second earring in reverse so that the finished pieces are symmetrical.

Stargazer Earrings

you will need

silver earring blanks, to fit the template, or 17 gauge/1.1mm/0.045in

silver sheet

PnP blue acetate film and iron

piercing saw

ring clamp

file

fine emery stick (board)

masking tape

centre punch

drill

wooden doming block

wooden doming punch

mallet

nitric acid

brass brush

washing-up (dishwashing) liquid

pestle and mortar

transparent enamels

enamel gum

fine artist's paintbrush or quill

trivet

kiln and firing equipment

diamond-impregnated paper

emery paper

general pickle solution

pumice powder or felt polishing mop (optional)

earring wires

pliers

◀ **1** Photocopy the template provided at the back of the book to produce a high contrast black-and-white design the size of the finished earrings. This design needs to be photo-etched on to the earring blanks or silver sheet (see Enamelling Techniques section). Now cut out the earring shapes with a piercing saw, place each earring in a clamp and file the edges straight.

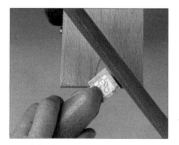

2 Polish the edges of the earrings with a fine emery stick to remove any scratch marks left after filing.

3 Secure each earring in turn on your work surface with masking tape. Centre punch and drill a hole in the top edge for the wires.

4 Place each earring in the doming block. Tap the silver with a doming punch and mallet to create the desired domed shape.

5 De-oxidize the earrings by placing them in nitric acid for a few minutes, then rinsing in cold water. Using a brass brush, brush with washing-up liquid solution until shiny. Hold by the edges only.

6 Grind and clean the enamels, then add a drop of enamel gum and water to cover. Apply the wet enamels, using a paintbrush or quill. Take care not to mix the colours.

7 Leave the earrings to dry, then fire in the kiln until the enamel is molten. Leave to cool. Apply further layers of enamel and fire each time until the cells of the design appear full.

8 Using medium-grade diamond-impregnated paper and water, abrade the enamel until you expose the silver design. Apply more enamel to any shiny areas, then repeat the firing, abrading and rinsing. Refire to glaze the surface.

9 Leave to cool. Abrade the back of the earrings with emery paper, and then place in pickle solution to remove oxidation.

10 Polish both sides of the earrings if desired. Carefully open the ear wires with the jewellery pliers and insert through the drilled holes. Squeeze the wires gently together to close.

This jaunty character is created by photo-etching the design on to a square brooch, leaving a generous frame of silver, then filling the etching with enamel. Follow the colours shown here or choose your own.

Pet Hound Brooch

you will need

silver brooch blank, to fit the template, or 17 gauge/ 1.1mm/0.045in silver sheet

PnP blue acetate film and iron

piercing saw

ring clamp

file

fine emery stick (board)

wooden doming block

wooden doming punch

mallet

nitric acid

brass brush

washing-up (dishwashing) liquid

pestle and mortar

transparent enamels

enamel gum

fine artist's paintbrush or quill

trivet

kiln and firing equipment

diamond-impregnated paper

emery paper

soldering equipment

brooch catch, joint and pin

easy solder

pickle solution

toothbrush

pumice powder

parallel (channel-type) pliers

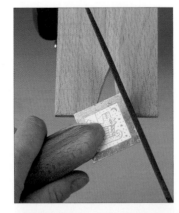

◀ **1** Photocopy the template at the back of the book to produce a high contrast black-and-white design. The design needs to be photo-etched on to the brooch blank or silver sheet (see Enamelling Techniques section) and the template should be copied at the actual size of the finished brooch. If you are using sheet silver, cut out the brooch shape with a piercing saw, place the silver in a clamp and file the edges straight.

2 Polish the edges of the brooch with a fine emery stick to remove any scratch marks left by the file.

3 Place the annealed brooch blank in the doming block. Tap lightly with the punch and mallet until the piece is slightly domed.

4 De-oxidize the silver by placing in nitric acid for a few minutes then rinsing in cold water. Using a brass brush, brush with water and washing-up liquid until shiny. Hold by the edges only.

5 Grind and clean the enamels, then add a drop of enamel gum and water to cover. Apply the wet enamels using a paintbrush or quill. Leave to dry on top of the kiln.

6 Fire in the kiln until the enamel is molten. Leave to cool. Apply further layers of enamel, firing in between each layer, until the cells appear full.

7 Using medium-grade diamond-impregnated paper and water, abrade the enamel until you expose the silver design. Apply more enamel to any shiny areas, then repeat the firing, abrading and rinsing. Refire to glaze the surface.

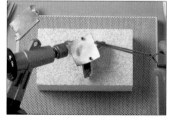

8 Leave to cool then remove the oxidation from the back of the brooch with emery paper.

9 Place the brooch upside down on a trivet so that only the edges touch. Solder on the brooch catch and joint with easy solder. Leave to cool, then place in pickle solution. Rinse, then clean using a toothbrush and a paste of pumice powder.

10 Polish the brooch if desired. Cut the brooch pin to length and place it in the ball joint. Using parallel pliers, squeeze the joint carefully to hold the pin in place.

Decorate this photo-etched pendant with as many transparent enamel colours as you like, including several shades of green, to evoke the atmosphere of a sunny summer garden in full bloom.

Flower Pendant

you will need

silver pendant blank, to fit the template, or 17 gauge/
1.1mm/0.045in silver sheet

PnP blue acetate film and iron

piercing saw

ring clamp

file

emery stick (board)

wooden doming block

wooden doming punch

mallet

nitric acid

brass brush

washing-up (dishwashing) liquid

pestle and mortar

transparent enamels

enamel gum

fine artist's paintbrush or quill

trivet

kiln and firing equipment

diamond-impregnated paper

fine-grade emery paper

small piece of silver wire

soldering equipment

easy solder

tweezers

pickle solution

pumice powder or felt

polishing mop (optional)

1 Photocopy the template at the back of the book to produce a high contrast black-and-white design. Photo-etch the design on to the silver. Cut out the shape with a piercing saw and file the edges until circular, then smooth with an emery stick.

2 Shape the pendant in a doming block, using a doming punch and mallet. To de-oxidize the silver, place it in nitric acid for a few minutes then rinse with water. Scrub with a brass brush and washing-up liquid solution.

3 Grind and clean the enamels, then add a drop of enamel gum to each and water to cover. Apply the wet enamels using a paintbrush or quill. Take care not to mix the colours. Leave to dry, then fire in the kiln. Leave to cool.

4 Using diamond-impregnated paper and water, abrade the enamel to expose the silver design, then rinse. Apply more enamel to the shiny areas, then repeat. Abrade the enamel and fire again.

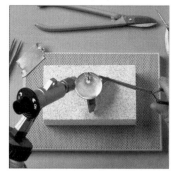

5 Leave to cool, then remove the oxidation from the back of the pendant by rubbing with fine-grade emery paper.

6 Bend the wire into a loop and melt easy solder on to the ends. To attach the loop to the pendant, hold it in tweezers against the back of the pendant and heat the ends until they join. Leave to cool, then pickle and polish the pendant as desired.

In *cloisonné* work, fine wires are laid down in a pattern to make cells for the enamels. The triangles in this design echo the outline of the silver mounts, and small curls of silver wire add a final flourish.

Cloisonné Earrings

ᵠᵠᵠᵠᵠ

you will need

piercing saw

18 gauge/1mm/0.04in silver sheet

tracing paper and pencil

24 gauge/0.5mm/0.02in silver sheet

double-sided tape

file

fine emery stick (board)

metal snips

16 gauge/1.2mm/0.05in round

silver wire

pliers

soldering equipment

hard solder

swage block

wooden doming punch

mallet

silver earring posts and backs

burnisher

glass fibre brush

scissors

28 gauge/0.3mm/0.013in silver

cloisonné wire

fine artist's paintbrush

enamel gum

trivet

pestle and mortar

transparent enamels: turquoise, light

amber, bright blue

quill (optional)

kiln and firing equipment

diamond-impregnated paper

silicon carbide (wet and dry) paper

nail buffer

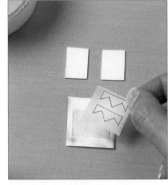

1 Cut two 16 x 22mm/⅝ x ⅞in rectangles from the thicker silver sheet. To create the earring tops, trace template 1 from the back of the book. Attach the tracing to the thinner silver sheet with double-sided tape. Cut out twice, using a piercing saw.

2 File the two cut-out earring tops and smooth the edges with a fine emery stick. Cut two lengths of round silver wire and bend into matching curls with pliers, following the shape of template 2.

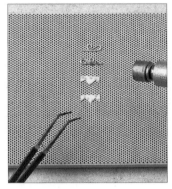

3 Melt hard solder on to the back of the earring tops and the straight part of the wire design.

4 Position the earring tops and the wire designs, solder side down, in place on top of the silver rectangles. Flux the metal and rerun the solder with the blowtorch.

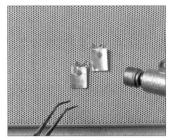

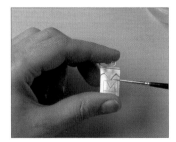

5 Place each earring face down in a swage block. Lay a wooden doming punch along its length and tap with a mallet to create a curved shape.

6 Solder the earposts to the earrings with hard solder. Burnish the edges of the earrings to provide a "grip" for the enamel to adhere to. Clean the metal with a glass fibre brush and water.

7 Cut the required lengths of *cloisonné* wire and lay on each earring in a geometric pattern, using a fine paint-brush dipped in a little enamel gum. Place on a trivet.

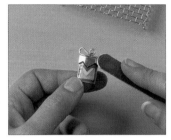

8 Grind and clean the enamels. Add a few drops of enamel gum and water to cover. Using a fine paintbrush or quill, apply the enamel to the cells between the *cloisonné* wires.

9 Allow to dry on top of the kiln, then fire. Apply two more layers of enamel, firing twice more. The enamel should now reach the top of the wire.

10 Abrade the enamel with diamond-impregnated paper and water to expose any covered *cloisonné* wire. Rinse and re-fire. Smooth the silver with silicon carbide paper and finish with a buffer.

A delicately textured surface is created by impressing silver with watercolour paper then applying two enamel colours and flux to create a marbled effect. Small shards of silver foil are fired between the layers.

Shield Earrings

you will need

scissors

rough-textured watercolour paper

20 gauge/0.8mm/0.03in silver sheet

blow torch

general pickle

rolling mill

tracing paper and pencil

double-sided tape

piercing saw

file

drill

burnisher

brass brush

washing-up (dishwashing) liquid

clean cotton cloth

pestle and mortar

transparent enamels: mauve and pale yellow-green

fine artist's paintbrush or quill

borax-based flux (auflux)

trivet

kiln and firing equipment

craft (utility) knife

scraps of fine silver foil

diamond file or carborundum stone

silicon carbide (wet and dry) paper

earring wires

round-nosed (snub-nosed) pliers

2 small domed silver discs

2 frosted beads

2 bead pins

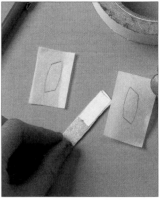

1 Cut a piece of watercolour paper slightly larger than the silver sheet. Anneal the silver and remove the oxidation (see page 204). Place the silver sheet on top of the paper and run them together through the rolling mill, with the rollers tightly clamped down.

2 Trace the templates at the back of the book to create the main body of both earrings. Attach the tracings to the silver with double-sided tape.

3 Using a piercing saw, cut out the shield shapes. File the edges. Drill small holes in two matching diagonally opposed corners of each shield. ▶

4 Burnish around the sides to raise an edge to contain the enamel. Now scrub the shields with a brass brush and washing-up liquid solution, rinse and dry.

5 Grind and clean the enamels. Using a fine paintbrush or quill, wet-apply the flux and mauve enamel randomly to create a marbled effect. Ensure that they do not run into the drilled holes.

6 Draw off any excess water with a clean cotton cloth. Fire the first layer in the kiln and leave to cool.

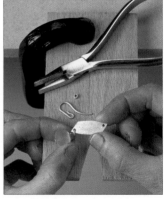

7 Using a craft knife, cut small jagged pieces of silver foil. Moisten the fired enamel with water and apply the pieces of foil in a broken S-shaped line, using a damp paintbrush. Draw off any excess water with a cloth. Wet-apply a spot of flux to one corner of each shield and fire. When the flux has fused, the foil will have adhered to the enamel.

8 When cool, wet-apply the yellow-green enamel over the foil. Apply flux to all other areas and fire. Finally, fire a last layer using flux only.

9 Abrade the fired surface using a diamond file, then rinse and fill in any low spots with more enamel, and re-fire. Remove excess enamel from the edges then finish all sides of the shields with fine-grade silicon carbide paper and rinse. Attach the earring wires to the holes at the top of the earrings and add discs, frosted beads and bead pins to the bottom.

The slender elegant shape of this pendant is reminiscent of Art Deco jewellery. A little *cloisonné* detailing has been added within the delicate silver frame, matching its geometric design.

Triangular Pendant

you will need

tracing paper, pencil and ruler

24 gauge/0.5mm/0.02in silver sheet

double-sided tape

piercing saw

drill

file

soldering equipment

hard solder

18 gauge/1mm/0.04in silver sheet

swage block

wooden doming punch

mallet

doming block

silver chain

glass fibre brush

trivet

small, sharp scissors

28 gauge/0.3mm/0.013in fine silver *cloisonné* wire

fine artist's paintbrush

enamel gum

pestle and mortar

transparent enamels: turquoise, light amber, bright blue and grey

quill (optional)

kiln and firing equipment

diamond-impregnated paper

silicon carbide (wet and dry) paper

nail buffer

silver necklace clasp

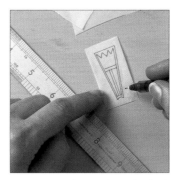

1 Trace template 1 from the back of the book on to tracing paper. Attach the tracing to the 24 gauge silver sheet with double-sided tape.

2 Cut out the outer shape with a piercing saw. Drill holes to allow access for the saw blade and cut out the inner parts of the design. File and smooth the inside edges.

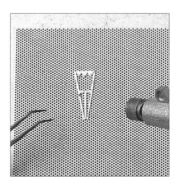

3 Melt some small pieces of hard solder on to the back of the pierced pendant shape.

4 Place the pierced shape, solder side down, on the 18 gauge silver sheet. Place hard solder around the outside and solder the pierced shape to the sheet. If any solder runs into the areas that are to be enamelled, it should be removed.

▶

5 Following template 2, saw off the excess silver sheet, leaving a tab at the top for a loop and a circle at the bottom. Do not file the edges. Drill a hole in the centre of both tab and circle.

6 Place the pendant face down in a swage block. Using the doming punch on its side, tap it into a curved shape using a mallet.

7 Cut out a circle of silver sheet fractionally larger than the circle at the bottom of the pendant. Place in a doming block and create a small dome. File the base of the dome flat.

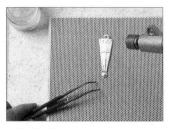

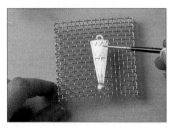

8 Solder the dome on to the circle at the bottom of the pendant with hard solder. Use a piercing saw to make the opening in the tab large enough to take your silver chain. Clean the metal with a glass fibre brush and water. Place on a trivet.

9 Cut the required lengths of *cloisonné* wire and place in the recesses in the pendant to form a geometric pattern, using a fine paintbrush dipped in enamel gum.

10 Grind and clean the enamels. Add a few drops of enamel gum and water to cover. Apply the enamel to the cells, using a fine paintbrush or quill.

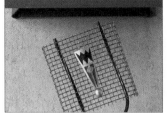

11 Leave the enamel to dry on top of the kiln, then fire. Apply two more thin layers of enamel, firing each time.

12 Abrade the enamel with diamond-impregnated paper and water. Clean with a glass fibre brush and water. Re-fire. File the pendant edges. Smooth the silver areas with silicon carbide paper. Finish with a buffer. Thread the chain through the loop. Solder on a clasp and polish.

Wirework

Available in a variety of thicknesses and strengths, wire can be used in a multitude of ways to create imaginatively decorative yet functional items for the home. You can make elegant candle sconces and candlesticks, unusual tablemats and napkin rings, charming kitchen accessories and even a hanging lantern for the garden. The decorative potential of wire is boundless.

You can buy wire from good jewellery, craft and sculpture suppliers, as well as some hardware stores. There are also specialist wire suppliers, and electrical stores may also stock the materials you need.

Wire

ideal for outdoor use. Galvanized wire is hard, so does not bend easily. This wire is springy, so needs to be used with caution. Available in five gauges.

Garden wire

This is easy to manipulate as it is plastic-coated. It is perfect for kitchen or bathroom accessories because it is waterproof, long-lasting and colourful.

Pipe cleaners and paper clips (fasteners)

These less obvious wirework materials are great fun to work with.

Silver-plated copper wire

This wire is particularly well suited to jewellery making and fine wirework.

Straining wire

This strong, textured wire is made of strands of galvanized wire twisted together. Take care when using it.

Tinned copper wire

This is shiny and does not tarnish, so it is suitable for kitchenware.

Twisty wire tape

This thin, flat tape with a wire core comes in green for gardening and blue and white for household use.

Wire coat hangers

These are cheap and widely available.

Aluminium wire

This is a dull blue-grey colour. It is the easiest to work with because it is so soft and easy to bend.

Chicken wire

This is made from galvanized steel wire. Usually used for fencing and for animal pens, it comes with different-sized holes and in a range of widths. The projects in the book call for the smallest gauge. Chicken wire is easy to manipulate and inexpensive.

Copper wire

This has a warm colour and comes in different tempers (hardnesses). Soft copper wire is easy to work with and is available in a broad range of gauges.

Enamelled copper wire

Used in the electronics industry, this is available in a wide range of colours.

Galvanized wire

This is zinc-coated steel wire. The zinc coating prevents rusting, making it

The most important tools for wirework are a good pair of wire cutters and some pliers. General-purpose pliers will be sufficient for some projects, although round-nosed pliers are a worthwhile investment.

Equipment

Parallel (channel-type) pliers – These are suitable for straightening bent wire and for bending angles.

Round-nosed pliers – Also known as snub-nosed jewellery pliers, these can be used for many different crafts, as well as for repairing broken jewellery. Use to bend wire into tiny circles.

Rolling pin, wooden spoon, pencil, broom handle

Many household objects are useful to coil wire around.

Ruler or tape measure

Many projects require very accurate measurements to ensure a good result.

Scissors

Use to cut through thin wire.

Wire cutters

Choose cutters with good leverage and long handles.

Gardening gloves and goggles

These protect your skin and eyes when working with scratchy wire. Wear goggles when manipulating long lengths of wire, especially if the wire you are using is under tension.

Hammer

A hammer is useful for flattening the ends of cut lengths of wire.

Hand drills

Useful for twisting soft wires together.

Permanent marker pens

Use to mark measurements on wire.

Pliers

General-purpose pliers – These often have serrated jaws to give a strong grip. Place a piece of leather between the pliers and the wire to prevent any marking.

Needle-nosed pliers – These are very useful for reaching into difficult places and are the best pliers for working with chicken wire.

Wooden coat hangers

These can be used to twist galvanized wire together. Make sure the handle is secure and will not unscrew.

Wooden form

To bend strong wire into small circles use a wooden mould. Drill a screw into a piece of wood, but leave the head protruding from the wood. Bend the wire around the screw.

These instructions will help you with the basic wirework techniques used to make the projects in this chapter. Try to familiarize yourself with this section before embarking on any of the projects.

Wirework Techniques

Twisting wire This is a simple and effective way of joining two or more wires to add strength and texture to a design. Soft wires, such as copper, are easiest to twist, and using a hand drill speeds up the process. The harder wires, such as galvanized wire, require more effort. If you use a coat hanger to twist wires, choose the wooden type with a wire hook that revolves, ensuring that the handle is securely attached and will not unscrew.

Twisting hard wire

1 Cut a piece of wire three times as long as the required twisted length. Double the length of wire and loop it around a door handle or other secure point. Wrap the loose ends on one side of the coat hanger hook. Make sure you hold the wire horizontally, otherwise you may get an uneven twist.

▶ **3** To release the tension in the wire, hold the hanger firmly in one hand and grip its hook in the other. Quickly release your hold on the hanger, which will spin around a bit. Remove the wire from the handle and cut off the ends.

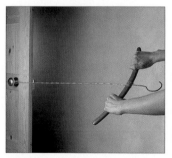

2 Keeping the wire taut, begin turning the coat hanger. Do not relax your grip as this may cause an uneven texture. Twist the wire to the degree required, taking care not to overtwist as the wire may snap.

Twisting soft wire

1 Double the lengths of wire to be twisted, by folding it in the middle. Two lengths have been used here, and you can use wires with different finishes. Loop the wires around a door handle and wrap the other ends with masking tape before securing them into the hand-drill chuck.

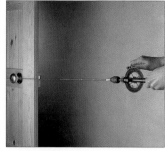

2 Keeping the wire taut, rotate the drill to twist the wire to the degree required. Start slowly at first so that you can gauge the tension. With soft wires there is no need to release the tension in the wire before removing them from the drill bit and trimming the ends.

Wrapping wire When wrapping wire, ideally the core wire should be both thicker and harder than the wrapping wire. Copper wire is the most suitable to use to wrap around a core. When cutting the core wire, remember to allow an excess length of at least 6.5cm/2½in to form a winding loop. The long lengths of soft wire used in wrapping can be unmanageable, so coil the wire first, as described in method B.

Method A

1 Using round-nosed (snub-nosed) pliers, make a loop at the end of the core wire. Neatly attach the wrapping wire to this loop.

2 Insert a pencil or other suitable object into the loop and use it as a winder. While winding, hold your thumb and index finger right up against the coil to ensure that the wire is closely wrapped.

Method B

1 Using round-nosed (snub-nosed) pliers, make a loop at the end of the core wire and bend the wire into the desired shape along half its length. Form a loop at the other end of the core wire and secure the wrapping wire to the loop. Insert a pencil into the loop and use it as a winder.

2 Wrap part of the wire, remove the pencil and coil the wire that has been wrapped. Now use this section as the winder. Use your hand to support the core wire from beneath, with the wrapping wire running between your fingers and thumb.

Tips for wrapping wire

When using wire from a skein, keep it on the floor with your foot holding it in place. This will help you achieve the necessary tension for wrapping the wire and prevent the wire skein from unravelling and knotting.

When using wire from a spool, it is easier if you insert a long stick through it and hold it in place with your feet. This will allow the spool to unwind quite freely while keeping the wire sufficiently taut.

Making coils

Coils are probably the most commonly used decorative device in wirework. They also have a practical use as they neaten and make safe what would otherwise be sharp ends. The flattened extended coil is a common structural and decorative device used in wirework. It is a quick and easy way to make the side walls of a container, for instance.

Open coils

1 Using round-nosed (snub-nosed) pliers, make a small loop at the end of the wire. Hold the loop in the pliers, place your thumb against the wire and draw the wire across it to form a curve. Use your thumb to supply the tension.

2 Use your eye to judge the space left between the rings of the coil. If the wire is thicker, you will need more tension to make the curve and it will be more difficult to make the curve evenly spaced.

3 Finally, carefully flatten the coil with parallel (channel-type) pliers. Bend the coil into shape carefully.

Closed coils

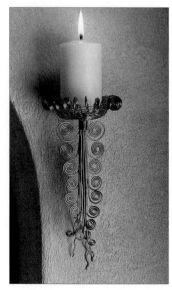

1 Using round-nosed (snub-nosed) pliers, make a small loop at the end of the wire.

2 Hold the loop securely with parallel (channel-type) pliers. Bend the wire around the loop until you have a coil of the size required. Keep adjusting the position of the pliers as you work.

Right: Ornate and stylish, wirework coils are surprisingly simple to make.

Flattened extended coils

1 Wrap the wire several times around a broomstick or other cylindrical object to give you a coil. If using galvanized wire, you need to brace your thumb firmly against it.

2 After removing the coil from the broomstick, splay out the loops one by one, holding them firmly between your fingers and thumbs.

3 Keep splaying out the loops until the whole coil has been flattened. The loops will now look more oval than round. You can stretch the coil further to open the loops if you wish.

Weaving Many basketwork and textile techniques can be applied to wirework. Knitting and lacemaking techniques can also be employed with great success. Fine enamelled copper wire is especially suitable for weaving as it is soft and pliable and comes in a wide range of colours. Of the techniques described here, methods B and C will give a more closely woven and tidier finish than method A. Method A is the simplest.

Method A

The quickest and easiest way to weave is to wind the wire in and out of the struts to create an open texture.

Method B

Pass the wire under each strut before looping it around the strut to create ridges in the weave.

Method C

Weave around the struts by passing the wire over each strut and looping it around the wire to create a smooth, closely woven surface. This result is similar to method B but the rib will be on the outside.

These monogrammed clothes hangers make lovely gifts, or a charming gesture in a guest's bedroom. The instructions show how to make the hanger as well as the decoration.

Monogrammed Clothes Hanger

you will need
galvanized wire, 2mm/¹⁄₁₃in,
1mm/¹⁄₂₅in and 0.3mm/¹⁄₈₃in thick
ruler or tape measure
wire cutters
large pliers
beads
round-nosed (snub-nosed) pliers

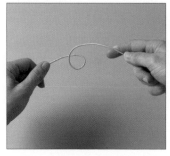

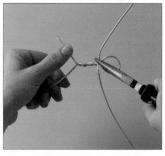

1 Cut a 140cm/55in length of the 2mm/¹⁄₁₃in galvanized wire. Bend it to form a loop 25cm/10in from one end, as shown.

2 Cross the two ends over at the loop and, holding them at the crossing-point with pliers, twist the two ends together for 5cm/2in.

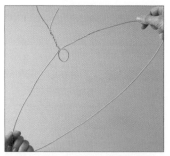

3 Above the twist, trim off the short end and shape the longer end to form the hook. Holding the circle of wire with the hook at the top, pull out the sides to form the hanger shape.

4 Using 1mm/¹⁄₂₅in galvanized wire, shape the initial letter for the centre of the hanger following the relevant template from the alphabet at the back of the book.

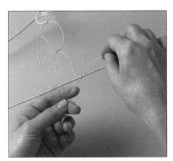

5 Bind the letter to the hanger at the top and bottom using the 0.3mm/⅙₃in galvanized wire.

6 With 1mm/½₅in wire, make the decorative shapes using the templates at the back of the book as a guide. Thread beads on to the ends of the wires, then twist into shape using round-nosed pliers.

7 Attach the shapes to the main frame in the order of the numbers shown on the template at the back of the book. Bind each one to the top and bottom of the hanger, using fine wire as before.

This unusual fly swatter is simple to make and extremely effective. It is designed to resemble a giant flower, and is an attractive addition to the kitchen or conservatory.

Flower Fly Swatter

you will need
straightened wire coat hanger
wire cutters
pliers
broom handle
ruler or tape measure
wooden ball, 2.5cm/1in diameter
paper
pencil
plastic mesh
scissors
cotton knitting yarn
needle

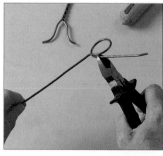

1 Cut the hook off the coat hanger. To form the flower centre, using pliers, bend one end of the wire and form a loop using a broom handle to bend the wire around. Trim.

2 To form the handle of the fly swatter, measure down 45cm/18in from the top of the loop and bend a 90° angle. Turn this end around the broom handle twice, then bend at 90° again and cut off, leaving a 4cm/1½in length parallel with the stem. Twist the end of the wire around the stem. Open the double loop and insert the wooden ball.

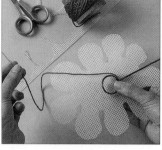

3 Enlarge the flower template at the back of the book to the required size. Trace it on to the plastic mesh, and cut out neatly. Centre the top loop of the wire stem on the flower shape and oversew firmly in place with cotton yarn.

A quirky design using coloured, plastic-coated wire makes a holder for a glass and four toothbrushes that will get you smiling in the morning. Glass beads add colourful decoration.

Toothbrush Holder

you will need

glass

plastic-coated steel wire, 1mm/¹/₂₅in thick

ruler or tape measure

wire cutters

glass beads, 5mm/¹/₅in

pen

all-purpose instant glue

1 Select a glass that is wider at the top than the bottom. Cut a 1m/40in length of wire and circle the glass with it, twisting the ends to secure. Twist one end of the wire firmly around the other, forming two loops on opposite sides to each other as you do so.

2 Thread eight glass beads on to the straight wire and twist the second wire between them to hold them in place and create a solid spine. Form two loops with the ends of the wires to make a heart. Twist the ends together at the base of the heart and trim off any excess wire.

3 To make the toothbrush holders, cut two 30cm/12in lengths of wire and then coil the central part of each one tightly around the glass.

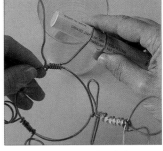

4 Coil the loose ends of the wires around a large pen to make four circles large enough to hold your toothbrush. Glue beads to the wire ends as a finishing touch.

Made from galvanized wire, this practical yet decorative accessory for the kitchen will co-ordinate with any style of kitchen decor. You could make a set of trivets in different shapes and sizes.

Heart-shaped Trivet

you will need
galvanized wire, 2mm/¹⁄₁₃in thick
wire cutters
ruler or tape measure
broom handle
pliers

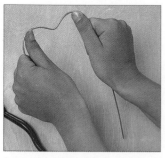

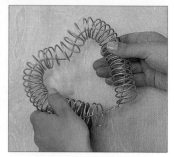

1 Cut a 50cm/20in length of wire, and form it into a heart shape by bending the wire in the centre to form the dip in the top of the heart. At the ends, make hooks to join the two ends of the wire together.

2 Make a coil by tightly and evenly wrapping more wire round a broom handle 50 times. Make hooks in the ends in the same way as before.

3 Thread the coil over the heart. Connect the ends of the heart by crimping the hooked ends together with pliers. Manipulate the coil, to make it sit evenly around the heart, before joining and crimping the ends together with pliers.

This clever little device made of two recycled coat hangers will give your rolling pin its own place on the kitchen wall, looking decorative as well as being out of the way.

Rolling Pin Holder

you will need
galvanized wire, 2mm/¹⁄₁₃in thick
wire cutters
ruler or tape measure
screwdriver
pliers
fine brass picture-hanging wire

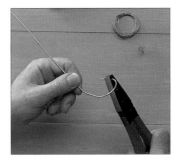

1 Cut two 75cm/30in lengths of the galvanized wire. Find the middle of one length and then bend it around a screwdriver handle to make a loop. Twist the two halves six times.

2 Using the pliers, curl the two ends of the wire forwards. The curls form the handle that holds the rolling pin, so check the fit as you work.

3 Twist the second length of wire into a heart shape – bend it sharply in the middle, then bring the ends down in opposite directions so that they cross over. Curl the ends.

4 Using short lengths of brass picture-hanging wire, bind the two lengths together at the points shown. Place your rolling pin between the curled hooks to judge the width needed.

Organize your desk with this smart wire stationery set. The pen pot and note holder are modern wire sculptures, and the notebook has a matching motif. Complete the set with designer paper clips.

Desk Accessories

you will need

paper

pencil

galvanized wire, 2mm/¹⁄₁₃in, 3mm/¹⁄₈in and 1mm/¹⁄₂₅in thick

wire cutters

long-nosed pliers

ruler or tape measure

soldering iron, solder and flux

florist's wire

scissors

thick cardboard

hardback notebook

craft (utility) knife

cutting mat

bradawl or awl

coloured paper

PVA (white) glue

1 Enlarge the spiral, triangle and flower templates from the back of the book to the required size. Cut lengths of the 2mm/¹⁄₁₃in galvanized wire with wire cutters and then use long-nosed pliers to bend the lengths of wire so that they match the spiral, triangle and flower designs. Set the wire shapes aside.

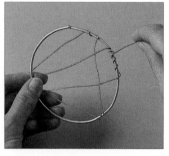

2 To make the pen pot, cut three 30cm/12in lengths of the 3mm/¹⁄₈in galvanized wire and bend them into circles. Use a soldering iron to join the ends. Stretch some lengths of florist's wire across the centre of one of the rings to form the foundations for the base of the pen pot. Wrap the ends of the florist's wire around the ring to secure.

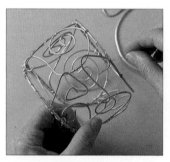

3 Using 1mm/¹⁄₂₅in wire, bind several shapes to the base and to each other to form the sides. Bind on another ring and repeat. Add the third ring to make the top and cut out and insert a circle of thick cardboard in the bottom.

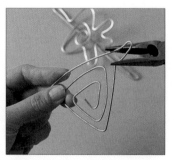

4 Repeat for the note holder, making two squares for the top and base. To make a paper clip, cut a 35cm/14in length of 3mm/¹⁄₈in wire and bend one end to match one of the template shapes.

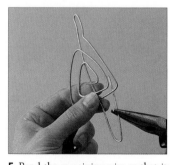

5 Bend the remaining wire so that it runs down behind the centre of the shape and extends below it, as shown. Take the end and bend it back on itself to form a large paper clip (fastener).

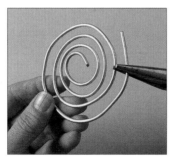

6 For the notebook, use a craft knife to cut a square from the front cover of a hardback notebook. Pierce a small hole halfway along each side of the window using a bradawl or awl.

7 Bend a length of 3mm/⅛in wire into a spiral shape to fit the window in the book cover.

8 Stick a sheet of coloured paper to the inside of the cover. Place the spiral inside the window then bind it to the book using florist's wire.

Extremely useful, bottle carriers can be quite hard to find. This version is made from thick galvanized wire formed into a clover leaf shape and holds three bottles.

Bottle Carrier

you will need

galvanized gardening wire, 2mm/¹⁄₁₃in
and 0.8mm/¹⁄₃₁in thick
ruler or tape measure
wire cutters
bottle
general-purpose pliers
permanent marker pen
nail, 5mm/¹⁄₅in long
large wooden bead
strong glue
hammer

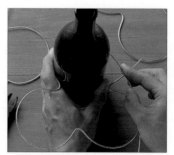

1 Cut three 80cm/32in lengths of the thicker wire. Leave 10cm/4in at one end of each wire and wrap the next section around a bottle. At the point of overlap, bend back the wire to form a second, then a third curve. Make a loop at each end of the wire and close together. Cut off any excess wire. Make two more clover shapes.

2 Cut seven 80cm/32in and two 91.5cm/36in lengths of thicker wire. Bundle them together so that the longest are in the centre and stick out at one end. This end forms the handle. Starting where the longer wires stick out, bind the bundle with thin wire for 42cm/16½ in.

3 To form the base of the bottle carrier, divide the wires into groups of three. Bend each group away from the central shaft at right angles. Arrange the wires in each group side by side. Measure 3cm/1¼in from the handle and bind together for 2cm/⁴⁄₅in. Bend out the outer two wires at right angles. Measure 5cm/2in from the bound section and mark each wire. Bend each wire up at a right angle so that it stands parallel to the handle. Make a hook at the end of each wire.

4 Slot the three clover shapes into the structure, and then close up the hooks around the top clover shape. Bind the bottom clover in place. Bind up each strut, securing the middle clover shape halfway up. Bind over the wire ends at the top of the structure.

5 Wrap a length of 2mm/¹⁄₁₃in wire around the nail to make a coil. Thread the bead on to the wires at the top of the central shaft. Apply strong glue to the coil and hammer on the bead.

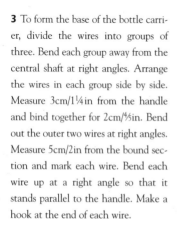

Simple copper coils with a random sprinkling of brightly coloured glass beads make attractive napkin rings. If you are designing a buffet table setting, scale up the design to make a paper napkin holder.

Spiral Napkin Holders

you will need
wire cutters
ruler or tape measure
copper wire, 0.8mm/¹⁄₃₁in and
1.5mm/¹⁄₁₉in thick
pen or wooden spoon
assorted glass beads
long flat-nosed pliers
cardboard tube from a roll of foil
or clear film (plastic wrap)

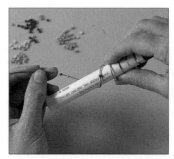

1 Cut a 1m/1yd length of 0.8mm/ ¹⁄₃₁in copper wire and wind it on to a pen or the handle of a wooden spoon. As you form each loop, add a few small glass beads in assorted colours.

2 Form 18 coils to make a tight spring, then slide it off the pen or wooden spoon. Twist the two ends of the wire tightly together using long flat-nosed pliers.

3 Add a small bead and pull the ends of the wire around it to secure.

4 To make a larger ring, use 1.5mm/ ¹⁄₁₉in copper wire and larger beads. Form the coils around a cardboard tube, such as the inside of a roll of foil or clear film.

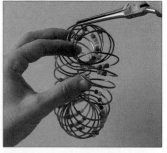

5 Make a small tight coil of 0.8mm/ ¹⁄₃₁in copper wire using long flat-nosed pliers and slide it over both ends of the ring. Pull the small coil tight. Add a bead to each end of the large ring and loop the ends of the wire over the bead to secure it.

Although it looks intricate, there is nothing more to this colourful tablemat than plain knitting and a simple double crochet stitch. Crystal seed beads add to the glittering effect.

Mesh Place Mat

you will need

50g/2oz each of enamelled copper wire in burgundy and pink, 0.4mm/¹⁄₆₃in thick

pair of knitting needles, 2.75mm/ size 12/US 2

ruler or tape measure

crochet hook, 2mm/size 14/B-1

wire cutters

crystal seed beads

sewing needle

1 Using the burgundy enamelled copper wire and knitting needles, loosely cast on 52 stitches. Knit every row with an even tension until the work measures 22cm/8½in. Use another combination of colours for the wire if you prefer.

2 When you reach this length, pull the work from the sides and from the top and bottom to stretch the mat out to the final measurement of 23 × 29cm/9 × 11½in. If necessary, add a few more rows to correct the length, then cast off loosely.

3 Using pink wire and a crochet hook, loosely chain crochet 165 stitches. Turn the work, miss one chain, then double crochet/single crochet into every chain. At the end of this length cut the copper wire, leaving a 2.5cm/1in tail.

4 Thread 82 crystal seed beads on to a length of pink wire. Holding several seed beads in your left hand, work along the edging strip again in double crochet, adding in one seed bead to every other double crochet stitch.

5 Work another two rows in double crochet and cast off. Measure the finished edging around the mat and stretch evenly if necessary to make it fit. Thread a sewing needle with pink wire. Starting in a corner of the mat, stitch on the pink edging.

Toasting English muffins over an open fire in winter is always a pleasant activity. This toasting fork is made from four coat hangers and is both light and strong.

Toasting Fork

1 To make an inner strut, measure 10cm/4in from the end of one of the straightened coat hangers and wind it around a wooden spoon at this point to create a loop. Measure 2cm/¾in before bending the remaining length of wire straight.

2 Make a second strut a mirror image of the first by winding the wire the other way around the wooden spoon.

3 Make the two outer struts in the same way. This time allow 12.5cm/5in for the prongs and bend a right angle 2cm/¾in beyond the prong loop.

4 Bind the struts together temporarily with tacking wire, loosely enough to allow movement.

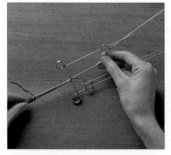

5 Slide the two outer prongs through the loops of the inner prongs. Measure up from the prongs and mark the handle at 4, 18, 4, 20, 4 and 2cm, or 1½, 7, 1½, 8, 1½ and ¾in intervals. Using galvanized wire, bind the 4cm/1½in sections. Do not trim the excess binding wire from the top section.

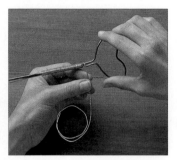

6 Cut off three of the remaining strut wires at the last mark. Form the fourth strut wire end into a heart shape, using pliers and bending it around a piece of copper piping to create the curves. Leave 2cm/¾in at the end. Bind it in with the other three wires, still using the binding wire.

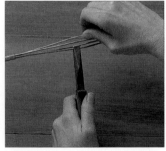

7 Using the pliers, grip each wire in turn halfway along the 20cm/8in section. Pull the wire so that it bows out. This will be the fork handle so test it in your hand for comfort and adjust if necessary. Trim the ends of the prongs so that they are even and hammer each tip flat.

These ingenious containers look like fat little pots, but are actually made of brightly coloured fabric stretched over wire frames. Use them as containers for cotton wool.

Fabric-covered Baskets

you will need
galvanized wire, 3mm/⅛in,
2mm/¹⁄₁₃in and 1mm/¹⁄₂₅in thick
ruler or tape measure
wire cutters
long-nosed pliers
masking tape
two-way stretch fabric
scissors
sewing-machine
sewing thread
needle

1 Measure and cut three lengths of 3mm/⅛in galvanized wire 45cm/18in long. Cross the wires at the centres and bind together using 1mm/¹⁄₂₅in wire so that the six prongs splay out evenly in a star shape. Using 2mm/¹⁄₁₃in wire, make a double ring 13cm/5in in diameter and bind it centrally to the framework to form a base.

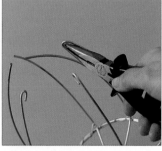

2 Use your fingers to bend each of the six prongs of the framework upwards where it joins the ring that forms the base. These prongs will form the structure for the sides of the container. Bend the end of each of the prongs into a tight loop using long-nosed pliers, as shown.

3 Make a second double ring of 2mm/¹⁄₁₃in wire to match the base, and then hold the two ends together temporarily using masking tape.

4 Slip the wire ring into the loops at the top of the framework, then bind in place using 1mm/¹⁄₂₅in wire.

5 Cut a 35cm/13¾in square of two-way stretch fabric. Fold in half and stitch down the long side to make a tube, using a machine stretch stitch.

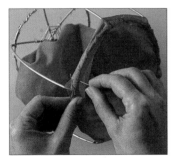

6 Place the fabric tube inside the wire framework. Hand stitch the raw edge to the top ring.

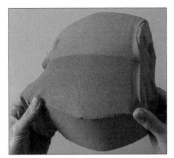

7 Pull the fabric up from inside the framework and carefully stretch it down around the outside of the tube. The fabric should be right side out.

8 Gather the raw edge under the base and stitch to the centre of the framework. Ease any remaining fabric up towards the top of the container, and secure it with curly clips made from galvanized wire.

This intriguing little basket is made using a simple wrapping technique. The tightly woven pipe cleaners give a softness that is irresistible to touch. Use this basket to hold jewellery.

Woven Pipe-cleaner Basket

you will need
galvanized wire, 1.5mm/¹⁄₁₉in and 0.5mm/¹⁄₅₀in thick
ruler or tape measure
wire cutters
50 lilac and 24 grey pipe cleaners, 30cm/12in long
flat-nosed pliers
round-nosed (snub-nosed) pliers

1 For the struts of the basket, measure and cut eight lengths of 1.5mm/¹⁄₁₉in galvanized wire, each 36cm/14in. Retain the curve of the wire as you cut the lengths from the coil. Cut one 30cm/12in length of the 0.5mm/¹⁄₅₀in galvanized wire.

2 Use the fine wire length to bind the struts together at the centre. Bind two pairs together at right angles, then place the remaining pairs diagonally. Wind the fine wire around all the individual struts to hold them in position, evenly spaced.

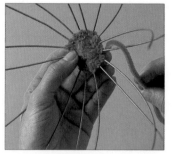

3 Weave a lilac pipe cleaner over the centre of the basket so that all the fine wire is covered.

4 Take the pipe cleaner under each wire, back around it and then on to the next, pushing the pipe cleaners in towards the centre to keep the weave tight. Adjust the wires as necessary to keep the shape and spacing even. Work in lilac until the woven piece measures 7.5cm/3in.

5 When you reach the end of a pipe cleaner or want to use a different colour, join the lengths by bending a small hook in the end of each. Hook them together and flatten the hooks with flat-nosed pliers.

6 Work two rows of weaving in the grey pipe cleaners, then three lilac, two grey, four lilac, two grey, five lilac, and four grey, to bring you to the top edge of the basket.

7 Take two lilac pipe cleaners and hook them together, and do the same with two grey pipe cleaners. Hold the two colours together at one end and twist them firmly together. Join the twisted length to the last grey length on the basket and arrange it around the top edge, outside the struts.

8 Trim the tops of the struts to 5mm/ ⅕in and use round-nosed (snug-nosed) pliers to bend them over the edging. Weave the ends of the twisted edge into its beginning.

Despite its ornateness, this medieval-looking candle sconce is quite easy to make. By making the base of the basket wider and weaving the sides deeper you can adapt the shape to fit a larger candle.

Decorative Candle Sconce

you will need
copper wire, 1.5mm/¹⁄₁₉in and 0.8mm/¹⁄₃₁in thick
ruler or tape measure
wire cutters
general-purpose pliers
masking tape
round-nosed (snub-nosed) pliers
parallel (channel-type) pliers

1 Cut 21 lengths of 1.5mm/¹⁄₁₉in wire, each 38cm/15in long. Bundle together so that they are even at the top and bottom, and grip them with the general-purpose pliers 16cm/6¼in from one end. Hold the pliers closed with masking tape so they act as a vice. Using the 0.8mm/¹⁄₃₁in wire, bind the bundle of wires for 2cm/¾in from the pliers. Do not cut off the wire. Release the pliers.

2 Using round-nosed pliers, bend a downward-curving loop at the end of each wire. Bend down the wires at right angles at the top of the bound section so they spread out in a circle. Using the 0.8mm/¹⁄₃₁in wire that is still attached to the bundle, weave around the wires to make a base with a diameter that measures 7cm/2¾in. This will form the base of the basket.

3 Bend up the wires at the edge of the circle and weave the side of the candle basket to a depth of about 2.5cm/1in.

4 Using parallel (channel-type) pliers, coil down the wires to the edge of the candle basket.

5 Using parallel pliers, make two columns of coils with the wires left under the candle basket. Make nine coils in each column, ensuring that the second column is a mirror image of the first. Trim the end of each wire, increasing the amount you cut off by 12mm/½ in each time, so that the coils decrease in size. Using round-nosed pliers, form waves in the remaining wires. Trim the ends of the outer wires, so that the central one is the longest.

6 Decide which is the back of the sconce. Using the parallel pliers, unwind the two coils at the back a little, cross them over each other and twist flat. Attach the sconce to the wall through the holes in these two coils. Bend back the wavy wires so that they support the sconce at the bottom, holding it away from the wall. Check the distance between the candle flame and the wall.

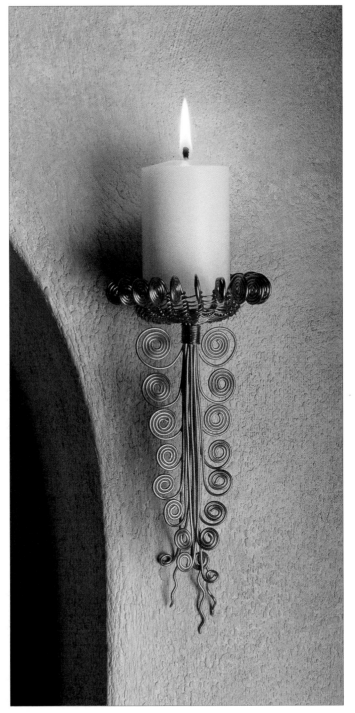

This sturdy basket is particularly suitable for gathering vegetables in from the garden. The mesh allows the soil to fall through and, because the wire is galvanized, the contents can be hosed down outside.

Vegetable Basket

you will need

small-gauge chicken wire

wire cutters

gloves

ruler or tape measure

straining wire

galvanized wire, 1.5mm/¹⁄₁₉in and 0.8mm/¹⁄₃₁in thick

round-nosed (snub-nosed) pliers

permanent marker pen

tacking wire

broom handle

1 To make the cylinder, cut a piece of chicken wire 28 × 89cm/11 × 35in. Form it into an oval and join the short edges together. Cut a 94cm/37in length of straining wire and form it into an oval that will fit snugly inside the chicken-wire cylinder. Bind the ends together with the 0.8mm/¹⁄₃₁in galvanized wire.

2 To shape the basket, count up ten holes from the bottom of the cylinder. This section will be the base. Use the round-nosed pliers to bend all the holes into heart shapes. To make the base support, cut a 70cm/28in length of straining wire and bind it into an oval.

3 Cut two 18cm/7in lengths and two 23cm/9in lengths of the 1.5mm/¹⁄₁₉in galvanized wire. Use round-nosed pliers to attach the wires to the oval to form a grid, binding where the wires cross.

4 Push the bottom edges of the basket together and bind with 0.8mm/¹⁄₃₁in galvanized wire to close up the base section neatly.

5 Position the base support on the bottom of the basket and bind it on to the chicken wire all the way around.

6 Place the large oval of straining wire inside the basket, 5cm/2in from the top. Fold the chicken wire over it, as shown. This will reinforce the top rim of the basket.

7 Mark a 54.5cm/21½in length of straining wire but do not cut it. Tack the end to one side of the basket and bend to form the handle. Secure the wire to the other side of the basket at the marked point. Wrap the next section of the straining wire around a broom handle to form ten loops. Bind these loops around the basket to the other side of the handle.

8 Bend the wire over the basket to double the handle. Bend the wire into a three-petalled decoration, as shown, and bind it to the basket. Loop the handle across again and make another three-petalled decoration on the other side.

9 Bend the wire back over the basket to form a fourth handle loop. Using the broom handle, make ten more loops in the wire and bind around the basket. Using 0.8mm/⅓₁in galvanized wire, bind the handle wires together, tucking the ends inside.

Twisted silver wire, sparingly threaded with beads, has a delicate yet sculptural quality. An assortment of decorative glass beads, following a colour theme, look wonderful entwining a pair of glass candlesticks.

Beaded Wire Candlesticks

you will need

ruler or tape measure

wire cutters

medium silver wire

round-nosed (snub-nosed) pliers

medium decorative glass beads in yellow, green, silver and clear

pencil

small glass rocaille beads and square beads in complementary shades

pair of glass candlesticks

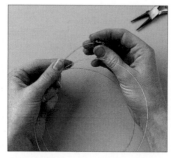

1 Cut four lengths of wire, each 1m/40in long for every candlestick. Bend a loop at the end of the first length with round-nosed pliers and thread on a decorative bead.

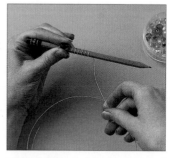

2 Wind the end of the first length of wire around a pencil six times to form a spiral. Make sure you leave some space between the coils, for threading more beads.

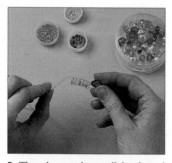

3 Thread on eight small beads and divide them along the spiral. Thread on a medium-sized bead and repeat, forming spirals and threading beads until you reach the end of the wire. At the end, twist the wire with pliers.

4 Thread on the final decorative bead and finish with a loop at the end of the wire. Make up the other three spirals in the same way, distributing the beads evenly along the spiral.

5 Wrap two spiral lengths around the stem of each candlestick to form an interesting shape. Secure the spirals in place by binding them gently to the candlestick stem with more of the silver wire.

Copper wire is naturally warm in colour, and the wrapping technique used here enhances its rich appearance. The bowl looks particularly soft and sumptuous when displayed by candlelight.

Copper Bowl

you will need

copper wire, 2mm/¹⁄₁₃in,
0.8mm/¹⁄₃₁in, 2.5mm/¹⁄₁₀in,
1mm/¹⁄₂₅in and 1.5mm/¹⁄₁₉in thick
ruler or tape measure
wire cutters
parallel (channel-type) pliers
bowls in two sizes
quick-drying glue
permanent marker pen
general-purpose pliers

1 Cut eight 42cm/16½in lengths of 2mm/¹⁄₁₃in copper wire. Wrap with 0.8mm/¹⁄₃₁in wire. Make a coil with a diameter of about 4cm/1½in at one end and one of 2.5cm/1in at the other, using parallel pliers.

2 Bend each wire to form the curved side struts of the bowl. To make the rims of the bowl, cut two lengths of 2.5mm/¹⁄₁₀in wire, one 80cm/32in and the other 50cm/20in. Wrap the longer length in 1mm/¹⁄₂₅in wire and the shorter in 1.5mm/¹⁄₁₉in wire.

3 Release 2cm/⅝in at each end of the coil. Bend the longer wrapped wire around the larger bowl and the shorter wrapped wire around the smaller bowl to make two wire hoops.

4 Insert a little quick-drying glue into the empty end of each coil and slot in the projecting end of wire. Hold it firmly in place until the glue is dry.

5 Lightly mark eight equidistant points around each of the hoops. Cut 16 lengths of 1mm/¹⁄₂₅in wire, each measuring 12.5cm/5in. Use these to begin binding the side struts to the hoops. Allow the struts to extend above the top rim by 6cm/2½in and below the bottom rim by 4cm/1½in.

6 Continue to bind the struts to the hoops, wiring alternate ones first. This gives the bowl stability. Bind the last four struts to the hoops, adjusting any that become misshapen in the process.

7 Make an open coil with a diameter of 15cm/6in, from the 2.5mm/¹⁄₁₀in copper wire. Hold the shape of the spiral by binding it with two lengths of 1mm/¹⁄₂₅in copper wire, leaving about 10cm/4in spare wire at each end.

8 To attach the base coil, bind the excess wire around four of the struts. Twist a 2.3m/2½yd double length of 1mm/¹⁄₂₅in wire and wrap it around the bowl. Make a zigzag between the struts and halfway between the top struts.

Chicken wire becomes an exotic material when used to make this lantern, which is perfect for hanging in the garden. Place long-lasting night-lights in the jam jars.

Garden Lantern

you will need
gloves
small-gauge chicken wire
wire cutters
ruler or tape measure
aluminium wire, 1mm/¹⁄₂₅in thick
galvanized wire, 1.5mm/¹⁄₁₉in thick
round-nosed (snub-nosed) pliers
general-purpose pliers
bottle with cone-shaped lid
jam jar
large beads
bath-plug chain
metal ring
flat-headed jewellery pins
narrow ribbon (optional)

1 Wearing gloves, cut one piece of chicken wire 18 × 61cm/7 × 24in and one piece 22 × 55cm/8½ x 21½in. Form two cylinders with the wire and join the short edges together with the aluminium wire. Cut one length of the galvanized wire 66cm/26in and one length 61cm/24in. Bend to form two hoops with the same diameter. Bind the ends with aluminium wire.

2 Use the aluminium wire to bind a hoop on to the edge of each cylinder. Carefully bend each of the holes in the chicken wire into heart shapes, by holding the centre of each strut in turn with the round-nosed pliers and twisting up to each side. Use round-nosed pliers and your hands to mould the cylinder into a bell shape.

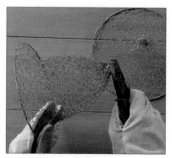

3 To make the lid, bend all the holes in the second cylinder into heart shapes, then mould the wire to form a curved lid shape. You will need to squash the holes together at the top.

4 Using the hollow section in the mouth of the general-purpose pliers, carefully crimp the chicken wire in the centre of each section to give you a central core.

5 Form a long cone for the lid. Wrap the aluminium wire around the tapered top of a paint or glue bottle. The bottom of the cone must fit over the central core of the lid.

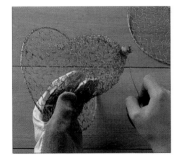

6 Secure a length of thin wire inside the centre of the lid and push it through the core. Thread the coiled cone on to the wire and slip over the core. Leave the length of wire hanging loose from the centre of the cone. Wrap another length of wire around the core of the lantern section to make a smaller coil.

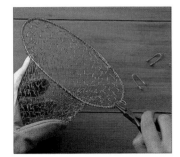

7 Cut four 10cm/4in pieces of the galvanized wire. Using round-nosed pliers, bend each piece into a loop with a hook at each end. Curve up the bend in each loop slightly. Position evenly around the rim of the lantern section and close up the hooks with pliers. Cut two lengths of galvanized wire and twist together around the neck of a jam jar so that the ends stick out on each side. Attach the wires to the lantern rim on each side of two opposite loops. This will hold the jam jar securely in place.

8 Thread a large metallic bead on to the loose wire in the lid. Bind the bath-plug chain on to the wire and trim any excess. Attach a metal ring to the other end for hanging. Thread beads on to flat-headed jewellery pins and hang evenly around the rim. Add a large bead to the lantern core.

9 Put the lid on the lantern and slot the four loops on the lantern rim through the chicken wire of the lid. Press them down firmly. It is very important for safety that the loops hold the bottom securely in place. Reinforce with extra pieces of wire or tie with narrow ribbon.

Keep your herb and spice jars neat in this heart-rimmed rack, which is designed to hold five standard-sized spice jars. It can be hung on the wall or used free-standing on a shelf or kitchen surface.

Heart Spice Rack

you will need

galvanized wire, 1.5mm/^{1}/₁₉in and 0.8mm/^{1}/₃₁in thick

ruler or tape measure

wire cutters

permanent marker pen

round-nosed (snub-nosed) pliers

general-purpose pliers

galvanized wire, 1.5mm/^{1}/₁₉in thick, doubled and twisted

tacking wire

broom handle

1 Cut five 45cm/18in lengths of the 1.5mm/^{1}/₁₉in wire. Mark at intervals of 5cm/2in, 5cm/2in, 25cm/10in, 5cm/2in and 5cm/2in.

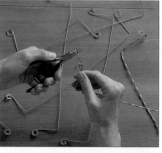

2 Using round-nosed pliers, carefully bend the 5cm/2in sections at the ends of each wire into coils. Using general-purpose pliers, bend each at right angles at the next 5cm/2in marks. Cut two 45cm/18in lengths of twisted wire and mark in the same way. Untwist 5cm/2in at each end and make two coils. Bend right angles at the next marks.

3 Cut two 9cm/3½in lengths of 1.5mm/^{1}/₁₉in galvanized wire. Make the box section of the spice rack by joining together the two twisted wire struts. Twist the ends of the 9cm/3½in lengths around the bent corners of the struts, leaving a distance of 6cm/2½in between the two struts.

4 Cut a 104cm/41in length of twisted wire and mark it at intervals of 20cm/8in, 12.5cm/5in, 6cm/2½in, 25cm/10in, 6cm/2½in, 12.5cm/5in and 20cm/8in. Bend at the marked points to form a rectangle and heart.

5 Attach the four corners of the heart rim to the top of the box section using tacking wire. Cut four 54.5cm/21½in lengths of twisted wire and mark each at intervals of 5cm/2in, 5cm/2in, 6cm/2½in and 38cm/15in.

6 Untwist the 5cm/2in end of each wire and make into two coils. Bend right angles at the next two marked points. Bend each 38cm/15in section into a coil. Bend a curve in the wire next to two of the coils.

7 Slot the box section inside these four pieces so that the four large coils are at the back beside the heart. Tack into place where the pieces touch.

8 Slot the plain wire struts made in step 1 inside the box structure. Space them evenly across the width of the box and tack into place.

9 Wrap a long length of 1.5mm/¹⁄₁₉in galvanized wire several times around a broom handle to make a loose coil. Flatten the coil and position it inside the front edge of the spice rack.

10 Using 0.8mm/¹⁄₃₁in galvanized wire, bind around the top rim of the box, securing each piece in position and removing the tacking wire as you go. Then bind from front to back along the bottom struts. Finish the spice rack by binding the heart closed at the top and bottom. Bind all of the decorative spirals where they touch.

A rack of hooks is always useful, and can be hung in the hall for keys, in the bathroom for towels and in the kitchen for utensils. This project is ideal to make with children, as the plastic-coated wire is safe to use.

Kitchen Hook Rack

you will need
green gardening wire
broom handle
ruler or tape measure
wire cutters
permanent marker pen
pencil
wooden spoon
screwdriver and 3 screws

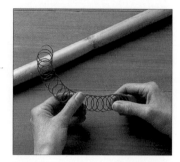

1 Tightly wrap the gardening wire 40 times around a broom handle. Leave 10cm/4in of wire at each end and cut off. Flatten the coil. The coil should be about 30cm/12in long.

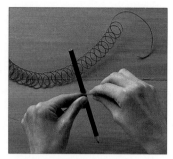

2 Cut a 56cm/22in length of wire. Mark the centre and the point 15cm/ 6in from each end. Form a loop at each of the points by wrapping the wire around a pencil. Thread the wire through the flattened coil, and then thread the circle at each end of the coil through the end loops on the wire.

3 Bend the 15cm/6in section at each end of the gardening wire around the handle of a wooden spoon to create a three-leaf clover shape, as shown. There should be about 2cm/¾in left at the end to bend back down the stem. Use the 10cm/4in of wire left at the ends of the coil to bind the stem.

4 Cut four 30cm/12in lengths of wire. Bend each in half and wrap the bend around the handle of a wooden spoon to make a circle. Twist to close. Bend small hooks in the ends of the wires. Bend each wire in half. Loop the hooks around the coil and bottom wire of the frame, and close tightly.

5 Cut a 2m/80in length of wire. Bend in half, wrap the bend around the handle of a wooden spoon to make a circle. Twist closed. Mark 15cm/6in from the circle. Ask a friend to hold this point while you twist the wires, then bend them around the broom to make a clover shape. Bind closed.

◀ **6** To finish, slot the clover hook through the middle of the coil, so that its shank lies on either side of the central loop in the base wire. Bend up the hook 5cm/2in from the circle end. Screw the rack to the wall through the three loops in the bottom wire. The central screw holds the hook firmly in place.

The shelf at the bottom of this simply designed rack is wide enough to hold four food cans. Stripped of their labels, the cans make useful storage containers that complement the design of the rack.

Utility Rack

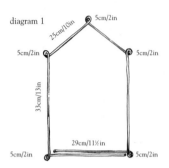

diagram 1

5cm/2in
25cm/10in
5cm/2in
5cm/2in
5cm/2in
33cm/13in
29cm/11½ in
5cm/2in
5cm/2in

1 To make the frame, cut a 2m/79in length of straining wire. Twist the ends to stop them from unravelling. Mark the wire at intervals of 29cm/11½ in, 5cm/2in, 33cm/13in, 5cm/2in, 25cm/10in, 5cm/2in, 25cm/10in, 5cm/2in, 33cm/13in, 5cm/2in, and 29cm/11½ in.

2 Using round-nosed pliers, make a loop with each 5cm/2in section, making sure that the pen marks match up and that all the loops face outwards (see diagram 1). Using the 0.8mm/¹⁄₃₁in wire, bind the 29cm/11½ in sections together to make the bottom of the frame.

diagram 2

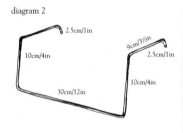

2.5cm/1in
9cm/3½in
10cm/4in
2.5cm/1in
10cm/4in
30cm/12in

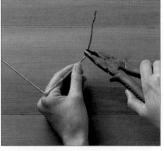

3 To make the shelf, cut a 73.5cm/29in length of straining wire and mark it at intervals of 2.5cm/1in, 9cm/3½ in, 10cm/4in, 30cm/12in, 10cm/4in, 9cm/3½ in and 2.5cm/1in.

4 Using general-purpose pliers, bend the wire at right angles at the marked points (see diagram 2).

5 Mark each side of the frame 10cm/4in from the bottom. Twist the 2.5cm/1in ends of the shelf wire tightly around the frame at these points.

6 For the rim and sides of the shelf, cut a 104cm/41in length of 1.5mm/¹⁄₁₉in galvanized wire and mark it at intervals of 2.5cm/1in, 12.5cm/5in, 9cm/3½in, 12.5cm/5in, 30cm/12in, 12.5cm/5in, 9cm/3½in, 12.5cm/5in and 2.5cm/1in. Using round-nosed pliers, make a loop with the 2.5cm/1in section at each end of the wire. Bend the wire at the 12.5cm/5in and 9cm/3½in points at each end at 45° angles to form the side crosses of the shelf. Bend the 30cm/12in section in the middle at right angles to form the top rim (see diagram 3).

diagram 3

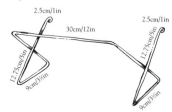

7 Tack the loops at the ends of the rim wire to the 10cm/4in markings on the sides of the main frame. Tack each corner of the side crosses to the frame.

◀ **8** Lay the frame on to a piece of chicken wire and cut around the frame. Allow 30cm/12in at the bottom for wrapping around the shelf, so that there is a double thickness of wire at the front of the shelf where it tucks inside. Using 0.8mm/¹⁄₃₁in galvanized wire, bind the edges of the chicken wire to the frame. Wrap any rough edges at the top around the frame before binding. Bind the shelf firmly to the frame as you bind on the chicken wire, and remove the tacking wire.

Tinwork

As well as being hardwearing, strong and durable, many metals are extremely versatile and attractive, making them ideal for crafting into a variety of decorative items around the home, from mirrors and candlesticks, to coat racks and spice racks, shelving and cabinets. Surfaces can be embossed, beaten, punched, painted or even studded with glass nuggets to create virtually any patterned finish you like.

For tin plate, metal foils and sheet metals, purchase materials from a specialist hardware store, or for recycled materials, a metal merchant or scrap yard. Always wear protective gloves, a work shirt and goggles.

Materials

Biscuit (cookie) tins

A good source of tin. Some tins have a plastic sheen so scrub with wire (steel) wool, if you intend to solder them.

Epoxy resin glue

This glue comes in two parts. Mix up as much glue as you need at one time. Once it has set the join is strong.

Flux

Used during soldering to make the area to be soldered chemically clean.

As the flux is heated, it runs along the metal preparing the surface. This helps the solder to flow and adhere.

Metal foils

These thin sheet metals usually come on rolls. Metal foil is so thin that it can be cut with household scissors. A variety of metal foils is available, and includes brass, aluminium and copper. The foil's thinness makes it very soft and it is easy to draw designs into the surface.

Silicon carbide (wet & dry) paper

This is abrasive. Fine-grade paper, when dampened, is useful for finishing off filed edges. Clamp the item in a bench vice and wrap the paper around a small wooden block.

S-joiners and jump rings

Use to join sections of an object together and to attach lengths of chain. They are very strong, and pliers are used to open and close the links.

Solder

This is an alloy, or mixture, of metals. Solder is a liquid metal filler that is melted, then used to join two pieces of metal together. Always use a solder that has a lower melting point than the metals to be joined. Follow the manufacturer's instructions.

Tin plate

This is a mild sheet steel that has been coated with tin. The plating will not tarnish in the open air or in humid conditions. Sheet metals are made in different thicknesses, or gauges. The higher the gauge, the thinner the metal. At 30 gauge (approximately 0.2mm/$\frac{1}{125}$in), tin plate can be cut by hand with tin snips and shears.

Zinc sheet

Thin zinc sheet has a matt (flat) surface and is fairly soft and easy to cut.

You may already have most of the basic tinwork tools. The more specialist items, such as punches, snips and shears, are available from good hardware stores.

Equipment

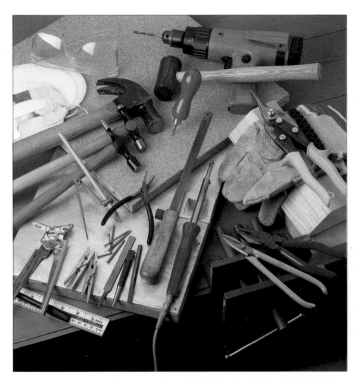

Bench vice

Use to clamp metal shapes when filing, sanding, and hammering edges.

Bradawl or awl

Use to make holes in metal.

Centre punch, chisel, nails

Use to punch decorative patterns.

Chipboard (particle board)

This is used as a work surface when punching tin and embossing foil.

Hammers

A variety of hammers are used. A medium-sized ball head hammer is used with nails or a punch to make a pattern in tin. A tack hammer is used to knock panel pins (brads) into wood. A heavy hammer is used with a chisel to make decorative holes.

Hand file

Use to remove any burrs of metal from the tin after a shape has been cut out.

Hide mallet

This is made from leather. It has a soft head so will not mark the tin.

Pliers

Use to hold tin when you are cutting it and for turning over edges. Round-nosed (snub-nosed) pliers are good for making small circles of wire.

Soldering iron

This is used to heat the solder that joins two pieces of metal together.

Soldering mats

Various fireproof soldering mats are available and may be purchased from good hardware stores and metal supply shops.

Tin shears

These are very strong scissors used for cutting sheet metal. Shears come with straight blades to cut a straight line, or blades curved to the left or right to cut circles and curves.

Tin snips

These are good for cutting small shapes from tin.

Wooden blocks

It is useful to have a wooden block with 90° edges and another with a 45° edge when turning over the sides of a piece of tin.

Only a few basic techniques are required for making simple tinwork items. Working with tin requires extra care so do read through this section before embarking on the projects.

Tinware Techniques

Cutting tin   It is not difficult to cut through thin sheets of tin plate or tin cans. It is important to get used to cutting smoothly to avoid making jagged edges, so practise first on scraps of tin. Cutting tin produces small shards of metal that are razor-sharp, so collect scraps as you cut and keep them together until you can dispose of them safely.

Cutting a section from a sheet

To cut a section of tin from a large sheet, use tin shears. To avoid creating a dangerous jagged edge when cutting, never close the blades of the shears completely. Instead, make a cut almost the length of the blades each time, open the shears, then guide the metal back into the blades and continue. Keep the blades in the cut, without removing them until the line of the cut is complete. If you are cutting a straight-sided shape, don't try to turn the shears around once you have reached a corner. Instead, remove the shears and cut across to the corner from the edge of the sheet of metal.

Cutting a small shape from a section of tin

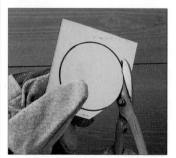

Use tin snips rather than shears to cut small shapes. They are easier to manipulate and control, especially if you are cutting an intricate shape. Again, don't attempt to turn the snips around in the metal; cut as much as you can, then remove the snips and turn the metal so that you can follow the cutting line more easily.

Safety advice

• Always wear a heavy work shirt and protective leather gloves when you are handling metal pieces or uncut sheet metal.

• Tin shears and snips are very powerful, being strong enough to cut through fairly heavy metal, and very sharp. They should be handled with respect and, like all tools, should always be kept in a safe place away from children.

• A protective face mask and goggles should always be worn during soldering as the hot metal, solder and flux give off fumes. Work should be carried out on a soldering mat and the iron put on a metal rest when not in use.

• All soldering should be carried out in a properly ventilated area and frequent breaks should be taken when working. Don't lean too near your work to avoid close contact with the fumes. Wear protective gloves when you are soldering as the metal is hot.

Cutting metal from an oil drum

1 The metal found in oil drums is very often thin and springy, and so care must be taken when cutting out panels from a drum. Protect your eyes with goggles for extra safety. To remove the top of the drum, make a cut in the side using a hacksaw blade. Open the cut slightly, then insert the blades of a pair of tin shears into the space and cut around the drum, removing the top.

2 Carefully cut down a side to within 18mm/¾in of the drum base using tin shears. Gently snip around the base of the drum, pushing back the panel as it is freed from the base. Once you have removed the panel, it may be used in the same way as a sheet of tin plate. Mop up any oil residue on the surface of the tin using tissue paper.

Finishing the edges

All tin items should be considered unfinished and unsuitable for use until all the edges have been smoothed or turned over. This should be done immediately to avoid any accidents. Long, straight edges may be folded and flattened with the aid of a hammer and wooden blocks with measured 90° and 45° edges. Irregularly shaped items may be finished with a hand file and silicon carbide (wet and dry) paper for complete smoothness. Tin cans should always be filed smooth around the rims before use to remove any jagged edges.

Filing cut metal

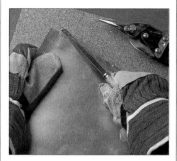

The raw, cut edges of a piece of tin plate are very sharp, and should be smoothed or finished immediately to prevent them causing harm to yourself or anyone else. Small shapes should be smoothed with a hand file while being firmly clamped in a vice. The file should be moved forwards at a right angle to the metal in one light stroke, then lifted and returned. This will remove most of the rough edges.

Using silicon carbide paper

To make a cut edge completely smooth after filing, finish with fine-grade silicon carbide (wet and dry) paper. This is dampened and wrapped around a small wooden block like abrasive paper. Sanding with this paper removes any remaining rough edges and leaves the metal smooth to the touch.

Turning over cut edges

The cut edges of straight-sided pieces of tin plate should be turned over immediately after cutting to avoid accidents. Mechanically made baking tins and boxes have their edges bent over to an angle of 45° by a folding machine. The edges are then pressed flat and made safe. It is simple to replicate this process at home using two blocks of wood.

1 Clamp a thick block of wood with an accurately measured 90° edge firmly in a bench vice. Draw a border around the cut edges of the tin plate. Place the piece of tin on the block with the borderline lying along the edge of the block. Strike the edge of the tin with a hide hammer to mould around the edge of the block.

2 Turn the piece of tin over and place a block of wood with a 45° edge inside the fold. Keep the wooden block firm with one hand while hammering down on the folded edge of tin with a hide hammer.

3 Once the metal has been folded over to this angle, remove the block then hammer the edge completely flat using a hide hammer. Fold each side of the piece of tin in turn and once all its edges have been hammered flat, file the corners to smooth any sharp edges. Straight edges should always be finished in this way to avoid accidents, even if the panel is to be set into a recess, for example in the case of a punched panel cabinet.

Soldering

Sections of metal may be joined together by soldering. It is essential that both surfaces to be joined are clean before they are soldered. Rubbing both areas with wire (steel) wool will help to remove any dirt and grease. All soldering should be done on a soldering mat, wearing protective gloves, masks and goggles, and the soldering iron should be placed on a metal stand when not in use.

1 Place together the two sections to be joined. Hold them in place with wooden pegs (pins) or masking tape. Smear the joint with flux. This is essential, as when the metal is heated, an oxide forms on the surface that may inhibit the adhesion of the solder. The flux prevents the oxide from forming on the metal.

◄ **2** The hot soldering iron heats the metal, which causes the flux to melt. Pick up a small amount of solder on the end of the iron. It will start to melt. The iron is drawn down the joint and the solder flows with it, and displaces the flux. The solder then cools and solidifies, joining the two pieces of metal together.

Punching tin Tin may be decorated in a variety of ways. Punching, when a pattern of indentations is beaten into the surface of the metal, is one of the most common methods. A centre punch or nail, plus a ball hammer, are used to produce the knobbly patterns, either on the front or back of the tin. Small chisels and metal stamps are also used. Opaque and translucent enamel paints are suitable for decorating tin plate and other metals. Thin metal foils, such as aluminium foil, are so soft that a design may be drawn on to the surface to leave a raised or "embossed" pattern.

Getting the design right

Nails or punches can be used to make indentations and holes in tin. If you want a sophisticated pattern, draw the design first on to a sheet of graph paper and punch through the paper into the tin following the lines. The paper should be taped to the tin, and the tin attached to chipboard using panel pins (brads) to keep it steady as you punch.

Punching tin from the front

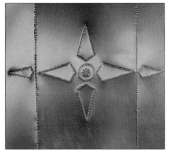

A design punched from the front will have an indented pattern. If an area of tin is punched from the front, and the indentations are made very close together, the punched area recedes and the unpunched area becomes slightly raised. This is one form of "chasing", where decorative patterns are punched into metal from the front and stand out in low relief.

Punching tin from the back

A design punched from the back will have a raised pattern and a pleasing knobbly effect on the surface. Patterns can be applied with nails of different sizes or punches to make a dotty texture. Short lines can be made by using a small chisel. It is also possible to buy decorative punches with designs engraved into the tip.

Embossing aluminium foil ▶

Aluminium foil is very soft thin metal. It can be cut with household scissors and bent or folded as desired. It is especially useful for cladding frames, books, boxes and other small items. Its softness makes it easy to emboss. This is done by drawing on to the back of the foil using a dry or empty ballpoint pen, which leaves a raised surface on the other side.

Right: *Many projects combine a range of decorating techniques.*

Make this exquisite embossed heart decoration to personalize a special gift. Metal stencils come in a variety of designs and make embossing foil simple, so this is an easy project to start with.

Embossed Heart

you will need
small, pointed scissors
pewter or aluminium foil, 36 gauge,
(0.1mm/¹⁄₂₅₀in thick)
metal stencil
double-sided adhesive tape
self-healing cutting mat
double-ended embossing stylus
sewing needle (optional)
pinking shears (optional)
album, box or greetings card

1 Cut a piece of foil large enough to fit the metal stencil plus a small border all around it. Tape the stencil on to the foil, then place on a cutting mat. Use the thin end of the embossing stylus to outline the stencil. Indent the pattern by drawing the outlines, then rubbing over the whole area. Use the thin end of the stylus for small shapes, and the wide end for large areas. For very small shapes, use the blunt end of a needle.

2 Remove the stencil and continue to work on the image to refine it. Cover the indented side of the foil with double-sided adhesive tape, then turn the foil over and cut out the heart shape. For a decorative border, use pinking shears.

3 Remove the adhesive backing and stick the tin motif on to an album, box or greetings card. To make it even more secure, work the stylus around the edge, pressing in between the raised dots.

Greetings cards decorated with aluminium foil motifs are quick and easy to make. The foil is soft and can be cut with scissors. Designs can be drawn into the back of the foil to make a raised, embossed surface.

Embossed Greetings Cards

you will need
tracing paper
soft pencil
masking tape
aluminium foil, 36 gauge
(0.1mm/^{1}⁄$_{250}$in thick)
thin cardboard
dry ballpoint pen
scissors
thick coloured paper
all-purpose glue

1 Trace the motifs from the templates at the back of the book, then tape the tracing to a piece of aluminium foil and place it on top of a piece of thin cardboard. Carefully draw over the motif with a dry ballpoint pen to transfer it to the foil.

2 Remove the tracing paper from the foil and redraw the lines to make the embossing deeper. Add detail to the design at this stage. Remember any mistakes will show so be sure to follow the markings of your paper template accurately.

3 Turn the sheet of foil over and cut around the motif, leaving a narrow margin of foil around the outline of the design. Cut a piece of thick coloured paper and fold it in half to make a greetings card. Carefully spread a little glue over the back of the foil motif and stick it to the card, raised side up.

You will have endless pleasure watching birds preening and cleaning themselves in this beautiful beaten copper birdbath. Keep a fresh water supply to ensure the health and happiness of the birds.

Copper Birdbath

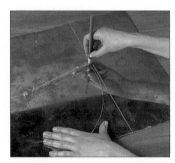

1 Using a chinagraph pencil and looped string, mark a 45cm/17¾in circle on the copper. Wearing gloves, cut out the circle with tin shears. File the sharp edges smooth.

2 Put the copper on a blanket and hammer it lightly from the centre. Spread the dips out to the rim. Repeat, starting from the centre each time, to get the required shape.

3 To make the perch, double a 1m/40in length of wire and hold the ends in a vice. Fasten a cup hook into the chuck of a hand drill and loop it through the wire. Twist the wire with the drill, then drill three 3mm/¹⁄₈in holes around the rim of the birdbath. Bend a knot into one end of three 1m/40in lengths of wire. Thread the wires up through the holes. Slip the perch over two of the straight wires.

Two small cake tins have been turned into a delightful wall decoration by the clever use of a metal angle bracket. The metal heart will reflect the flickering flame of a small candle or night-light.

Heart Candle Sconce

you will need
6-holed angle bracket
heart-shaped cake tin (pan), 7.5cm/3in
circular cake tin (pan), 7.5cm/3in
permanent marker pen
clamp and masking tape
drill
2 nuts and bolts
spanner (US wrench)
wall plugs (plastic anchors)
screwdriver and screw
candle or night-light

1 Place the angle bracket against the back of the heart tin and one edge of the circle tin. Mark through the holes in the bracket with a pen.

2 Drill through the marked holes. The photograph is styled for clarity – the drill would be perpendicular to the taped and clamped tin.

3 Use nuts and bolts to join the round tin to the bracket. Pre-drill and plug the wall, and then screw through the hole in the heart and the bracket into the wall behind. Add the candle to complete the project.

Aluminium flashing, traditionally used in roofing, takes on an unusual, pitted appearance that resembles pewter when it is hammered. It can be used to cover simple shapes such as this shelf.

Pewter-look Shelf

you will need

paper

pencil

ruler

scissors

sheet of MDF (medium density fiberboard), 18mm/³⁄₄ in thick

hand saw

drill

wood glue

2 screws

screwdriver

aluminium flashing

craft (utility) knife

ball hammer

1 Mark the two shelf pieces on MDF, using the templates at the back of the book. Cut them out with a hand saw. Draw a line down the centre and mark two points for the drill holes. Mark corresponding points on the long edge of the stand. Drill holes at these points, then glue and screw the shelf and stand together.

2 Cut lengths of aluminium flashing roughly to size using a craft knife. Peel away the backing and stick them to the shelf top, trimming the rough edges at the side with a craft knife and ruler as you go. Join each new length of flashing very closely to the last, so that no MDF is visible beneath the covering.

3 When the top is covered, place the shelf face down on a large piece of scrap MDF and trim away the excess flashing using a craft knife.

4 Cut lengths of flashing to cover the back and sides of the shelf, and stick them in place.

5 Using a ball hammer, tap the surface of the flashing to make indentations close together. Vary the force with which you strike the flashing, to make an interesting and irregular pattern.

This jewel box is made from a combination of thin zinc sheet, which has a subtle sheen rather like pewter, and brass shim, which is a fairly soft metal used mostly by sculptors.

Heart Jewel Box

you will need
work shirt and protective leather gloves
tin shears and snips
thin zinc plate
old cigar box
file
pencil
thin cardboard
scissors
brass shim
sheet of chipboard (particle board)
hammer and nail
soldering mat
protective mask and goggles
soldering iron and solder
strong glue

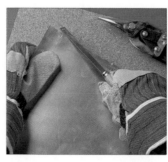

1 Wearing a work shirt and protective gloves, use tin shears to cut a piece of zinc to cover the lid of the cigar box. The zinc should be slightly larger than the box lid, to allow for a rim to cover the edges of the lid. File any rough edges. Draw a diamond and two different-sized hearts on a sheet of thin cardboard and cut them out.

2 Place the templates on a piece of brass shim and draw around them – six small hearts, one large heart and two diamonds. Draw some small circles freehand. Draw one small heart on a scrap of zinc. Cut out all the shapes and file the edges smooth. Place them on the chipboard and stamp a line of dots around the edge of each using a hammer and nail. Do not stamp the circles and zinc heart.

◀ **3** Cut four strips of shim to make a border around the zinc lid cover. Place all the pieces on a soldering mat and, wearing a protective mask and goggles, drop a blob of liquid solder in the centre of the circles, small hearts and diamonds. Cover the zinc heart with solder blobs. Add a line of blobs to each piece of the shim border.

4 Turn down a narrow rim around the zinc panel at 90° to turn down over the sides of the lid. Glue all the shapes and the borders to the panel.

5 Cut a strip of zinc the width of the box side and long enough to fit all around. File the edges smooth. Cut circles of shim, decorate each with a blob of solder and glue in place.

6 Glue the zinc strip around the sides of the box. Glue the zinc panel to the top of the lid. Gently tap the edges of the panel to make them flush with the sides of the lid.

Inspired by European folk-art motifs, these foil birds make very pretty ornaments for hanging on the Christmas tree, where their embossed decorations will catch the light as they twirl.

Embossed Birds

you will need
tracing paper
pencil
paper
small, pointed scissors
aluminium foil, 36 gauge
(0.1mm/¹⁄₂₅₀in thick)
adhesive tape
self-healing cutting mat
dry ballpoint pen
dressmaker's tracing wheel
hole punches, 5mm/¹⁄₅in and 3mm/¹⁄₈in

1 Trace and transfer the templates from the back of the book and cut out of paper. Place the templates on the aluminium foil and secure with tape. Place the foil on a cutting mat and draw around the shapes using a dry ballpoint pen.

2 Remove the templates. Draw in the top of the head and the beak of each bird with the ballpoint pen. Use a dressmaker's tracing wheel to mark the dotted lines on the body, tail, neck and crown, following the guidelines on the templates.

3 Draw the eye and the large dots on the wing and neck using the pen. Cut out the birds, cutting just outside the indented outline. Make the hole for the eye with a 5mm/¹⁄₅in hole punch, then use a small punch to make a hole in the bird's back for hanging.

There's more than one way to recycle empty cans: these light-hearted designs turn tin cans into insects to decorate the garden. Use cans that have the same logos so that your insects are symmetrical.

Tin-can Insects

you will need

tracing paper

pencil

strong scissors with small points

large steel beer can, top and

bottom removed

adhesive tape

large paintbrush with a tapered handle

small long-nosed pliers

1 Trace the template from the back of the book and cut it out. Cut up the side of the beer can opposite the bar code and open it out. Place the template in position and secure with adhesive tape. Cut all around the template carefully with sharp scissors.

2 Place the body of the insect over the handle of a paintbrush, with the fat part near the head. Bend the body around the handle. Fold the lower wings slightly under the body and the upper wings forwards, folding them slightly over the top of the body.

3 Using long-nosed pliers, twist the antennae back on themselves and curl the ends.

Aluminium cans are easy to recycle into attractive and useful objects such as this candle sconce. The shiny interior of the can makes a most effective reflector for the candle flame.

Beer-can Candle Sconce

you will need

tall aluminium beer can

craft (utility) knife

protective gloves

small, pointed scissors

paper

adhesive tape

permanent marker pen

hole punches, 5mm/⅛in and 3mm/⅛in

1 To cut off the can top, make a slit in the metal using a craft knife and wearing protective gloves, then cut through the slit with scissors. Enlarge the template at the back of the book to fit your can, and cut it out of paper. Wrap it around the can and secure with adhesive tape. Draw around the shape using a marker pen.

2 Remove the paper template and cut around the design using small, pointed scissors. Make a short slit between each scallop.

3 Use the larger hole punch to make a hanging hole at the top, a hole on either side of the heart shape, and one in each scallop. Use the smaller punch to make a border all round the heart shape. Fold over each punched scallop shape to form a decorative rim for the candle sconce.

These plant markers will lend an air of elegant order to any flower garden. They are simple to construct and will hold together without any glue. Punch the plant name into each marker.

Plant Markers

you will need
tracing paper
soft pencil
thin cardboard
scissors
sheet of copper foil, 36 gauge
(0.1mm/¹⁄₂₅₀in thick)
permanent marker pen
sheet of chipboard
bradawl or awl
pliers

1 Trace the template at the back of the book. Transfer to thin cardboard. Cut out the template and draw around it on the copper foil with a permanent marker pen. Cut the plant marker from the foil using a pair of scissors.

2 Place the copper marker on the cardboard on top of the chipboard. Punch the design and plant name into the front of the marker using a bradawl or awl. Cut all the way up the stem directly under the flowerhead. Using pliers, pleat the middle sections of the plant marker.

3 Hold the cut strips of the stem together so that the two halves of the bottom petal are joined. Make a fold along the two outer lines of the stem. Wrap the stem around the cut section to hold the marker together.

Adapted from the simple paper angels that we all made as children, this embossed pewter design will add a touch of elegance to the top of your Christmas tree or provide a festive ornament on the mantelpiece.

Treetop Angel

you will need

pencil

paper

masking tape

pewter shim

self-healing cutting mat

dressmaker's tracing wheel

dry ballpoint pen

pinking shears

craft (utility) knife

permanent marker pen

1 Enlarge the template at the back of the book to the required size. Tape to the pewter shim. Place the sheet on a self-healing cutting mat and use a dressmaker's tracing wheel to trace over the double outlines.

2 Draw over all the solid lines using a dry ballpoint pen. Indent the dots using a pencil.

3 Cut around the shape using pinking shears. Be very careful when cutting around the halo and wing tips. If you bend some of the zigzag edging, smooth back into shape with your fingers.

4 Turn the angel over. Following the paper pattern, complete the remaining embossed markings from the reverse side, pressing in dots for the eyes and at the centre point of each star.

5 Use a craft knife to cut a slit around the head, inside the halo. Be careful not to cut too near the neck so as not to weaken it. Cut the two slits beside the wings where marked.

6 Roll the head and neck slightly around a cylindrical object such as a marker pen.

7 Bend the angel's body into a curve and slot together as shown.

This punched tin cabinet is based on those of the American settlers, who produced a wide range of household artefacts using tin plate, and in doing so raised the decorative punching process to an art form.

Punched Panel Cabinet

you will need

small wooden cabinet with a recess in the door

ruler

sheet of tin plate, 30 gauge (0.3mm/⅛₃in thick)

permanent marker pen

work shirt and protective leather gloves

tin shears

90° and 45° wooden blocks

bench vice

hide hammer

file

pair of compasses (compass)

pencil

graph paper

scissors

sheet of chipboard (particle board)

panel pins (brads)

tack hammer

masking tape

centre punch

ball hammer

small chisel

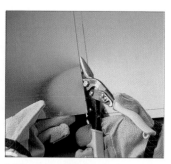

1 Measure the recess in the door of the cabinet. Mark out the dimensions of the recess on the tin using a marker pen. Draw a 1cm/⅖in border inside the rectangle. Mark points along the sides 2cm/⅘in from each corner of the outer rectangle. Draw diagonal lines from these points to the corners of the inner rectangle.

2 Wearing a work shirt and protective leather gloves, cut the panel from the sheet of tin using tin shears. Cut along the diagonal lines at the corners. This will allow the border to be folded behind the panel to give it a smooth edge.

3 Firmly clamp the 90° block of wood in the bench vice. Place the panel on the wooden block with the ruled edge of the tin resting on the edge of the block. Using a hide hammer, tap along the edge of the panel to turn it over to an angle of 90°.

4 Turn the panel over. Position the 45° wooden block inside the turned edge and hammer the edge over it. Remove the block and hammer the edge flat. Finish the remaining sides of the panel in the same way. File the corners to remove any sharp edges.

5 Using a pair of compasses and a ruler, measure out and draw the panel design on graph paper. Cut the paper to the same size as the panel.

6 Place the panel face up on a sheet of chipboard and secure each corner to the board with a panel pin. Tape the paper pattern to the front of the panel with masking tape.

7 Place the centre punch on one of the lines. Tap it with the hammer to indent the tin. Move the punch along the line and tap it to make the next mark. Complete the design.

8 Remove the paper pattern and add extra decoration to the front of the panel using a small chisel. Unpin the panel from the board.

9 Place the decorated panel in the recess on the front of the cabinet. Use panel pins at each corner to attach the panel securely to the cabinet.

Pewter shim is simple to emboss. For this project, a wooden block is wrapped like a parcel with the embossed pewter to make an attractive doorstop – you could also use it as an unusual bookend.

Scrollwork Doorstop

1 Place the pewter shim on a cutting mat. Following the template at the back of the book, use a marker pen and ruler to draw the foldlines on to the metal. Using a dry ballpoint pen, score a line 3mm/⅛in from one end and fold over. Score along all the solid marked lines. Turn the pewter over and score the remaining dotted lines.

2 Turn the sheet back again and use a permanent marker pen to draw the pattern in freehand on the areas shown on the template. Vary the design according to your personal taste. If you are using a more formal design than these freestyle curlicues, plan it on paper first. This is the back of the design.

3 Score the pattern on the pewter with a stylus. Use an ice lolly stick end for thick lines and a pencil for fine ones.

4 Turn the sheet over and complete the design by indenting dots around the lines using the stylus or pencil.

5 Wrap the shim around the wooden block, allowing the neatened, folded edge to overlap the other edge. Make sure you place the block centrally, with equal amounts for folding.

6 Fold along the scored lines and wrap up the block as if it were a present.

7 Place a metal washer centrally on the end of the block and hammer a roofing nail through it to secure the pewter and give it interesting detail. Repeat at the other end of the block.

The rising sun has been incorporated into the design of this number plaque. Small indentations are punched into the front of the plaque to create a densely pitted surface and to raise the unpunched areas.

Number Plaque

you will need

sheet of tin plate, 30 gauge
(0.3mm/¹⁄₈₃in thick)

permanent marker pen

ruler

work shirt and protective
leather gloves

tin shears

90° and 45° wooden blocks

bench vice

hide hammer

file

graph paper

scissors

pencil

masking tape

sheet of chipboard (particle board)

panel pins (brads)

tack hammer

centre punch

ball hammer

wire (steel) wool

clear polyurethane varnish

varnish brush

1 Draw a rectangle on a sheet of tin. Draw a 1cm/²⁄₅in border around the inside of the rectangle. Measure a point 2.5cm/1in from each corner of the outer rectangle. Draw diagonal lines across all the corners. Wearing protective clothing, cut out the plaque with tin shears.

2 Firmly clamp the 90° block of wood in a bench vice. Place the plaque on the wooden block with the ruled edge of the tin resting on the edge of the block. Using a hide hammer, tap along the edge of the plaque to turn over all the marked border areas to an angle of 90°.

3 Turn the plaque over and position the 45° wooden block inside the turned edge. Hammer the edge over it, remove the block and then hammer the edge completely flat. Finish the remaining three sides of the plaque in the same way. Carefully file the four corners to make them smooth.

4 Cut a piece of graph paper the same size as the plaque. Draw your pattern and desired numbers, then tape the pattern to the front of the plaque. Secure it to the chipboard with a panel pin in each corner.

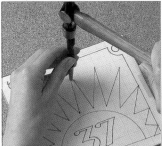

5 Place the centre punch on a line and tap it with a ball hammer to make an indentation. Move the punch about 3mm/⅛ in along the line and tap it again to make the next mark. Continue to punch along the lines until the design is completed.

6 Remove the paper pattern, then randomly punch the surface around the sunburst and inside the numbers. Scour the surface of the panel with wire wool before sealing the plaque with varnish. Allow to dry before screwing in place.

Unwanted food containers are a good source of tin and are perfect for making items such as this handsome spice rack, as they are already partly formed into the right shape.

Tin Spice Rack

1 Wearing protective clothes, cut the base of the biscuit tin in half carefully using tin shears. File all the cut edges of the tin smooth. You will only need one half of the tin for this project. Dispose of the other half of the tin safely.

2 Draw the curved shape of the back panel of the spice rack on to the lid of the tin. Cut out using tin shears and file all the cut edges smooth. Place the curved back panel against the cut edge of one half of the biscuit tin. Hold the two together with masking tape.

3 Place the spice rack on a soldering mat. Wearing a protective mask and goggles, apply flux to the join, then solder the two parts together. Using pliers, fold in the filed edges of the back panel and the base to flatten them completely. File any remaining rough edges smooth.

4 Measure the dimensions of the inside of the spice rack. Cut lengths of fine wire and solder them together to make a grid to form compartments for the spices. Place the grid inside the spice rack and solder it in place.

5 Place the top edge of the rack on a block of wood and pierce a hole in it using a bradawl or awl. Open the hole slightly using a pair of pliers. File the rough edges from the inside hole. Turn over the edges around the hole and squeeze them flat with pliers.

6 Cut a length of fine wire and form a spiral at each end. Cut six lengths of wire and form two large and two small curves and two small circles. Solder the spiral to the back of the rack and the curves to the front. Shape a wire to fit around the edges of the back of the rack and solder in place.

7 Cut a small circle of brass shim and glue it to the centre back of the rack. Apply decorative blobs of solder to the shim circle, along the edge of the rack, around the spiral and in the small circles. Make a wire circle to go around the shim and solder in place.

The appearance of a special book can be dramatically enhanced with an embossed metal panel. The panel covering this book imitates the ornate leather and metal bindings adorning early prayer books.

Embossed Book Jacket

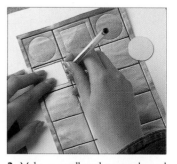

1 Cut a piece of aluminium foil the same size as the front of the book. Using a marker pen and a ruler, draw a 6mm/¼in border all the way around the edge of the foil. Divide the area within the border into squares. Draw over the lines to emboss the foil using a dry ballpoint pen. This is the back of the design.

2 Make a cardboard rectangle and circle template. Make them small enough to fit into the grid. Make another circle and rectangle, slightly smaller. Cut out the shapes. Place the large circle in the centre of the first square. Draw around it using a dry ballpoint pen. Repeat with the large rectangle in the next square. Repeat over the whole jacket.

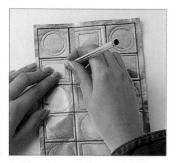

3 Place the small circle inside an embossed circle and draw around it. Place the small rectangle inside a large rectangle and emboss all the shapes in the same way.

4 Draw small double circles and also double semicircles in each circle. Draw a double oval and radiating lines inside each rectangle. Emboss a dotted line around each rectangle and around the edge of the jacket.

5 Turn the foil over so that it is right side up. Using a fine brush, highlight small areas of the design with the gold lacquer paint. When it is dry, glue the jacket to the front of the book.

You don't need metal-working skills to make this cheerful weathervane, as the shapes are cut out of rigid plastic sheet and covered with strips of roof-flashing, which is given a densely pitted texture.

Hammered Weathervane

you will need

paper

pencil

ruler

scissors

permanent marker pen

Perspex (Plexiglas)

coping saw, jigsaw or band saw

scrap wood

drill

craft (utility) knife

small paint roller

galvanized wire

aluminium flashing

metal straight edge

hacksaw

file

brass screw

screwdriver

metal rod or broom handle

newspaper

small hammer

blue glass paint

paintbrush

1 Scale up the template at the back of the book and cut out paper patterns for the rooster and an arrow 24cm/ 9½in long. Draw around these shapes on to the plastic sheet.

2 Cut out the shapes using a coping saw, jigsaw or band saw. Using a piece of scrap wood to protect your work surface, drill a row of small holes as shown. Drill the rooster's eye.

3 Use a craft knife to cut the central plastic tube from a small paint roller and use galvanized wire to attach it to the rooster.

4 Cut strips of aluminium flashing long enough to cover the plastic shapes. Trim the edges of the strips using a craft knife and straight edge, so that you can make neat joints.

5 Apply the strips of flashing to both sides of the rooster, trimming the edges with a craft knife as you stick them on. Wrap the lower strips on the rooster around the roller.

6 As you apply further strips, join the long edges together carefully. Cut out the eye of the rooster. Cover the arrow with flashing, then drill a small hole for the screw.

7 Using a hacksaw, remove the bent section of the paint roller handle. File the sawn edges smooth.

8 Screw the arrow to the plastic roller handle. Fit the roller handle to the metal rod or broom handle to make a mount for the weathervane.

9 Working on newspaper, tap gently all over the bird to give it texture. Colour the section marked on the template blue. Attach the rooster.

A coat rack will keep coats, umbrellas and hats tidy, avoiding clutter in halls. The rich purple background and the slightly matt tones of the metal foils give this rack a touch of splendour.

Regal Coat Rack

you will need

pencil

graph paper

ruler or tape measure

scissors

sheet of MDF (medium-density fiberboard), 5mm/¼in thick

hand saw or jigsaw

fine-grade abrasive paper

wood primer

paintbrush

satin-finish wood paint

tracing paper

soft pencil

thin cardboard

copper foil, 40 gauge (0.08mm/¹⁄₃₀₀in thick)

dry ballpoint pen

aluminium foil, 36 gauge (0.1mm/¹⁄₂₅₀in thick)

centre punch

epoxy resin glue

drill

3 ball end hooks

2 mirror plates

1 Draw the basic shape for the coat rack on to graph paper to make a pattern. This rack is 60cm/24in wide by 20cm/8in high at its highest point. Cut out and draw around it on to the MDF. Saw out the shape with a hand saw or jigsaw. Smooth the edges with abrasive paper.

2 Seal the surface of the coat rack with one coat of wood primer. When it is dry, lightly sand the surface, then paint it with satin-finish wood paint. Allow to dry thoroughly. Trace the crown, fleur-de-lys and star templates from the back of the book. Transfer them on to a sheet of thin cardboard. Cut out the shapes to make templates.

3 Place the crown on the copper foil and draw around it using a dry ball-point pen. Repeat. Draw around the fleur-de-lys and stars on aluminium foil. Draw two stars. Cut out all of the shapes using scissors.

4 Rest each shape on a piece of thin cardboard. Make a line of dots around the edge of all the shapes by pressing into the foil using a centre punch.

5 Cut a 5cm/2in-wide strip of the aluminium foil the same length as the bottom edge of the rack. Cut a wavy line along the top edge of the strip and then mark a row of dots along it with the punch.

6 Place the wavy edging and the stars, crowns and fleur-de-lys on the front of the rack with the raised side of the dots facing upwards. Use epoxy resin glue to stick the pieces in place.

7 When the glue is thoroughly dry, drill three holes at equal distances 2.5cm/1in from the bottom edge of the coat rack. Screw a hook into each hole. Attach a mirror plate to both sides of the coat rack for hanging.

Add a touch of fairy-tale romance to your garden with this whimsical tower. Secure it to a tray on top of a tree stump or post, and sprinkle nuts and seeds all around to attract the birds.

Rapunzel's Tower

you will need

paper

pencil

garden twine

ruler or tape measure

scissors

metal tubing, 15cm/6in diameter

45 x 45cm/18 x 18in copper sheet, 0.9mm/¹⁄₂₇in thick

chinagraph pencil

protective gloves

tin shears and snips

file

drill, 3mm/¹⁄₈in bit

blind rivet gun and 3mm/¹⁄₈in rivets

glue gun and glue stick

2.5 x 5cm/1 x 2in copper foil, 0.2mm/¹⁄₁₂₅in thick

nail or wire, 6.5cm/2½in long

twigs

1 Make a pattern for the cone-shaped roof to fit around the metal tubing; add a 2cm/⅘in overlap for joining the edges. Transfer on to the copper sheet with a chinagraph pencil. Wearing protective gloves, cut out the shape using tin shears. File off any sharp edges. Bend the copper into a cone shape with an overlap. Check the fit on the tubing.

2 Drill 3mm/⅛in holes at intervals through both layers of copper along the overlap and fasten the overlap using blind rivets. Squeeze the handle of the rivet gun until the rivet shaft snaps off, securing the overlap firmly. Use a glue gun to glue the cone-shaped roof in place on top of the metal tubing. Allow the glue to dry.

3 Cut a wavy flag for the roof from copper foil. Cut a sideways "V" in one end of the flag and bend the other end around a nail or short piece of wire as a flagpole. Glue to the tip of the roof.

4 Make a rope ladder by knotting cut lengths of small twigs between two lengths of twine. Cut an entrance hole in the tubing with tin snips and glue the ladder in place.

The idea of decorating metal objects with raised punched patterns has been around ever since sheet metal was invented about 300 years ago. Bare metal buckets are ideal for this sort of pattern-making.

Punched Metal Bucket

you will need
permanent marker pen
bare metal bucket
piece of wood
blunt nail or centre punch
hammer
rag
lighter fuel (or similar solvent)

1 Using a permanent marker pen, draw your pattern on the inside of the bucket. Any repeated curves or shapes are suitable.

2 Rest the bucket on a piece of wood to protect the work surface. Following the pattern, tap the nail or centre punch with a hammer, keeping the dents about 1cm/⅖in apart. Hammer the pattern all over the inside.

3 Use a rag and lighter fuel to clean off the marker pen pattern that is left between the punched marks.

Inspired by Mexican folk art, this brilliantly painted and punched mirror frame will give your room a touch of exotic colour and warmth. Use the brightest paints or pens you can find.

Mexican Mirror

you will need
paper
permanent marker pen
scissors
aluminium sheet
glue gun and glue stick
self-healing cutting mat
hammer
small and large centre punches
tin snips
protective gloves
chisel
blue glass paint
paintbrush
permanent felt-tipped pens or
glass paints: turquoise, green,
orange and pink
circular mirror, 15cm/6in diameter
circular cake board, 25cm/10in
diameter
double-sided adhesive pads
nail or fine drill bit
galvanized wire
wire cutters
pliers
7 short screws
screwdriver

1 Enlarge the template at the back of the book to a diameter of 30cm/12in and then cut it out. Stick the paper pattern to the aluminium sheet using a glue gun, and trace around this with a permanent marker pen.

2 With the aluminium sheet resting on a cutting mat, make indentations along the lines of the pattern using a hammer and small centre punch. Just two taps of the hammer at each point should be sufficient.

3 Cut out the shape with tin snips, wearing gloves to protect your hands. To cut out the central area, first punch a hole through the centre using a chisel, and cut from there.

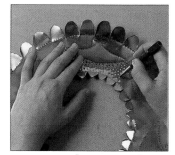

4 Using the small centre punch, hammer indentations at random all over the inner section of the frame to give it an overall texture.

▶

5 Paint the indented section using translucent blue glass paint. Leave to dry. Colour the rest of the frame as shown using permanent felt-tipped pens or glass paints.

6 Draw and cut out a five-petalled flower template with a diameter of 5cm/2in. Trace all around it on to an aluminium sheet using a permanent marker pen to make seven flowers. Cut them out using tin snips.

7 Colour the individual flowers using permanent felt-tipped pens or glass paints in bright colours.

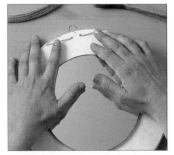

8 Place all the flowers on a cutting mat and use a large centre punch to hammer a hole through the centre of each, big enough for a screw to pass through. If the flowers buckle, bend them back into shape. Make similar holes at all the points on the frame, following the template.

9 Attach the mirror to the bottom of the cake board using double-sided adhesive pads. Pierce two holes near the edge of the board using a nail or fine drill bit. Cut a piece of galvanized wire and bend into a hanging loop. Thread the ends through the holes and bend them flat against the board.

10 Place the frame over the mirror and backing board. Place the flowers in position so that holes correspond with those in the frame and screw them on through the frame into the backing board. Colour the screws to match the flower centres.

Painted tinware is a popular art form in many countries, including India, where fine-gauge tin is stamped with highly decorative patterns and often highlighted with translucent paints.

Painted Mirror

you will need
sheet of tin plate, 30 gauge
(0.3mm/¹⁄₈₃in thick)
marker pen
ruler
work shirt and protective
leather gloves
tin shears
90° and 45° wooden blocks
bench vice
hide hammer
file
graph paper
scissors
saucer
pencil
masking tape
sheet of chipboard (particle board)
panel pins (brads)
tack hammer
centre punch
ball hammer
chinagraph pencil
soft cloth
translucent paints
paintbrush
square mirror tile
aluminium foil, 36 gauge
(0.1mm/¹⁄₂₅₀in thick)
epoxy resin glue
copper foil, 40 gauge
(0.08mm/¹⁄₃₀₀in)
D-ring hanger

1 To make the frame, draw a 30cm/ 12in square on a sheet of tin. Draw a 1cm/⅖in border inside the square. Measure 2cm/⅘in from the outer corners along each side. Connect these points by drawing diagonal lines, as shown. Wearing protective clothes, cut out the square with tin shears. Cut along the diagonal lines.

2 Firmly clamp the 90° block of wood in a bench vice. Place the mirror frame on the wooden block with the ruled edge of the tin square resting on the edge. Using a hide hammer, tap along the edge of the tin to turn it over to an angle of 90°.

3 Turn the frame over. Hold the 45° block of wood inside the turned edge and hammer the edge over. Remove the block and hammer the edge flat. File the corners of the mirror frame to remove any sharp edges. Cut a piece of graph paper the same size as the frame.

4 Draw the decorative corner lines on to the paper, drawing around the saucer. Draw the centre square slightly larger than the mirror tile. Tape the pattern to the back of the frame, place it face down on the chipboard and secure with panel pins.

5 Place the point of the centre punch on a line of the inside square and tap it with the ball hammer to make an indentation. Move the punch about 3mm/⅛in along the line and tap it to make the next mark. Continue punching along all the lines until the design is completed.

6 Unpin the frame from the board and remove the pattern. Turn the frame over, so the raised side faces up. Using a chinagraph pencil, draw a square halfway along each side. Draw a heart in each square. Pin the frame to the board again and punch an outline around each square and heart. Punch the area between the heart and the square to make a densely pitted surface. Remove the frame from the board. Wipe over the surface of the metal with a clean, soft cloth to remove any grease.

7 Paint the embossed areas and the border. Leave to dry and apply a second coat if the first is patchy. Place the mirror tile on aluminium foil and draw around it, then draw a 1.5cm/⅗in border around that. Cut out the foil. Clip the corners to make folding the edges over easier. Glue the mirror to the centre of the foil. Glue the edges of the foil over the tile.

8 Cut four small squares of copper foil, mark your choice of design on each, then glue one square in each corner of the tile. Glue the mirror to the centre of the frame. Glue the hanger to the back of the frame. Allow the glue to dry thoroughly.

Because of its softness, fine-gauge aluminium foil is just perfect for cladding frames. Coloured and clear glass nuggets combine with the subdued tones of the foil to give this frame a Celtic air.

Photograph Frame

you will need
photograph frame
ruler
aluminium foil, 36 gauge
(0.1mm/¹⁄₂₅₀in thick)
scissors
epoxy resin glue
pencil
thin cardboard
marker pen
dry ballpoint pen
coloured and clear glass nuggets

1 Carefully remove the glass and the backing from the frame. Cut foil strips to cover. Make the foil long enough to wrap around to the back of the frame. Mould the foil strips around and glue them in place.

2 Cut pieces of foil to cover the four corners. Mould to the contours of the frame and glue them in place.

3 Draw a circle on to cardboard and cut out to make a template. Draw around the cardboard on to the foil using a marker pen. Cut out the foil circles. Draw a design on to one side of each circle using a dry ballpoint pen. This is now the back of the circle.

4 Turn the foil circles over so that the raised side of the embossing is face up. Glue coloured glass nuggets to the centre fronts of half of the foil circles. Glue clear glass nuggets to the centres of the other half.

5 Glue the foil circles around the frame, spacing them evenly. Alternate the circles so a coloured glass centre follows one with clear glass. When the glue is thoroughly dry, replace the glass and backing in the frame.

This chandelier is made from eight small tin cans and a tin flan ring. The chandelier is suspended from strong beaded chain; buy the kind with forged links that can withstand the weight of the chandelier.

Tin-can Chandelier

you will need

tape measure

marker pen

tin flan ring, 30cm/12in in diameter

wooden block

bradawl or awl

file

can opener

8 small cans

length of wooden pole

bench vice

8 nuts and short bolts

screwdriver

pliers

4 S-joiners

strong beaded chain

wire cutters

4 jump rings (wires)

key ring

epoxy resin glue

coloured glass nuggets

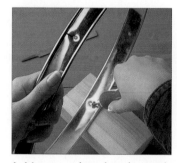

1 Measure and mark eight evenly spaced points around the flan ring. Rest the ring on a block of wood and pierce a hole at each point using a bradawl or awl. File away the rough edges at the back of the holes.

2 Mark three equally spaced points near the top edge of the ring. These holes will be used to suspend the chandelier from the beaded chain for hanging. Pierce them with a bradawl as before and file away the rough edges.

3 Remove the top from each can and file the edges smooth. Mark a point halfway down each can (avoiding the seam). Clamp a length of wooden pole in a bench vice. Support each can on the pole and pierce a hole in the side at the marked point using a bradawl. File any rough edges at the back of the holes.

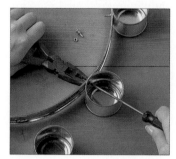

4 Place each can against a hole in the flan ring. Join the cans to the ring using short bolts. Screw the nuts on to the bolts as tightly as they will go so the cans are kept firmly in position.

5 Attach an S-joiner through each of the three holes in the top of the flan ring. Using pliers, close the joiners as tightly as they will go.

6 Cut three lengths of beaded chain each 30cm/12in. Attach a jump ring to the end of each length of chain. Attach a length to each S-joiner. Tightly close the jump rings with pliers.

7 Hold the free ends of the chains together and join them using a jump ring. Join the jump ring to an S-joiner and close the ring very tightly. Attach a key ring to the top of the S-joiner to make a hanger.

8 Glue green glass nuggets around the outside of the chandelier. Glue a red glass nugget to the outside of each can.

This aluminium candlestick has a cartoon-like appearance that is very appealing. The small sections are constructed first and then joined together. Each section is attached to the next using pop rivets.

Rocket Candlestick

you will need
tracing paper
soft pencil
thin cardboard
glue
scissors
thin aluminium sheet
work shirt and protective
leather gloves
tin snips
file
drill
pliers
90° wooden block
hammer
pop riveter and rivets
black oven-hardening clay
epoxy resin glue

1 Trace the rocket templates from the back of the book. Enlarge the pieces if required using a photocopier. Stick the tracings on to thin cardboard, allow to dry, then accurately cut out each shape.

3 Mark the drilling points on each piece and drill the holes. Hold the metal with a pair of pliers to stop it spinning around while you drill.

◀ **5** Place the side sections on the edge of the wooden block and hammer over the edges. Hold each section and gently curve it outwards.

▶ **6** Hold two side sections with the tabs to the inside. Join the sections with pop rivets at the middle and the bottom holes. Join two more pairs.

2 Cut out the templates and draw around them on to the aluminium. Draw six side sections, three fins and one top shelf. Wearing protective clothes, cut out all the pieces using tin snips and file the edges smooth.

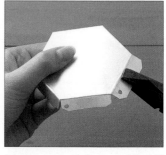

4 Using a pair of pliers, carefully fold down all the sides of the top shelf to make an angle of 90°. Bend the metal over a right-angle object.

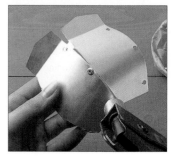

7 Place a fin between two separate side pairs and pop rivet all three layers together at the middle and bottom holes. Pop rivet the remaining side pairs together, with a fin in-between.

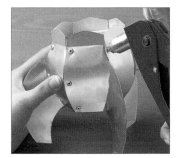

8 Position the shelf at the top of the candlestick with the sides pointing downwards. Join the shelf to the base with pop rivets through the top holes.

9 To make the feet, roll three balls of black clay. Flatten the base of each and make an indentation in the ball top. Bake the clay according to the manufacturer's instructions. When cool, glue a foot to each fin.

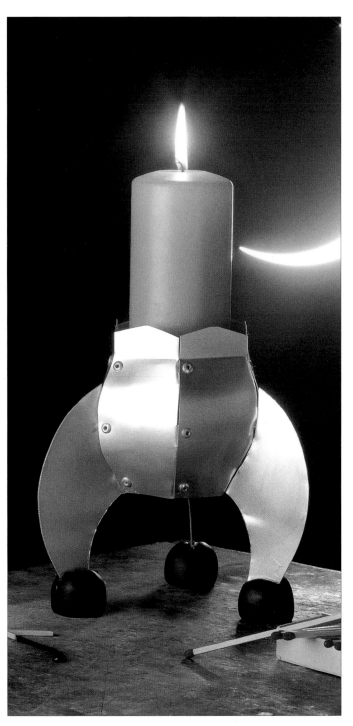

Picture Framing

In this chapter you can learn the basics of making an attractive frame and use a wide range of paint effects to brighten and transform existing picture frames. A simple coat of colourwash or woodstain will add instant colour, or you could go for a more dramatic look, such as gilding or a tortoiseshell effect, to create sumptuous style. Add extra decoration with stencils or stamps, and finish with wax or varnish to protect your work.

Most of the items listed below are basic frame-making equipment, which you will use many times, so it is worth investing in any you do not already have. Specialist tools are available from framing suppliers.

Materials and Equipment

is a metal fixture, usually bolted to a workbench, in which moulding lengths are cut at a 45° angle.

Corner gauge

When decorating mounts (mats), this fits into the corner of the window to allow pencil corner marks to be positioned accurately.

Craft (utility) knife

This has multiple uses in picture framing. There are several varieties so choose one that feels comfortable.

Cutting mat

Essential when cutting with a craft knife, as it protects the underlying surface. Self-healing cutting mats stay smooth and free from score marks.

Drill and drill bits

Both electric and hand drills are suitable for frame making.

D-rings

Picture wire is threaded through these for hanging. D-rings are available as single or double. Attach them to the backing board with butterflies (rivet-like fixings), or screw into the back of the frame.

Frame clamp

Frames are clamped to hold the joints together while the glue dries.

Acid-free hinging tape

Water-soluble gummed tissue tape is used to make tab hinges to secure artwork to a backing board. It should be weaker than the paper of the artwork so that it tears first if the assembly is broken up.

Blade

When cutting windows in mounts (mats) a blade is needed to release the cut corners to avoid tearing and give a neat, sharp finish.

Bradawl or awl

Used for making initial holes in hardboard or wood.

Burnishing tools

A burnishing bone is for smoothing the cut edges of a mount (mat). The traditional gilder's agate burnisher is used to polish water-gilded surfaces.

Clamps

These come in all shapes and sizes and have various uses. A mitre clamp

Framer's point gun

This specialist tool is used for fitting up picture frames. It inserts flat pins horizontally into the moulding to hold the backing board in place.

Glass cutter

Diamond-headed and tungsten types for heavy-duty glass cutting can be quite expensive, but cheaper alternatives are available for domestic use.

Glue

PVA (white) glue is used to hold the mitre joints in frames. Two-part **epoxy resin glue** forms a very strong bond for joining metal and stone. **Rubber solution glue** is used for attaching fabrics to mounts (mats).

Hacksaw

Used in a mitre clamp to cut wooden or manufactured mouldings. There are various types of blade, including blades for cutting metal mouldings.

Heatgun

Normally intended for stripping painted wood, an electric heat gun can be used to scorch patterns in wooden mouldings.

Mitre box

This two-sided wooden box has deep slots at a 45° angle to take a tenon saw for cutting moulding lengths. Its high sides keep the saw vertical and help to steady the moulding.

Mount (mat) board

The wide range of mount boards available fall mainly into two categories: regular and conservation.

Regular boards are cheaper but the acid from the wood pulp used to make them will damage artwork over the years. Conservation boards are acid-free and will not damage artwork.

Mount (mat) cutter

A tool for cutting a bevelled window out of mount (mat) board. You can buy hand-held versions from good art stores and framing suppliers.

Paintbrushes

Use flat-face oil and sable brushes, approximately 1cm/½in and 2.5cm/1in wide, for detailing and pointing. Use stencil brushes for stencilling.

Panel pins (brads)

Thin pins are used for joining frames and tacking the backing board to the frame in the final assembly stage.

Safety gloves

Wear rubber (latex) gloves when painting, and protective cotton or leather gloves when handling metal foils or cutting glass.

Safety mask

Use with any paint or varnish sprays to avoid inhaling the mist, and when sawing MDF, which creates a large amount of fine dust.

Straight edge rule

Use for marking and cutting lines.

Tack hammer

A lightweight hammer is used for tapping in panel pins (brads); it can be used as an alternative to the V-nail joiner when assembling frames.

Tape measure

Used for measuring artwork, mounts and moulding.

Tenon saw

A 30cm/12in-wide flat saw used with a mitre box to cut wooden or manufactured mouldings. The reinforced upper edge keeps the blade rigid to allow very accurate straight cuts.

T-square

A measuring tool used to give a true square or rectangle. Used for marking up mounts (mats) and cutting glass.

V-nail joiner

When the frame is being joined together it is used to push V-shaped nails across the mitres to hold them together. It can also be used to secure the backing board to the frame.

V-nails

Used with the V-nail joiner to underpin the frame.

Wire cutters

Used to cut picture wire.

Wood

Mouldings are available in both soft and hardwoods in many designs. Those sold for framing have a ready-cut rebate to take the picture and glass. **Plywood** is an ideal material for making frames. It consists of thin sheets of wood glued together; the grains of wood in adjacent sheets are arranged at right angles to each other, which makes it exceptionally strong. It can be used to make backing boards as an alternative to **hardboard**.

A picture frame serves a dual purpose: it is designed both to display and to protect the painting or photograph within it, and all its various components contribute to these functions.

The Parts of a Frame

The component parts of the frame form a multi-layered sandwich, with the picture or photograph as the filling. The backing board, which is usually made of hardboard, gives rigidity. If delicate artwork is being framed, the backing board should be overlaid by an acid-free barrier to give extra protection. The image itself can be secured to the backing board using tab hinges of acid-free paper tape.

When a picture is to be displayed within a window mount (mat), it is customary to allow a slightly larger margin at the bottom of the mount than at the top or sides, to correct an optical illusion which occurs when the picture is hung on the wall. If all the margins were the same width, the bottom one would appear smaller than the others.

It is very important to take precise measurements before making a mount, and it is usually worth checking all your measurements before you begin to cut anything.

If a mount is not used, narrow wooden fillets should be inserted in the frame between the glass and the picture, to prevent the glass from touching the surface of the artwork. These will be visible when the picture is hung, so the wood should be selected to coordinate well with the image and the frame.

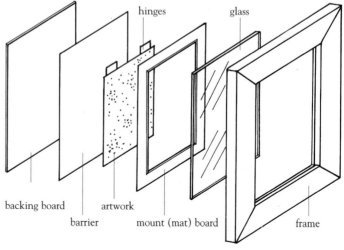

backing board · barrier · artwork · hinges · mount (mat) board · glass · frame

Glass suppliers will cut glass to size for you at the time of purchase, but you may also need to cut pieces yourself if you are doing a lot of framing. The skill needs a confident but careful approach.

Cutting Glass

you will need

frame
tape measure
protective cotton gloves
fine black marker pen
picture glass
T-square
glass cutter
piece of board
pencil

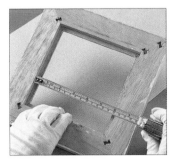

1 On the reverse side of the frame, measure the horizontal from rebate to rebate. Wear protective cotton gloves when you are handling glass.

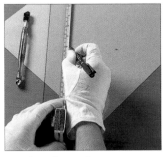

2 Reduce the window measurement by 2mm/¹⁄₁₆in, then mark the measurement on the glass using a fine black marker pen.

3 Place a T-square on the glass and line up the glass cutter so that it is on top of the marks. Holding both the glass cutter and T-square, firmly score the glass with the glass cutter in one long smooth stroke. Do not cut again over the same line, as this will make the glass shatter and splinter.

4 Hold the glass over a board so that the score line is on the edge. Gently tap the glass below the score mark, using the round end of the cutter.

5 Place a pencil directly beneath the cut. Using both hands placed on each side of the pencil and score mark, gently but firmly press the glass down. The glass will break cleanly along the score line. Repeat for the vertical measurement. When the glass is cut, clean it, then gently insert it in the rebate at the back of the frame.

Covering a mount (mat) with fabric adds richness and depth to a background, especially if you use a luxury fabric such as silk or velvet. Traditionally, Persian and Indian textiles were framed in a fabric mount.

Fabric-covered Mount

you will need
pre-cut mount (mat)
fabric
cutting mat
tape measure
craft (utility) knife
ruler
fabric glue
glue brush
ink roller

1 Place the pre-cut mount (mat) face down on the fabric, on a cutting mat. Cut out the fabric 2.5cm/1in larger all around to allow for overlaps. Trim the corners of the fabric to make folding over easier.

2 Apply a thin, even coat of fabric glue to the face of the mount. Centre the fabric on top of the mount, press down and rub gently with a clean ink roller to ensure good adhesion.

3 Turn over the covered mount so that the fabric is face down. Cut out the window, leaving a 2.5cm/1in border of fabric for the overlaps.

4 Cut mitres in the overlap fabric in the window. Apply fabric glue to the mount where the overlaps will lie, then fold over the fabric edges and press down firmly.

5 Fold down the overlaps on the side edges of the mount. At the corners, hold the fabric firmly and cut a mitre with a craft knife, then apply fabric glue and press the fabric down.

There are several ways of cutting a length of moulding to make a basic frame, but the ends must always be cut at a precise angle. You can use either a mitre clamp or a wooden mitre box to guide the saw.

Basic Wooden Frame

you will need

tape measure

moulding

mitre clamp or box

saw

pencil

PVA (white) glue and brush

frame clamp

cloth

V-nail joiner and V-nails or vice,

panel pins (brads) and tack hammer

woodfiller

cork sanding block

medium- and fine-grade abrasive paper

1 Measure the mounted artwork to give you the inside rebate measurement for the frame. Hold the length of moulding in a mitre clamp or box and cut the first end at a 45° angle. The edge of the moulding with the rebate should be the furthest from you.

2 Measure along the inside rebate of the moulding and mark the position for the next mitre cut on the face of the moulding.

3 Insert the moulding in the mitre clamp or box and saw at a 45° angle along the marked line.

4 Place the moulding in the mitre clamp or box. To make the next section of the frame, cut away the triangular "offcut" as in step 1 with the same 45° angle. Do this before you measure the second cut.

5 Measure and mark the second cut on the moulding. Repeat the steps until all four lengths are cut. Check that each pair – the two side lengths and the lengths for the top and bottom – is an exact match.

6 Using PVA glue, secure two sections of the moulding together to make a right angle. Repeat with the other sections, then join them all together to make the frame.

9 Turn the frame right side up and fill the mitred corners with woodfiller. Wipe away any excess woodfiller with a damp cloth. Allow to dry.

10 Use a cork block and medium-grade abrasive paper to sand all over the frame and the rebate. Repeat with finer-grade sandpaper.

7 Secure the frame clamp around the frame to hold the glued pieces together. Wipe away any excess glue with a damp cloth before it begins to set, otherwise it will form a waterproof barrier sealing the wood and any colourwash or woodstain you choose to use will not stain the wood around the joints.

8 Turn the frame right side down and insert V-nails into the corners of the back of the frame using a hand-held underpinner tool. Or, place the right-angled corners of the frame in a vice, and hammer panel pins into the corner edges of the moulding using a tack hammer. Once all four corners have been pinned, leave the frame to dry completely.

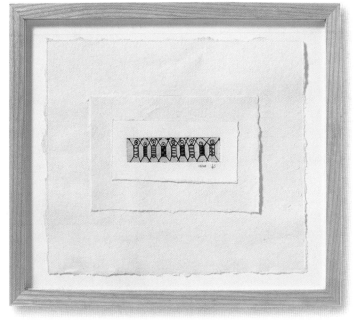

Above: *A light-coloured wood frame is a good choice for contemporary art.*

If your wooden frame has an attractive grain, this simple technique allows you to introduce colour without obscuring the wood's natural qualities. Gouache, acrylic or emulsion (latex) paints are suitable.

Colourwashed Frame

you will need
gouache paint: spectrum violet
bowl
2.5cm/1in flat sable paintbrush
ash or oak frame, prepared
and sanded
fine-grade abrasive paper
cloth
clear wax
hardboard offcut (scrap)

1 Place a walnut-sized amount of violet gouache in a bowl, add a little water and blend in thoroughly. The more water you add, the more translucent the wash will be; if you want a strong colour, add less water. Test the strength of the wash on the back of the frame. When you have the correct dilution, dip a paintbrush into the paint then wipe it against the side of the bowl, removing excess paint.

2 Apply the wash to one section of the face of the frame in one smooth, even stroke, from mitre to mitre. Then paint the side section of the frame. Continue all around the frame. Leave to dry for at least 15 minutes. The more coats of wash applied, the more opaque the colour will appear. Two coats are recommended. Allow to dry.

◄ **3** Lightly sand the frame with fine-grade abrasive paper to distress the wash and give a smooth finish. For a wax finish, cover your finger with a cloth, dip it in wax and work it in on a small piece of hardboard to soften the wax. With one long, smooth stroke lightly apply the wax to the frame; do not rub it in as it may remove the wash. Continue all around the frame. Once finished, lightly rub in the wax from where you began. Two or three coats of wax may be necessary.

This project combines all the creative possibilities of stamping. It involves four processes: painting the background, stamping in one colour, over-printing in a second colour and rubbing back.

Stamped Star Frame

1 Paint the frame blue and leave to dry. Put some red-brown paint on a palette and run a foam roller through it until evenly coated. Use the roller to ink a small star stamp and print it in the middle of each side of the frame.

2 Using the red-brown paint, stamp a large star over each corner of the frame. Leave to dry.

3 Ink the large stamp with gold and over-print the corner stars. Allow to dry before rubbing the frame gently with fine-grade abrasive paper.

The stylish raised leaf patterns around this pair of frames are simple to create using white interior filler to fill in stencilled shapes. Why not make several matching frames using different combinations of motifs?

Leaf-stippled Frames

you will need

2 wooden frames, prepared and sanded

acrylic paint: dark green

paintbrush

fine-grade abrasive paper

paper

pencil

stencil card

scissors

ready-mixed interior filler

stencil brush

1 Paint the frames dark green. When dry, gently rub them down to create a distressed effect. Enlarge the templates at the back of the book to fit the frames, transfer them to stencil card and cut them out.

2 Position a stencil on one of the frames and stipple ready-mixed filler through it using a stencil brush. Reposition the stencil and repeat. Continue all round the frame, spacing the leaves evenly. Leave to dry.

3 Repeat with a different combination of motifs on the second frame. When the filler is completely hard, gently smooth the leaves with fine-grade abrasive paper.

Good, clean driftwood can be hard to find even if you live near the sea, but you can make your own "driftwood" from old boards or packing crates. Break up the wood and distress the lengths with a chisel.

Driftwood Frame

you will need
packing crate or wooden board
chisel
hammer
surform file
coarse-grade abrasive paper
watercolour paints: green, crimson
and blue
paintbrushes
epoxy resin glue
coping saw
hardboard
chalkboard paint
masking tape
drill
sisal string, 1m/1⅛yd
scissors
thick sisal rope, 1m/1⅛yd

1 Split the wood into narrower lengths using a chisel and a hammer.

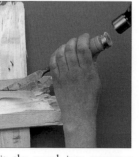

2 Select four suitable lengths of similar width for the sides of the frame. Gouge chunks from the sides of the wood to make it look weatherbeaten.

4 Sand the wood down with coarse-grade abrasive paper to remove any splinters, and round off the edges.

5 Mix a thin colourwash using green, crimson and blue watercolour paints and brush it on to the wood. Allow the wood to dry.

3 Use a surform to file away the edges of the wood until they are smooth.

6 Glue the frame together with epoxy resin glue and allow to dry. Cut a piece of hardboard to fit the back of the frame and paint the smooth side with chalkboard paint.

7 Tape the chalkboard to the back of the frame. Drill a hole in each corner through all the layers. Thread each end of a length of sisal string through the holes at the bottom of the frame, working from the back to the front. Knot the ends on the front of the frame. Trim any excess string.

8 Enlarge the two holes at the top of the frame and pass thick sisal rope through the holes as before, leaving enough excess rope to hang the frame. Tie a knot in each end on the front of the frame.

Three-dimensional motifs applied on the face of a picture frame are simple to create using interior filler. Tint the filler any colour you choose by adding pigment, gouache or watercolour paint.

Raised Motif Frame

you will need
bowls
gouache paint: cobalt blue
2.5cm/1in flat sable paintbrush
wooden frame, prepared and sanded
fine-grade abrasive paper
tracing paper
pencil
stencil card
cutting mat
craft (utility) knife
interior filler
pigment
stencil brush

1 In a bowl, blend one part cobalt blue gouache paint with three parts water. Paint this wash on to the frame in long, even strokes, working from mitre to mitre. Leave to dry for approximately 15 minutes.

2 Lightly distress the face and edges of the frame by rubbing them with fine-grade abrasive paper.

3 Trace the design for the frame using the template at the back of the book, then transfer on to stencil card. Place this on a cutting mat and cut out the design with a craft knife.

4 Mix two parts interior filler with one part water and mix to an ice cream consistency. Add pigment to tint the filler. Place the stencil on the frame and hold securely. Apply the filler by stippling with a stencil brush.

5 Lift off the stencil and repeat all round the frame. Leave the filler to dry for approximately 30 minutes, then lightly smooth the surface using fine-grade sandpaper.

Adorn an old gilded frame with gilded and coloured seashells to give it a baroque look. Shells are ideal objects for gilding, as the added lustre brings out their beautiful natural detail.

Gilded Shell Frame

you will need
assorted seashells
red oxide spray primer
1cm/½in paintbrushes
water-based size
Dutch metal leaf: gold and aluminium
soft brush
amber shellac
acrylic varnish
acrylic paints: pale blue, pink
and orange
soft cloths
gilded frame
strong clear glue

1 Spray the shells with an even coat of red oxide spray primer and leave to dry for 30–60 minutes. Paint on a thin, even coat of water-based size and leave for 20–30 minutes, until it becomes clear and tacky.

2 Gild the shells with gold or aluminium Dutch metal leaf, dabbing the leaf into place with a soft brush. Use the brush to remove any excess leaf.

3 Seal the gold shells with a thin, even coat of amber shellac and leave to dry for 45–60 minutes. Seal the aluminium-leaf covered shells with acrylic varnish and leave to dry for at least an hour.

4 Mix some pale blue acrylic paint with a little water. Paint on to the shells, then rub off most of the paint with a cloth, allowing only a little paint to remain in the recessed areas. Colour some of the shells in pink and orange. Leave to dry for 30 minutes.

5 Arrange the shells on the gilded frame and attach in place with strong clear glue. Leave to dry thoroughly before hanging the frame.

Liming wax is usually applied to attractively grained wood such as oak or ash. The white pigment in the mixture settles into the grain of the wood, while the wax on the surface remains translucent.

Lime-waxed Frame

you will need
wooden frame, prepared and sanded
coarse- and fine-grade abrasive paper
liming wax
wire (steel) wool
cloth

1 Sand the frame all over, initially with coarse-grade then with fine-grade abrasive paper, to give a smooth surface.

2 Pick up some liming wax on a piece of wire wool and apply it to the frame in long even strokes, continuing all around the frame. Work the wax into the wood grain as you go. Apply a second coat of liming wax to achieve a deeper effect.

3 When you have covered the frame completely, gently polish the liming wax with a cloth. Do not use excessive pressure as this will wipe off too much of the wax.

Woodstain penetrates the wood but allows the grain to show through, giving a translucent finish. Brushes should be cleaned with methylated spirits (methyl alcohol) when using a spirit-based stain.

Woodstained Frame

you will need

wooden frame, prepared and sanded

spirit (alcohol)-based woodstain

methylated spirits (methyl alcohol)

glass bowl

rubber gloves

2.5cm/1in flat sable paintbrush

acrylic varnish and brush

1 For an opaque result, use pure undiluted woodstain. For a translucent finish, dilute the woodstain with methylated spirits. Decant the mixture into a glass bowl. Wear rubber gloves when working with woodstain.

2 Dip the paintbrush into the solution, wiping off the excess. Apply the stain, working from mitre to mitre, in a single long, even stroke. Repeat all around the sides of the frame. Leave to dry for 10–15 minutes. Two or three coats may be required.

3 When the woodstain is dry to the touch, apply a coat of acrylic varnish. Leave to dry before applying one or two more coats as required.

Transform a wooden frame into a gleaming gilded one using Dutch gold leaf, varnish and orange acrylic glaze. Flicking enamel varnish over the frame creates an effective antiqued look.

Gold Leaf Frame

you will need

wooden frame, prepared and sanded

red oxide spray primer

paintbrushes

water-based size

Dutch metal leaf: gold

soft brush

wire (steel) wool

methylated spirits (methyl alcohol)

clear shellac

old stiff brush

French enamel varnish

rubber gloves

acrylic paint: orange

soft cloth

1 Prime the wooden picture frame with the red oxide spray primer. (Use the spray in a well-ventilated room.) Obtain an even coverage and ensure that the wood is completely covered.

2 Apply a thin, but even, coat of water-based size, painting out any bubbles that appear. Leave the size to get tacky, following the manufacturer's instructions on the bottle of size.

3 Place sheets of metal leaf on the size, dabbing them into place with a soft brush. Work around the frame adding leaf, then fill in any tears or gaps.

4 When the surface is completely covered, remove any excess leaf with the soft brush. Using wire wool and methylated spirits, rub over the raised areas to reveal some of the base coat.

5 Apply a coat of shellac to seal the metal leaf and prevent tarnishing.

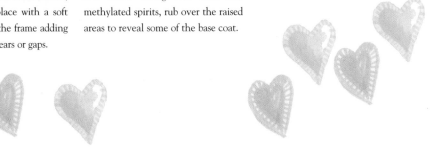

6 Dip an old, stiff brush into some French enamel varnish and, wearing rubber (latex) gloves, flick the bristles to spray enamel over the frame.

7 When the varnish is dry, dilute some orange acrylic paint with a little water to make a glaze. Paint the glaze all over the frame.

8 While the glaze is still wet, wipe off the excess with a soft cloth so that some paint remains in the detail areas. Allow to dry.

This modern picture frame is decorated using a simple stencilling technique and treated with a crackle glaze. The brightly coloured paintwork is distressed slightly to give a very attractive finish.

Crackle-glaze Frame

1 Paint the frame with two coats of yellow ochre emulsion paint, allowing each to dry. Brush on a coat of crackle glaze. Leave to dry according to the manufacturer's instructions.

2 Place strips of masking tape in a pattern on two opposite sides of the frame, using the finished photograph as your guide.

3 Where the ends of the tape overlap, carefully trim off the excess with a craft knife to leave a straight edge.

4 Brush turquoise paint on some unmasked sections of the frame, working in one direction. The crackle effect will appear almost immediately.

5 Brush orange paint on alternate sections of the pattern in the same way. Paint the remaining sections lime green. Leave the paint to dry, and then carefully peel away the masking tape.

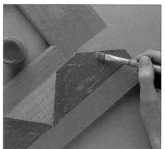

6 Using a flat artist's paintbrush, apply bright pink paint to the areas that were covered by the masking tape. Do this freehand to give the frame a hand-painted look. Leave to dry.

7 Rub coarse-grade abrasive paper over the crackled paint surface to reveal some of the yellow ochre paint beneath.

8 Seal the frame with two coats of acrylic varnish. Apply the first coat quickly, taking care not to overbrush and reactivate the crackle glaze.

Combine two or three picture-framing mouldings to make your own made-to-measure frame. Two treatments are given to the mouldings chosen for this project: black stain, and a clear polyurethane varnish.

Using Decorative Mouldings

Black frame

1 Using a tenon saw, cut 20cm/8in lengths from each piece of moulding. Using wood glue, join a barley twist and a semi-circular moulding strip to each side of the flat moulding. (The semicircular moulding will form the rebate of the frame.) Allow the glue to dry completely.

2 Mitre the lengths of assembled moulding using a mitre clamp or box and tenon saw, and make up the frame (see Basic Wooden Frame pp334–5). Mitre the remaining barley twist moulding and glue around the centre front of the frame. Allow to dry.

3 Stain the frame with black ink or woodstain applied with a paintbrush.

4 When the stain is dry, seal the wood and add a sheen with black shoe polish, applied with a soft cloth. Buff it up with a shoe brush.

Natural Frame

1 Using a tenon saw, cut four 20cm/ 8in lengths of square moulding. Cut four pieces of flat moulding to the same length. Glue a piece of square moulding to one edge of each piece of flat moulding.

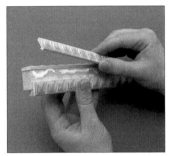

2 Cut 12 pieces of decorative moulding, each 20cm/8in long. Glue two decorative mouldings to the front surface and one on the side. Leave the glue to dry thoroughly.

3 Mitre the ends of the assembled pieces, using a mitre block and tenon saw. Glue and clamp the corners accurately together.

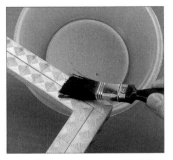

4 Apply one or more coats of clear polyurethane varnish to seal the wood and enhance the natural colours and grain of the wood.

Similar in effect to a multi-window mount (mat), this frame is ideal for collections of objects – in this case, pressed leaves – and creates a dramatic three-dimensional effect. Finish the surface with Danish oil.

Multi-window Frame

you will need

tape measure

T-square

pencil

18mm/³⁄₄ in birch plywood:

2 front verticals, 60 x 6cm/

24 x 2¹⁄₂ in; 4 front horizontals,

13 x 7cm/5 x 2³⁄₄ in;

back, 60 x 25cm/24 x 10in

jigsaw

tenon saw

medium- and fine-grade abrasive paper

cork sanding block

PVA (white) glue and glue brush

self-adhesive sealing tape

scissors

soft cloths

Danish wood oil

dish

rubber gloves

sheer fabric

metal ruler

craft (utility) knife

heavy weights or G-clamps

tack hammer

large-headed nails, 2.5cm/1in long

epoxy resin glue and brush

pressed leaves

1 With a tape measure, T-square and pencil, mark the lengths and widths of the plywood and saw the pieces to size. Butt the plywood pieces together to check that they fit. Cut the back of the frame and set aside. Sand down all the edges.

2 Apply PVA glue to the ends of the horizontals and assemble the frame. Wrap self-adhesive sealing tape around the frame, both front and back. Wipe off the excess glue at once with a damp cloth and leave overnight to dry.

3 Once the glue has set, remove the tape. Use medium-grade abrasive paper with a cork sanding block to sand the face and all edges of the frame. For a smooth finish, sand again with fine-grade sandpaper.

4 Place some Danish wood oil in a dish. Wearing rubber gloves, apply the oil over the wood in a circular motion using a soft cloth. Work the oil into the wood. Buff up with a clean soft cloth.

5 Apply a line of glue to the front of the backing board, approximately 3cm/1¼ in in from the edge. Stick the fabric on to it. Leave to dry.

6 Trim the excess fabric using a metal ruler and craft knife.

7 Apply glue to the back of the frame front, then align the frame front and backing board and stick the two halves together.

8 Place heavy weights or G-clamps on each corner and the middle section of the frame. Place a cloth below the weights or clamps to prevent damage to the face of the frame. Wipe away excess glue with a damp cloth and leave to dry overnight.

9 Apply a coat of oil to the side edges of the backing board. Find the centre of each window and hammer in a large-headed nail, leaving approximately 1cm/½ in showing. Mix a small amount of epoxy resin glue and apply this to the nail heads. Place a leaf on each nail and leave to set.

A deep-sided, sectioned frame is the perfect way to display a collection of small objects such as ornaments, jewellery or badges. Custom-build the sections to suit the size of the objects in your collection.

Multi-box Frame

you will need

length of batten, 30 x 5mm/1¼ x ¼in

pencil

metal ruler

junior hacksaw

wood glue

panel pins (brads)

hammer

hardboard

jigsaw or coping saw

white acrylic primer

paintbrush

length of batten, 30 x 2mm/1¼ x ¹⁄₁₆in

masking tape

PVA (white) glue and brush

tissue paper in assorted colours

acrylic paint: yellow and blue

artist's brushes

small Indian shisha glass

1 Using the thicker battening, measure and cut four sides of the rectangular frame, then glue them together with wood glue and fully secure with panel pins.

2 Cut a piece of hardboard to fit the frame and paint the smooth front side with acrylic primer. When dry, glue and pin it to the back of the frame.

3 Measure and draw out all the compartments. Cut the dividers from the length of thinner battening.

4 Assemble the compartments inside the box frame with wood glue, taping them in position with masking tape until the glue has set.

5 Coat the inside of each compartment with PVA glue and cover with pieces of torn tissue paper. Work the tissue paper into the corners and keep applying the glue. Use light colours over strong colours to create depth.

6 Carefully retouch any areas of the compartments that need more colour, using yellow acrylic paint. Allow the paint to dry.

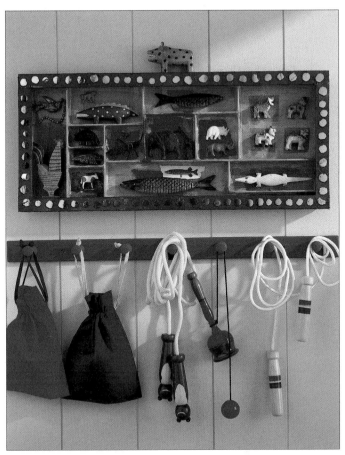

7 Use wood glue to attach lengths of the thinner battening to the outer edge of the frame, in effect creating a rebate. Leave the glue to dry.

8 Cover the edge of the frame with a collage of blue tissue paper, using PVA glue.

9 Using an artist's brush, lightly brush over the tissue paper with blue acrylic paint. Leave to dry.

10 Glue small Indian shisha glass all around the frame. Arrange your collection in the compartments, securing the pieces with glue.

Reclaimed timber has a natural distressed and heavy appearance. This frame requires no finish, relying instead on its natural characteristics for its rugged, contemporary appeal.

Reclaimed Timber Frame

you will need

reclaimed timber:

2 verticals, 62 x 10cm/25 x 4in

2 horizontals, 18 x 10cm/7 x 4in

tape measure

pencil

tenon saw

abrasive paper

hardboard, 54 x 28cm/22 x 11in

coping saw

fabric glue and brush

black felt

decorative paper

PVA (white) glue and brush

chalk

bradawl or awl

14 screws, 2.5cm/1in long

screwdriver

4 reclaimed brackets

8 galvanized nails, 2.5cm/1in long

hammer

fillets, 5mm/¼in deep

natural objects for framing

1 On the timber, measure and mark with a pencil the length and width of the frame verticals and horizontals. Use a tenon saw to cut the timber to the correct sizes. Lightly sand the sawn edges. Cut the hardboard backing board to size. Apply fabric glue to the back, then stick a piece of black felt on top. Glue decorative paper to the face of the backing board.

2 Mark out corner holes for the screws, using chalk. Turn the cut lengths of timber face down and butt them together at the corners. Place the felt-covered hardboard on the back of the timber. Make initial holes in the hardboard with a bradawl or awl, then screw into the back of the frame. The screws will hold the frame together.

3 Turn the frame the right way up and nail in the reclaimed brackets, using galvanized nails.

4 Cut small fillets to size, coat with PVA glue, and use them to mount the framed objects to give a three-dimensional effect.

In this type of frame, the artwork sits flush with the face of the frame. A gap is left around the edge of the canvas to give it depth. Here the frame is colourwashed to match the colours in the painting.

Framing a Canvas

you will need

tape measure
painted, stretched canvas
pencil
wooden frame, prepared and sanded
gouache paint: ultramarine and black
paintbrush
bowl
cloth
batten, 2.5cm/1in wide, 5mm/¼in deep
tenon saw
hardboard
jigsaw or coping saw
emulsion (latex) paint: black
PVA (white) glue and brush
framer's point gun
panel pins (brads) and tack hammer
(optional)
bradawl or awl
screws, 1cm/½in long
screwdriver
self-adhesive backing tape
craft (utility) knife

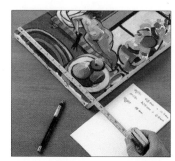

1 Measure the canvas and add on 1cm/½in to the vertical and horizontal measurements. This will give a 5mm/¼in gap around the canvas when it is eventually inserted into the frame. Measure the depth of the canvas and choose a frame that is deep enough to allow the canvas to lie flush with the face of the frame.

2 Mix two parts ultramarine gouache with one part black gouache in a bowl. Blend together and add four parts water. Mix well with a paintbrush. This is a very opaque colourwash solution. Apply the wash in long, smooth strokes on the face and then the side edges of the frame. Leave to dry.

3 Place the frame face down on a piece of cloth. Measure the inside vertical and horizontal edges of the frame. These measurements are for the fillets and the backing board. Mark and saw the fillets and the hardboard to fit inside the rebate.

4 Using black emulsion paint, paint one face and edge of all the fillets and a strip approximately 5cm/2in wide around the edge of the face of the hardboard. Leave to dry. Neatly paint the edge of the canvas.

5 Once the fillets have dried, apply PVA glue to the unpainted side of each one and place them around the sides of the frame.

6 When the fillets are secure, place the backing board, painted side facing inwards, in the frame and pin in position, using a framer's point gun. Alternatively use panel pins and a tack hammer.

7 Place the canvas in the frame and hold it in place. On the back make a hole aligning with each corner of the canvas using a bradawl or awl. Screw the hardboard to the canvas. Tape up the back of the frame.

If the image you are going to frame is simple and plain, you can add decorative interest by insetting objects into the frame. Choose a wide moulding with enough depth to allow shapes to be chiselled out.

Decorative Insets

1 Mark out oblongs and squares on the face of the frame with a ruler and soft pencil. Centre the shapes between the rebate and outside edge.

2 Score the pencil marks on the frame using a craft knife and a metal ruler. Chisel out the shapes quite deeply, so that the glass will not protrude from the face of the frame.

3 Sand the frame with medium-grade abrasive paper and a cork sanding block, then with a finer grade of sandpaper.

4 Using a soft cloth and wearing rubber gloves, apply olive green oil paint over the frame. Cut pieces of black cardboard for the background of each inset, and glue in place in the chiselled-out spaces.

5 Cut the glass for all the inserts to the sizes required using a glass cutter and a T-square. Decorate the under-side of some pieces of the insert glass with Dutch metal leaf for an opaque effect. Spray a few of the glass pieces with a little glass etching spray, ensuring that the objects underneath will remain visible. Wear a protective face mask and work in a ventilated area.

6 Select the objects to be inserted in the inset panels. To decorate the glass for the slate pebbles, place masking tape in two strips over the glass and spray on the etching spray in a line down the centre, holding the can about 20cm/8in away. When the spray is dry, remove the tape to reveal a neat line of mottled glass.

7 Mark and cut out cardboard fillets to the appropriate size. Glue the fillets into the chiselled oblongs.

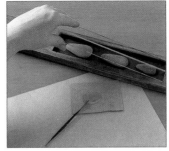

8 Glue the slate pebbles on to the black cardboard background using epoxy resin. Glue the glass on to the fillets using epoxy resin.

9 Add other decorative elements to the frame as desired. If the objects are flat, attach them to the glass with PVA glue, which will dry transparent.

A craquelure effect is created using two varnishes. One is slow-drying, while the other is fast-drying. As the slow-drying lower layer contracts it causes cracking in the dry layer of varnish above.

Craquelure Frame

you will need
2.5cm/1in flat sable paintbrush
gouache paint: white
wooden frame, prepared and sanded
fine-grade abrasive paper
clear spray lacquer
2.5cm/1in flat oil paintbrush
two-stage crackle varnish
cloths
palette or plate
oil paint: olive green

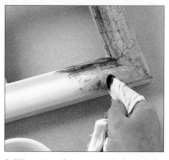

1 With a flat sable paintbrush, apply four coats of white gouache paint to the frame, allowing each to dry before applying the next. Rub over the frame with abrasive paper. Spray with clear spray lacquer to make the surface less absorbent.

2 Using a flat oil paintbrush, apply a coat of stage-1 crackle varnish sparingly over the frame. When the varnish has become slightly tacky, apply the stage-2 crackle glaze. Cracks should begin to appear in about an hour. Leave the frame to dry overnight.

3 Wrap your finger in a cloth and dip it into olive green oil paint. Apply the paint all over the frame, working the colour into the cracks. Then wipe the paint off with a cloth; this will remove paint from the surface but leave the colour in the cracks.

Verre eglomisé is glass that has been mirrored using gold or silver leaf, creating a magical, mysterious effect. The technique is named after an eighteenth-century art dealer, Jean-Baptiste Glomy.

Verre Eglomisé Frame

you will need

2.5cm/1in flat oil paintbrush

rubber gloves

metal polish

wooden frame, prepared and sanded

sponge

black patina

burnishing tool

glass to fit frame

cloths

methylated spirits (methyl alcohol)

gelatine capsules

glass bowl

deep tray

white gold leaf (loose)

gilder's knife

gilder's cushion

2.5cm/1in flat sable paintbrush

gilder's tip

kettle

cotton wool (balls)

pumice powder (0003 grade)

safety mask

black lacquer spray

1 Using a flat oil paintbrush and wearing rubber gloves, apply metal polish to the frame. Dab the sponge over the polish as you work along the frame for a textured finish. Leave for 30 minutes. Apply a second layer in the same way. Leave overnight to dry.

2 Apply a coat of black patina over the frame, wiping it off as you work. The patina will remain in the recessed areas, giving the impression of age. Leave the frame to dry overnight.

3 Polish the frame with a burnishing tool to give a soft sheen.

4 To create the mirror, clean the glass thoroughly to remove all dirt and grease, using a cloth dipped in methylated spirits.

▶

5 Place half a gelatine capsule in a glass bowl and add a little boiling water. When the capsule has completely dissolved, add 300ml/½ pint/ 1¼ cups cold water.

6 Place the glass at an angle of 45° in a deep tray, so that the solution can run down freely. Cut the gold leaf into small squares with a gilder's knife. Using a flat sable paintbrush, apply the solution to the glass and immediately lay a piece of gold leaf on the solution using a gilder's tip.

7 Work from the top to the bottom of the glass. Continue until you have gilded the entire glass, then leave to dry. When the gold leaf looks shiny, it is dry. If it is matt, it is not yet dry.

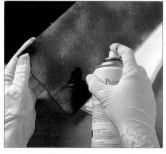

8 To seal the leaf, hold the gilded glass approximately 20–25cm/8–10in away from the steam of a boiling kettle. Leave to dry. Once dry, gently brush off any excess leaf with cotton wool.

9 A more distressed, antiqued look can be achieved by gently rubbing pumice powder into the gold leaf with your fingertips. When the desired effect has been achieved, brush away the excess powder.

10 Wearing a mask and rubber gloves, spray black lacquer over the gilded side of the glass. Hold the spray about 20–25cm/8–10in away for an even coat. Leave to dry. Insert the gilded glass in the frame.

Penwork was one of many artistic amusements popular at the end of the eighteenth century. This elaborately detailed black decoration is traced from a copyright-free book on to a white frame using black ink.

Ink Penwork Frame

you will need
paintbrushes
acrylic gesso
wooden frame, prepared and sanded
medium- and fine-grade abrasive paper
white acrylic paint
tracing paper
design
masking tape
hard and soft pencils
fine black marker pen
emulsion (latex) paint: black
safety mask
clear spray lacquer
2.5cm/1in flat lacquer brush
shellac

1 Apply four coats of acrylic gesso to the frame, allowing it to dry between layers. Sand the gesso with medium-, then fine-grade abrasive paper. Apply four layers of white paint to the frame, allowing each coat to dry for 5–10 minutes before applying the next. Place tracing paper over the design. Hold in place with masking tape and trace with a soft pencil.

2 Place the tracing, pencil-side down, on the frame, and secure with masking tape. Using a hard pencil, draw over the design. This will transfer the pencil design on to the frame.

3 Remove the tracing paper and ink over the design with a fine black marker pen. Paint the rebate with black emulsion paint.

4 When the penwork is completed, spray clear lacquer over the frame to seal it. Wear a safety mask and hold the can approximately 20–25cm/ 8–10in from the frame. Leave to dry.

5 Using a flat lacquer brush, apply four layers of shellac to the frame, allowing each coat to dry for about 30 minutes before applying the next. This will give an aged, ivory appearance.

This technique involves burning a design into a frame with a heat gun. A close-grained wood, such as oak or ash, is recommended to stop the design spreading. Polish the frame with tinted wax to finish.

Scorched Frame

you will need
kitchen foil
white chinagraph pencil
craft (utility) knife or tin snips
oak or ash frame
heat gun
safety gloves
coarse- and fine-grade abrasive paper
raw sienna pigment
clear wax
soft cloths

1 Draw your design on foil using a white chinagraph pencil. Cut out the design using a craft knife or tin snips. Place the foil template on the bare frame. Using a heat gun and wearing safety gloves, scorch the design into the wood, holding the gun 10–15cm/ 4–6in away from the wood.

2 Using coarse-grade abrasive paper, sand off any over-burns. Repeat with fine-grade abrasive paper.

3 Mix raw sienna pigment with wax in the proportion of 1.5ml/¼tsp of pigment to 15ml/1 tbsp of clear wax.

4 Apply the pigmented wax to the frame using a soft cloth. Work all around the frame.

5 Using a dry, clean cloth, polish up the wax to a soft sheen.

Decorating Tiles
and Ceramics

Ceramics and tiles can be decorated in a myriad ways, using different techniques and finishes depending upon their intended use. Plain white glazed plates, bowls and tiles offer a perfect canvas for painting. You do not need to be an expert artist or have trained in drawing techniques to paint beautiful designs on ceramics and tiles. All you need is the enthusiasm to have a go, and a design or a colour palette that will inspire you to follow through your ideas.

A variety of materials are needed for painting on ceramics, all of which are available from craft stores. Many items can be improvised, but some materials, such as paints, have to be specially purchased.

Materials

surfaces that may come in contact with foodstuffs or the mouth such as serving plates, bowls and cups.

Solvent-based ceramic paints

These come in a huge range of colours and lend themselves well to varied painting styles such as wash effects. White spirit (paint thinner) can be used to dilute the paint and to clean paintbrushes after use. Solvent-based paints take approximately 24 hours to dry. They can then be varnished to protect the finish.

Water-based ceramic paints

Sold under various trade names and specially made for painting glazed ceramics, these paints are available in a range of colours. They produce a strong, opaque, flat colour and can be diluted with water. Wash paintbrushes in warm water immediately after painting. Water-based paints dry in around 3 hours; do not attempt to bake them until they are completely dry or the colour may bubble. Baking the painted item will make the colour durable enough for a dishwasher. Put the item in a cold oven and do not remove it after baking until it has completely cooled. Always follow the paint manufacturer's instructions for the temperature and baking time, and do a test first as over-firing can turn the colour slightly brown.

Enamel paints

These paints are not made exclusively for china and ceramics. They are available in a range of colours and dry to a hard and durable finish. They contain lead and should only ever be used for decorative purposes and not on items that will contain food.

Masking fluid

Watercolour art masking fluid is used to mask off areas of the design while colour is applied to the surrounding

area. Apply to a clean, dry surface. Always allow the masking fluid to dry before filling in the design with paint.

Polyurethane varnish and glazes

Apply varnish evenly, using a large, flat brush and stroking in one direction over the ceramic. The more coats you apply, the more durable and washable the surface, but keep each of the coats thin, allowing a minimum of 4 hours' drying time between coats. Polyurethane varnish is unsuitable for

No expensive specialist equipment is required for painting ceramics. In fact, you probably already have much of the equipment needed among your normal household supplies.

Equipment

Paintbrushes
Use a fine brush for details, and a broad soft brush for covering larger areas.

Paint palette
Use to mix and hold paints.

Pencils and pens
A hard pencil is good for transferring designs; a soft for direct marking.

Printing blocks
Use for printing repeated patterns.

Ruler or straightedge
Plastic rules measure adequately. For cutting, metal ones are better.

Scissors
Use to cut paper patterns.

Self-healing cutting mat
This protects the work surface when cutting paper with a craft knife.

Stencil card
This is manila card (cardboard) water-proofed with linseed oil.

Tracing paper
Use with carbon paper to transfer designs on to the object to be painted.

White spirit (paint thinner)
Use to clean brushes, to remove paint mistakes and to thin paint.

Carbon paper
Use to transfer designs on to ceramic. Place it carbon side down, on the object. Stick the image drawn on tracing paper on top. Draw over the image to transfer it to the ceramic.

Clear adhesive tape
Use for sticking designs to ceramic.

Craft knife
Use with a metal ruler and cutting mat for cutting papers and cardboard.

Masking film (frisket paper)
This self-adhesive transparent paper has a waxed paper backing, which peels away. Use it to mask out areas you want to keep blank.

Masking tape
Use to hold stencils in place and to mask off areas of ceramic.

Natural and synthetic sponges
Use to create paint effects for anything from an even to a textured finish.

The projects in this chapter do not require any specialist skills but it is worth practising a few painting techniques before you start. The tips suggested below will prove useful as you work through the ideas.

Basic Techniques

Cleaning china

Clean china before painting it to remove invisible traces of dirt. Good cleaning agents are cleaning fluid, turpentine, methylated spirit (methyl alcohol), lighter fuel or white spirit (paint thinner). Keep these materials away from naked flames.

Safe drinking vessels

To ensure that there is no possibility of any paint being swallowed when drinking from a mug or glass, adapt designs so that any colour you paint is at least 3cm/1¼in below the rim of drinking vessels. Otherwise the piece should be fired in a kiln.

Working with paints

Paints suitable for applying to china are available in water or oil-based types. When mixing up a shade of your own, remember that the two types of paint cannot be intermixed. Always thoroughly clean brushes as directed by the paint manufacturer.

Using paintbrushes

Always use an appropriately sized paintbrush for the task in hand. Larger areas should always be painted with a large brush using bold strokes, while small, fine brushes are best for all detailed work.

Watery effects

You can achieve a watery effect in oil-based colours by diluting paints with white spirit (paint thinner). Water-based paints can be diluted by adding water.

Transferring a design

Cut a piece of tracing paper the same size as the tile. Centre the design, then trace it. Centre the paper design-side down on the tile, matching the edges. Scribble over the lines to transfer to the tile.

Creating white lines

If you want to leave thin lines of china showing through areas of colour, paint them in first with masking fluid. This can be gently peeled off when the paint is dry to reveal the white china beneath. Use an instrument with a sharp point such as a craft knife or compass to lift off the dried masking fluid.

Using masking fluid

Add a drop of water-based paint to masking fluid before use when you are working on plain white china. This will help you to see where the masking fluid has been applied, enabling you to wipe it off easily when you are ready to do so.

Preparing a sponge

Use a craft (utility) knife to cut cubes of sponge for sponging paint. Hold the sponge taut as you slice down into it to make cutting easier and the lines straight. Keep several sponge cubes to hand when sponging as you may need to change them frequently.

Testing a sponge

Before sponging on to your china after loading the sponge with paint, test the print on a scrap piece of paper. The first print or two will be too saturated with paint to achieve a pleasing effect.

Sponging variations

To add interest, vary the density of the sponging within the image or add more than one colour. Allow the first coat of paint to dry partially before the application of the second.

Printing blocks

Test the print on scrap paper before you print on the china. When using printing blocks, roll the block lightly on to the surface to ensure you get a good, even print.

Cutting tiles Tiling a wall with your completed painted tiles can be challenging depending on the size of area you are tiling and the number of tiles that have to be cut. The following tips will help the beginner.

1 To use a hand-held tile cutter, first measure the width required and deduct 2mm/¹⁄₁₆in to allow for grout. Mark the cutting line on the tile. Place the cutting wheel against a short metal ruler and score the line once only to pierce the glaze.

2 Wearing protective leather gloves and safety goggles, place the tile as far as it will go into the jaws of the cutter with the scored line positioned in the centre, then close the handles of the cutter to snap the tile in two.

3 Manual tile-cutting machines will cut tiles up to about 5mm/¹⁄₄in thick quickly and accurately, and they have a useful measuring gauge. Adjust the gauge to the correct width, then pull the wheel once down the tile to score a cutting line. Snap along this line.

4 Wearing protective leather gloves, a face mask and safety goggles, use a tile file to smooth along the cut edge of the tile if desired.

Right: Tile cutters, grout, tiles and a straightedge are just a few of the items you will need to tile an area.

Mixing grout

When colouring grout, mix enough for the whole project, as it is difficult to match the colour in a second batch.

1 When mixing up powdered grout, add the powder to a measured amount of water, rather than the other way round, otherwise the mixture may be lumpy. Mix the powder thoroughly into the water. Always wear rubber gloves, a protective face mask and goggles.

2 Grout colourant can be added to the powdered grout before mixing it with water. Wear protective clothing as for powdered grout, and then mix with water in the proportion advised by the manufacturer.

Removing grease

You many wish to decorate tiles that are not in pristine condition. It is essential to start with a clean surface to ensure an even application of paint. To remove grease and fingerprints from the surface of tiles before you paint them, wipe with a solution of 1 part malt vinegar to 10 of water.

Below: *Single painted tiles can be used to break up a plainly tiled wall.*

These cheerful tiles are based on simple Mexican designs. The motifs are easy to do so you can paint a set quite quickly. They will add a colourful touch to a kitchen wall, as an all-over design or a border.

Mexican Folk Art Tiles

you will need
soft pencil
clean, off-white glazed ceramic tiles
medium and fine paintbrushes
non-toxic, water-based, cold-set
ceramic paints
paint palette

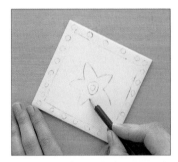

1 Using a soft pencil, draw a simple flower and spotted border design on one of the tiles.

2 Fill in the petals, using a medium paintbrush. Add a dot of contrasting paint for the flower centre.

3 Paint the border in a dark colour, leaving the spots blank. Using a fine paintbrush and various colours, paint a small spot in the centre of each blank spot. Leave to dry.

Children will love these chunky letter tiles. Use them to make a panel or a frieze around a bedroom or playroom wall, mixing the letters at random or spelling out a name. Use non-toxic ceramic paints.

Alphabet Tiles

you will need
fine black felt-tipped pen
clean, plain white glazed ceramic tiles
fine and medium artist's paintbrushes
non-toxic, water-based, cold-set
ceramic paint: black
paint palette

1 Using a fine felt-tipped pen, draw the outline of the letter on to one tile, extending the lines right to the edges of the tile. Using a fine paintbrush, go over the outlines with black paint. Leave to dry.

2 Using a medium paintbrush, paint bold black stripes down one side of the tile, as shown.

3 Leaving the letter white, fill in the rest of the design with dots, spots and fine lines. Leave to dry thoroughly.

Stencilling offers a quick and easy method of decorating china. The simple shapes of these limes look terrific adorning a fruit bowl. Choose just two or three bold colours for maximum effect.

Citrus Fruit Bowl

you will need
soft pencil
tracing paper
masking tape
stencil card
self-healing cutting mat
craft (utility) knife
plain fruit bowl
cleaning fluid
cloth
yellow chinagraph pencil
water-based ceramic paints: citrus green, mid-green, dark green and yellow
paint palette
artist's paintbrushes
acrylic varnish (optional)

1 Draw a freehand lime shape on to tracing paper. Using masking tape to hold the tracing paper securely in place, transfer the lime outline to a piece of stencil card. Working on a self-healing cutting mat, carefully cut all around the shape of the lime using a craft knife with a sharp blade.

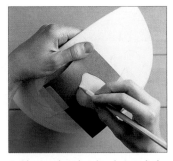

2 Clean a plain fruit bowl. Attach the stencil to the bowl using masking tape. Draw inside the stencil outline on to the bowl using a yellow chinagraph pencil. Repeat to draw several limes all over the bowl.

3 Fill in all the lime shapes with citrus green paint using an artist's paintbrush. Allow the paint to dry completely. Add highlights to each of the fruits using the mid-green paint and allow the paint to dry thoroughly as before.

4 Paint a stalk at the end of each lime shape in the dark green paint. Allow to dry. Paint the background all over the outside of the bowl yellow, leaving a thin white outline around each of the lime shapes to help them stand out.

5 To complete the bowl, either use a clean brush to apply a coat of acrylic varnish over the painted section, or bake the bowl in the oven, following the paint manufacturer's instructions.

Imagine the effect produced by a whole set of this delightful sponge-ware design, set out on your kitchen shelves. Painting your own mugs in this lovely decorative style is an easy way of transforming plain china.

Stamped Spongeware Mugs

you will need
ballpoint pen
cellulose kitchen sponge
scissors
all-purpose glue
corrugated cardboard
ceramic paints: dark blue and
dark green
paint palette
kitchen paper
clean, white china mugs
masking tape
craft (utility) knife
fine black felt-tipped pen
stencil brush or small
cosmetic sponge

1 Draw a crab on the sponge. Cut out and glue to the corrugated cardboard. Trim as close as possible. Press the sponge into the blue paint and blot any excess on kitchen paper. Stamp the crab evenly on to the mugs.

2 Allow the paint to dry. Stick the masking tape around the bottom edge of the mug. Draw the border freehand on the tape with black felt-tipped pen. Carefully cut away the bottom edge of the masking tape using a craft knife.

3 Use the cosmetic sponge to decorate the border. Use both the blue and green paints, to add depth. Sponge the handles and stamp more mugs with related motifs. Peel off the masking tape. Set the paints.

A set of delicately frosted plates would look terrific for winter dinner settings and this snowflake design is child's play to achieve. Make up as many differently designed snowflakes as you like.

Sponged Snowflake Plate

you will need
plain china plate
cleaning fluid
cloth
pencil
cup
masking film (frisket paper)
scissors
craft (utility) knife
self-healing cutting mat
sponge
paint dish
water-based ceramic paints: ice blue, dark blue and gold

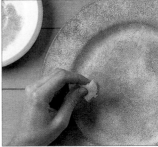

1 Clean the plate. Draw round an upturned cup on to the backing paper of masking film to make eight circles. Cut out the circles with scissors. Fold each circle in half. Crease each semi-circle twice to make three equal sections. Fold these sections over each other to make a triangle with a curved edge.

2 Draw a partial snowflake design on to one triangle and shade the areas that will be cut away. Ensure that parts of the folded edges remain intact. Cut out the design using a craft knife and self-healing cutting mat. Repeat to make seven more snowflake shapes. Unfold them, peel away the backing paper and position them on the plate.

3 Load a sponge cube with ice blue paint and dab it all over the plate. When dry, sponge darker blue around the outer and inner rims. Allow to dry, then dab a sponge loaded with gold paint around the edge of the plate, the inner rim and dark areas to highlight them. Remove the film snowflakes and then set the paint following the manufacturer's instructions.

Ceramics with low-relief decorative motifs are ideal for painting. Like children's colouring books, the shapes are all set out ready to colour in and, as there are no clearly defined outlines, mistakes will go unnoticed.

Low-relief Ceramic Pitcher

you will need

clean, white glazed pitcher with a low-relief fruit motif

medium and fine artist's paintbrushes

solvent-based ceramic paints: acid yellow, golden yellow, light green, medium green and dark green

polyurethane varnish or glaze

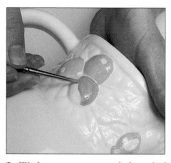

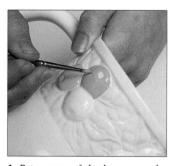

1 Paint some of the lemons on the pitcher acid yellow. Vary them so that one group has two acid yellow lemons, the next group one, and so on. Leave a narrow white line around each lemon, and leave the seed cases and the small circles at the base of the fruit white. Allow to dry.

2 Work your way around the relief pattern at the top of the pitcher, painting the remaining fruit a rich golden yellow. Using two yellows for the fruit creates a sense of depth and variety. Once again, leave a narrow white line around each fruit, and leave the paint to dry.

3 Starting with light green, paint roughly a third of the leaves, evenly spaced apart if possible, but don't worry about being too exact. Leave the central midrib of each leaf and a narrow line around each leaf white. Allow to dry. Paint the small circles.

4 Paint a third of the leaves medium green, spacing them evenly. Paint a narrow green line around the base of the pitcher and leave to dry. Paint the remaining leaves dark green and leave to dry.

5 Paint the rim (or the handle) of the pitcher in acid yellow, leaving a narrow white line at the lower edge. Once the paint is dry, varnish the pitcher with polyurethane varnish or the glaze provided specially by the ceramic paint manufacturer for this purpose.

This quirky cherub tile panel will add cheery individuality to any wall. Decorated in the style of Majolica ware, with bright colours and a stylized design, this romantic cherub is easy to paint.

Cherub Tiles

you will need
pencil
tracing paper
4 clean, plain white, glazed, square ceramic tiles
fine artist's paintbrushes
non-toxic, water-based, cold-set ceramic paints: dark blue, yellow and red
paint palette

1 Trace the template from the back of the book. Enlarge the design on to a piece of tracing paper. Use a pencil to transfer a quarter of the design to each ceramic tile.

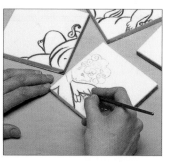

2 With a fine brush, and dark blue paint, paint over the main outline on each tile. If required, heat the tiles in the oven for the time specified by the paint manufacturer, to set the outline.

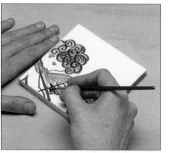

3 Fill in the wings, hair and drapery with yellow paint. Allow the paint to dry. Mix yellow with red to add darker tones, using the finished picture as a guide. Bake the tiles again, to prevent the colours from smudging.

4 With diluted blue paint, mark in the shadows on the cherub's face and body. Go over any areas that need to be defined with more blue paint. Paint the corner motifs freehand and then bake for the final time.

This delightful vase of flowers is based on a tile design from the Urbino area of northern Italy, where the Majolica style of pottery decoration developed in the 15th century.

Majolica Tile

you will need
tracing paper
pencil
clean, plain white glazed ceramic tiles
fine artist's paintbrushes
non-toxic, water-based, cold-set
ceramic paints: yellow, orange,
royal blue, white, light green
and dark green
paint palette
water-based acrylic varnish

1 Trace the vase of flowers design from the back of the book, enlarging it if necessary, and transfer it on to the tile. Begin to paint the design with a fine paintbrush, starting with the palest tones of each colour.

2 Carefully paint in the foliage with light and dark green paint, leaving each colour to dry before applying the next. Add white to orange paint to create a paler shade. Use this to paint the top and bottom of the vase. Using darker orange, fill in the flower centres and emphasize the shape of the vase.

3 Using royal blue paint, outline the shapes of the flowers and vase. Add the vase handles and decorative details to the flowerheads. Leave the tile to dry, then seal the surface with two coats of acrylic varnish, allowing the first coat to dry before applying the second, if required.

Translucent ceramic paints give this exotic tile the rich, glowing colours associated with Byzantine art. The decorative bird motif is taken from a *cloisonné* enamel panel originally decorated with precious stones.

Byzantine Bird Tile

you will need
tracing paper
pencil
clean, plain white glazed ceramic tile
non-toxic, water-based, cold-set
ceramic paints in a variety of
rich colours
fine artist's paintbrushes
paint palette
gold felt-tipped pen

1 Trace the bird design from the back of the book, enlarging it if necessary, and transfer on to the tile. Paint the bird's head and legs, then start to paint the features, using bright colours.

2 Paint the plants, using your choice of colours. Leave to dry completely.

3 Using a gold felt-tipped pen, draw an outline around every part of the design. As a final touch, add decorative gold details to the bird's feathers and the plants.

Coffee cups handpainted with broad brush strokes and lots of little raised dots of paint are simpler to create than you would think…with the help of a little self-adhesive vinyl.

Leaf Motif Cup and Saucer

you will need

white ceramic cup and saucer
cleaning fluid
cloth
cotton buds (swabs)
pencil
paper
scissors
self-adhesive vinyl
green water-based ceramic paint
medium artist's paintbrush
hair dryer (optional)
craft (utility) knife
pewter acrylic paint with nozzle-tipped tube

1 Clean any grease from the china to be painted using cleaning fluid and a cloth or cotton bud. Draw leaves and circles freehand on to paper. Cut them out and draw around them on the backing of the self-adhesive vinyl. Cut out. Peel away the backing paper and stick the pieces on the china, evenly spaced.

2 Paint around the leaf and circle shapes with green water-based ceramic paint, applying several coats of paint in order to achieve a solid colour. Leave the centre circle of the saucer white. Leave each coat to air-dry before applying the next, or use a hair dryer for speed.

3 To ensure that the design has a tidy edge, cut around each sticky shape carefully with a craft knife, then peel off the sticky-backed plastic.

4 Clean up any smudges with a cotton bud dipped in acetone or water. Paint fine green lines out from the centre of each circle.

5 Using pewter paint and the nozzle-tipped paint tube, mark the outlines and details of the leaves with rows of small dots. Leave for 36 hours, then bake, following the manufacturer's instructions. The paint will withstand everyday use, but not the dishwasher.

Jazz up herb containers to match your kitchen decor. Each of these jars bears a coloured panel which can be used to display the name of the herb contained within.

Kitchen Herb Jars

you will need
tracing paper
soft pencil
carbon paper
masking tape
6 plain china herb jars
cleaning fluid
cloth
blue chinagraph pencil
water-based enamel paints: blue, lime green, dark green and turquoise
paint palette
artist's paintbrush
dried-out felt-tipped pen

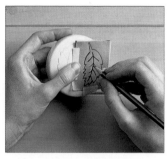

1 Draw one large and one small leaf design, each on a separate piece of tracing paper. Attach the tracing paper to carbon paper, carbon side down, with masking tape.

2 Clean the jars. Attach the tracing of the larger leaf on to the lid of a jar, to one side, and trace the outline with a pencil to transfer the design. Replace the tracing in another position on the lid and repeat.

3 Attach the smaller tracing to the side of a jar and trace the leaf outline on to the jar. Repeat the process to transfer the outline several times in different places around the jar, leaving a large space in the centre of one side for the "lozenge".

4 Using a blue chinagraph pencil, draw a freehand oval shape in the large space you have left. Fill in the oval with blue paint.

5 Before the paint dries, draw a design, pattern or a word on the oval shape, using an old dried-out felt-tipped pen. The felt tip will remove the blue paint to reveal the white china beneath.

6 Paint the herb leaves lime green. Allow the paint to dry completely. Add detail to the leaves in a darker green paint. Allow to dry.

7 Fill in the background in turquoise, leaving a thin white outline around each image. Paint the background of the lid in the same way. Leave the paint to dry. Paint the remaining jars in complementary colours.

Four plain ceramic tiles combine to make a striking mural, reminiscent of Japanese art in its graphic simplicity and clear, calm blue-and-white colour scheme.

Maritime Tile Mural

you will need
soft and hard pencils
tracing paper
masking tape
4 clean, plain white glazed 15cm/6in square ceramic tiles
chinagraph pencil
non-toxic, water-based, cold-set ceramic paints: mid-blue, dark blue and black
paint palette
small and fine artist's paintbrushes

1 Trace the template from the back of the book and enlarge, if necessary. Tape the tracing to the four tiles, positioning it centrally. Transfer the outline to the tiles with a hard pencil.

2 Trace over the outline again with a chinagraph pencil. Draw the border freehand, and add any extra details to the fish. Follow the finished picture as a guide.

3 Keep the tiles together as you paint. Using the ceramic paints, fill in the fish shape. First, paint the main part of the fish mid-blue.

4 Paint the detail and the border dark blue. Highlight the scales with black. Set the paint following the manufacturer's instructions. The painted tiles will withstand gentle cleaning.

Imaginative seaside designs applied to a plain ceramic soap dish and toothbrush holder will transform the look of your bathroom, giving it an underwater theme.

Seashore Bathroom Set

you will need

plain china soap dish and
toothbrush holder or mug
cleaning fluid
cloth
tracing paper
soft and hard pencils
plain paper
adhesive spray
carbon paper
scissors or craft (utility) knife
masking tape
medium and fine artist's paintbrushes
water-based ceramic paints: mid-blue,
ivory, turquoise, lemon, pink,
white and dark blue
paint palette

1 Clean the china well. Trace the templates at the back of the book, enlarging if necessary. Transfer the designs on to plain paper. Spray the back of the paper with adhesive and stick to the back of a sheet of carbon paper. Cut out the designs, leaving a margin all round. Tape on to the china; transfer the lines with a hard pencil. Remove the carbon.

2 Using a medium paintbrush, paint a border around the soap dish, and then paint the background in mid-blue. When it is dry, paint the fish and shells, using the ivory, turquoise, lemon and pink paints. Paint the toothbrush holder in the same way.

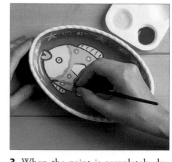

3 When the paint is completely dry, add the final touches to the soap dish and toothbrush holder. Paint on white dots and fine squiggles to create the effect of water. Using a fine paintbrush and the dark blue paint, carefully sketch in any detailing on the fish and shells. Allow to dry.

This cheerful sun design would be particularly welcome on the breakfast table for milk, orange juice or a simple posy of flowers. The colours could be adapted to suit your other china.

Sunshine Pitcher

you will need
white ceramic jug (pitcher)
cleaning fluid
cloth
tracing paper
hard and soft pencils
scissors
masking tape
acrylic china paints: black, bright yellow, ochre, blue, red and white
paint palette
fine artist's paintbrushes
hair dryer (optional)

2 Go over the sun's outlines with black paint and allow to dry; a hair dryer can speed up the process. Paint the main face and inner rays in bright yellow and then paint the cheeks and other parts of the rays in ochre.

3 Paint the background blue, then add fine details to the sun's face. Highlight each eye with a white dot. Set, following the manufacturer's instructions. The paint will withstand everyday use, but not the dishwasher.

1 Clean the china to remove any grease. Trace the template at the back of the book, try it for size and enlarge it if necessary. Cut it out roughly then rub over the back with a soft pencil. Make several cuts around the edge of the circle, so that the template will lie flat, and tape it in place. Draw over the outlines with a hard pencil to transfer the design.

Imagine the delight this painted tea set featuring playful rabbits will bring to a child you know. This fun design is easy to accomplish using the templates provided; they can be enlarged as necessary.

Playful Fun Tea Set

you will need
plain china mug, plate and bowl
cleaning fluid
cloth
tracing paper
soft pencil
plain paper
adhesive spray
carbon paper
scissors
clear adhesive tape
felt-tipped pen
cotton bud (swab)
water-based enamel paints: yellow, turquoise, red, green and blue
paint palette
medium and fine artist's paintbrushes

1 Thoroughly clean the china mug, plate and bowl with cleaning fluid and a cloth. Trace the templates for the rabbits and flower at the back of the book and transfer them to a piece of plain paper. Spray the back of the paper with glue and place it on top of a sheet of carbon paper, carbon side down. Cut out around the drawings, leaving a narrow margin.

2 Arrange the cut-out drawings around the china mug, plate and bowl, securing them in place with clear adhesive tape. Go over the designs with a felt-tipped pen to transfer the designs to the china pieces. Remove the cut-outs and clean any smudges carefully with a cotton bud.

3 Paint the background areas of the centre of the bowl in yellow.

4 Paint the remaining background areas, around the rim of the bowl, in turquoise. Leave to dry.

5 Begin to paint in the details. Here the flowers are painted red, turquoise and green.

◀ **6** Using a fine paintbrush, paint over the outlines of the large rabbits and flowers with blue paint. Paint over the outlines of the smaller rabbits on the rim of the plate with blue paint.

▶ **7** Paint the mug handle turquoise. Allow to dry. The pieces should be fired in a kiln to make them foodsafe.

Kitchen storage jars are always useful, and when adorned with bold designs such as these colourful vegetables they add quirky visual detail to your kitchen.

Vegetable Storage Jars

you will need
tracing paper
soft pencil
plain paper
adhesive spray
carbon paper
scissors
plain china storage jars
cleaning fluid
cloth
clear adhesive tape
felt-tipped pen
medium and fine artist's paintbrushes
water-based enamel paints: turquoise, coral, ivory, blue and yellow
paint palette

1 Trace the templates at the back of the book and enlarge if necessary. Transfer the designs on to a piece of plain paper. Spray the back of the paper with glue and stick it on to a sheet of carbon paper, carbon side down. Cut out the designs leaving a margin all round.

2 Clean the china storage jars, using cleaning fluid and a cloth. Tape some of the designs on to one of the jars. Go over the outlines lightly with a felt-tipped pen to transfer the designs to the jar. Remove the carbon paper designs and repeat the process for the other jars.

3 Using a medium paintbrush, paint in the turquoise background colour between the vegetable designs on the sides of the storage jars and their lids. Allow the paint to dry completely before proceeding to the next stage – this may take several days.

4 Mix up some red paint from the coral and ivory and paint the chillies. Mix the blue and yellow paint and paint the green of the vegetable leaves. Allow to dry.

5 Using a fine paintbrush and the blue paint, sketch in the detailing for the vegetables.

6 Paint the jar rims with the yellow paint and add some small ivory dots in the turquoise background area for decoration. Allow the paint to dry completely before using the jars.

Decorating Glass

A wide range of glass paints in a glorious array of colours is now available to the amateur. These paints can be applied easily to glassware and do not require kiln firing to set them. Glass is a versatile medium to work with and can be used to create all sorts of accessories and decorations from bottles and vases to outdoor lanterns. If you need to cut glass yourself, learn to do it safely and accurately.

A variety of materials are needed for painting glass including glass paints and etching paste, available from specialist glass shops, and self-adhesive vinyl, which is available from craft shops.

Materials

colour. They are not washable, and are designed purely for decorative use. Oil-based and water-based glass paints are available: the two types should not be combined. Ceramic paints can also be used on glass for an opaque effect.

Masking tape
This is ideal for making straight lines for etching and painting.

Paper towels
These are useful for cleaning glass and brushes, and wiping off mistakes.

Reusable adhesive
This is useful for holding designs in place on the glass.

Self-adhesive vinyl
Vinyl is used to mask off large areas when painting and etching the glass.

Acrylic enamel paints
These are ideal for use on glass.

Clear varnish
Mix with glass paints to produce lighter hues.

Contour paste
Use to create raised lines on glass. This gives the look of leaded windows and also acts as a barrier for paints. It can be used to add details within a cell of colour, such as the veins on a leaf.

Epoxy glue
Use this strong, clear glue to attach hanging devices to glass. It takes just a few minutes to go hard.

Etching paste
This acid paste eats into the surface of glass to leave a matt "frosted" finish. Use on clear and pale-coloured glass.

Glass paints
Specially manufactured, glass paints are translucent and give a vibrant

Toothpicks
Use to scratch designs into paintwork.

Ultraviolet glue
This glue goes hard in daylight. Red glass blocks ultraviolet rays, so you should let the light shine through the non-red glass when sticking two colours together, or use epoxy glue.

White spirit (paint thinner)
Use as a solvent to clean off most paints and any errors.

A well-lit workplace and a paintbrush are all that is needed for many of the projects in this chapter. However, the items listed below will make the job easier.

Equipment

Paintbrushes
Use a selection of artist's paintbrushes for applying paint and etching paste. Always clean brushes as directed by the paint manufacturer.

Paint palette
Large quantities of glass paint can be mixed in a plastic ice-cube tray.

Pencils and pens
Use a pencil or dark-coloured felt-tipped pen when making templates. A chinagraph can be used to draw guide-lines on the glass and wipes off easily.

Rubber gloves
A pair of gloves is vital to protect your hands from etching paste.

Ruler or straightedge
These are essential for measuring, or when a straight line is needed.

Cloth
A piece of cloth or towel folded into a pad is useful to provide support for items such as bottles or bowls while they are being painted. Paint one side of a vessel first, then allow it to dry thoroughly before resting it on the cloth while you paint the rest.

Cotton buds (swabs)
Use these to wipe away any painted mistakes and to remove chinagraph pencil marks.

Craft (utility) knife
A craft knife is useful for peeling off contour paste in glass-painting and etching projects. Ensure the blade is sharp and clean.

Nail polish remover
Before painting, always clean the glass on both sides to remove all traces of grease or fingerprints. Household glass-cleaning products can be used but nail polish remover is just as good. Use with paper towels.

Scissors
A pair of small, sharp scissors is useful for various cutting tasks, including cutting out templates.

Sponges
Cut sponges into pieces and use them to apply paint over a large area of glass. A natural sponge can be used to give the paint a decorative mottled effect, whereas a synthetic sponge will give a more regular effect.

On the following pages you will find useful step-by-step descriptions of some of the basic glass-painting techniques. They will help you to perfect your skills and achieve beautiful and successful results.

Glass Painting Techniques

Using templates and stencils

There are many different templates and stencils suitable for using on glass. Choose the type that is most useful for the size and style of glassware you are decorating.

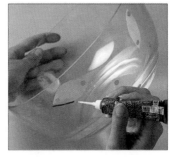

1 If you are working on a flat piece of clear glass, a template can simply be taped to the underside or attached using pieces of reusable putty adhesive, to ensure it does not move.

2 When you are decorating a curved surface, such as a bowl, small paper templates can be attached to the inside, following the curve. Use adhesive tape.

3 When working on a small, curved surface, such as a drinking glass, it may be easier to apply the template to the outside and then draw around it using a chinagraph pencil to make a guide.

Preparing the glass

It is essential to clean the surface of the glass thoroughly to remove any traces of grease or fingermarks, before beginning glass painting.

Clean both sides of the glass thoroughly, using a glass cleaner or nail polish remover and a paper towel.

4 Cut straight-sided stencils using a craft (utility) knife and metal ruler and resting on a cutting mat. Always keep your fingers well away from the blade and change the blade frequently to avoid tearing the paper.

5 When you are cutting a stencil that includes tight curves, cut what you can with a craft knife, then use a small pair of sharp-pointed scissors to cut the curves smoothly.

Transferring a design

In addition to using templates and stencils, there are several other ways of transferring a design on to glass. You can trace it, sketch with a pen, use carbon paper or even use water.

Tracing through the glass

Stick the design in position on the back of the article you wish to transfer it to with reusable putty adhesive or masking tape. For curved vessels cut the design into sections. Trace the design directly on to the surface of the vessel with the tube of contour paste.

Felt-tipped pens

A water-based overhead-projection pen is ideal for sketching freehand on to glass. Many felt-tipped pens will also work. When you are happy with your design, apply contour paste over the lines.

Water-level technique

To draw even lines around a vase, bowl, or other circular vessel, fill with water to the height of the line. Turn the vessel slowly while tracing the waterline on to the surface of the glass with contour paste.

Using carbon paper

Place a sheet of carbon paper over the article and then put the design on top. With a ballpoint pen, trace over the lines of your design, pressing it fairly firmly. Some carbon papers will not work on glass – handwriting carbon paper is the most suitable.

Using contour paste

Contour paste is easy to use, but it takes a little practice to get the pressure right. As it is the basis of much glass painting, it is worth persevering.

1 Squeeze the tube until the paste just begins to come out, then stop. To draw a line, hold the tube at about 45° to the surface. Rest the tip of the tube on the glass and squeeze it gently while moving the tube.

2 Occasionally air bubbles occur inside the tube. These can cause the paste to "explode" out of the tube. If this happens, either wipe off the excess paste straight away with a paper towel, or wait until it has dried and use a craft knife to remove it.

Mixing and applying paint

Glass paints come in a range of exciting, vivid colours, and produce beautiful translucent effects. Practise painting first on a spare piece of glass to get used to the consistency of the paint.

1 Mix paint colours on a ceramic palette, old plate or tile. To make a light colour, add the colour to white or colourless paint, a tiny amount at a time, until you reach the required hue. Use a separate brush for each colour so that you do not contaminate the paint in the pot.

2 If you want the finished effect to be opaque rather than translucent, add a small amount of white glass paint to the transparent coloured paint on the palette, plate or tile.

3 Always use an appropriately sized paintbrush for the job. A large, flat brush will give a smooth and even coverage over larger areas of glass, as well as making the job quicker.

4 Use a very fine brush to paint small details and fine lines. Let one coat of paint dry before painting over it with another colour.

5 To etch a design into the paint, draw into the paint while it is still wet using a toothpick or the other end of the paintbrush. Wipe off the excess paint after each stroke to keep the design clean.

Applying paint with a sponge

Sponging produces a mottled, softened effect on glass surfaces. Experiment first on scrap paper.

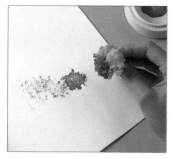

1 Use a dampened natural sponge to achieve a mottled effect. Dip the sponge in the paint then blot it on a sheet of paper to remove the excess paint before applying it to the glass.

2 Use masking tape or small pieces of reusable putty adhesive to attach the stencil to the glass for sponging.

3 Add texture and interest to sponged decoration by adding a second colour when the first has dried. This is most effective when both sides of the glass will be visible.

4 Sponge a neat, decorative band around a drinking glass by masking off both sides of the band with strips of masking tape.

Free-styling

Rather than using contour paste to define individual cells of colour, apply a coat of varnish over the article and brush or drop colours into the varnish, allowing them to blend freely.

Flash drying with candles

It is possible to flash dry paintwork over a heat source. A candle is ideal, but take care not to burn yourself. Turn the article slowly about 15cm/6in above the flame.

Cutting glass   Before you begin to tackle any of the projects in this chapter, look through this section, which acts as an introduction to the basic skills you will need for working with glass with assurance. Measure accurately the area of glass you want to cut. There is no margin for error and mistakes cannot be rectified.

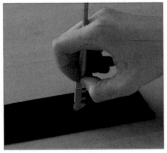

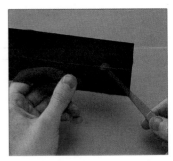

1 Hold the cutter so that your index finger is on top, your thumb and second finger grip each side, and the grozing teeth face towards your elbow. When you cut correctly with the cutter at a right angle to the glass, this position will give you movement in your arm.

2 Always cut the glass from edge to edge, one cut at a time. So start at one edge of the glass, with your cutter at right angles. Make it one continuous cut from one edge to the other.

3 Break the glass where you have made the score mark. Hold the cutter upside down between your thumb and first finger. Hold it loosely so that you can swing it to hit the underside of the score mark with the ball on the end of the cutter. Tap along the score mark. The glass will break.

4 Alternatively, hold the glass at each side of the score mark. Apply firm pressure pulling down and away from the crack. Use this method for very straight lines.

5 You could try putting the cutter on the table with the glass on the cutter and score mark over the cutter. With the base of your thumbs put pressure on both sides of the score mark.

6 Break the glass along the score mark as shown. Smooth the edges and remove any sharp points with a scythe stone. Use a little water to lubricate the stone.

Foiling glass Edging glass with copper foil allows you to solder pieces of glass together to create stained-glass effects. This technique is simple to do.

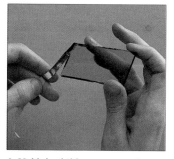

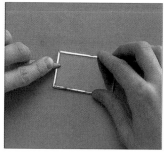

1 Hold the foil between your fingers, and use your thumb to peel back the protective backing paper as you work around the glass. Try not to touch the adhesive side of the tape – it will not stick if it is greasy or dusty.

2 Stick the foil to the edge of the piece of glass, working all the way around it, and overlapping the end of the foil by 1cm/½in.

3 Using two fingertips, press the foil down on to both sides of the glass, all the way around. Now use the fid to flatten the foil on to the glass to ensure it is stuck firmly all the way around.

Soldering glass Soldering is the technique of joining pieces of metal together, in this case copper foil-edged glass. This is a technique that requires some practice to achieve a neat, professional finish.

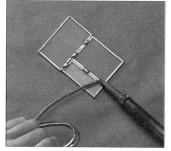

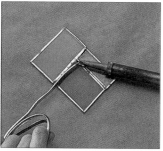

1 Using a flux brush, apply the flux to all the copper foil showing on the first side. Take the soldering iron so the tip of the iron side faces side to side and the thin side faces up and down. Hold the solder in the other hand with 10cm/4in uncoiled. Tack the pieces together by melting blobs of solder on to each joining edge. This holds the pieces while you solder them together.

2 Melt the solder, and allow it to run along the copper. Do not let it go too flat, but make sure you are always working with a small drop of solder. This makes it look neater and, even more importantly, is stronger. Turn the piece over and flux and solder the edges on the other side.

3 Tin all around the outer edges of the glass by firstly fluxing, and then running the soldering iron along the edges. There is usually enough solder from joining the inner edges to spread around the outside.

Using self-adhesive lead

Using self-adhesive lead is quick and easy. The skill is in the preparation: always ensure that the surface of the glass is scrupulously clean.

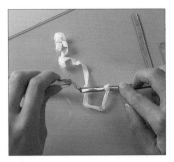

1 Clean the glass. Peel off the backing from the lead and press one end of it down gently with your fingers. Use one hand to hold the end while you bend the lead to fit the design. Always wash your hands after handling lead.

2 Trim the end with scissors. It is important that the lead strip is firmly stuck to the glass so that paint will not leak underneath it. After applying the strip, burnish it using a boning peg or the back of an old teaspoon.

Above: *Simple, yet effective, self-adhesive lead adds a stylish finish to this glass vase.*

Using lead came

This technique requires skill, but it is within everyone's reach. As special tools are needed for this technique, it can be expensive.

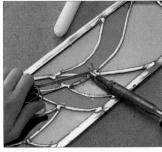

1 Draw the outline of each piece of glass that makes up the design. This outline represents the central point of the lead. Cut each piece of glass on the inside of the outline. To stretch the lead came to remove any kinks and make it easier to shape and cut, secure a spring-loaded vice to your bench and place one end of the came in it. Pull the other end with flat-nosed pliers. Do not break the lead.

2 Using a lead knife, bend the came to the shape of the edge of the glass. Using the knife blade, mark across the leaf where it will be cut (leave it a little short to accommodate the leaf of the piece crossing it). Place the came leaf on a flat surface. Position the knife and push down in a gentle but firm rocking motion until you are right through the came. Cut directly down and not at an angle.

3 Soldering wire for leaded panels contains lead, so wear barrier cream to protect your hands. Holding the soldering wire in your left hand, lower the tip of the soldering iron for a few seconds to melt the solder and join the separate pieces of lead came securely together.

Craft suppliers stock a range of glassware especially for painting, and these small glass hearts would look beautiful catching the light as they twirl in a window.

Heart Decoration

you will need
clean, clear glass heart shapes
nail polish remover or glass cleaner
paper towels
etching paste
medium artist's paintbrush
sponge
contour paste: light gold, dark gold and bronze

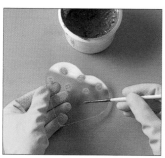

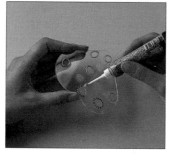

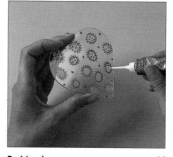

1 Clean both sides of the glass shapes to remove grease. Paint etching paste in small circles all over one side of the glass. Leave to dry, then wash off the paste with warm water and a sponge.

2 Outline alternate etched circles using light gold contour paste. Leave to dry. Add short "rays" all round each outline using dark gold contour paste, then add rays in light gold. Leave the contour paste to dry.

3 Use bronze contour paste to add a few dots between the circles. Turn the heart over and cover the etched areas in dots of bronze contour paste. Leave to dry. Bake the glass to harden the paint if necessary, following the manufacturer's instructions.

Stained glass is made for sunlight, and this sunlight catcher can hang in any window to catch all of the available light. Gold outliner separates the brightly coloured areas of orange, yellow, red and blue.

Sunlight Catcher

you will need
clean, 20cm/8in diameter clear glass roundel, 4mm/³⁄₁₆in thick
paper
pencil
tracing paper
indelible black felt-tipped pen
gold contour paste
glass paints: orange, yellow, red and blue
fine artist's paintbrush
73cm/29in length of chain
pliers
epoxy glue

1 To make a template of the sun motif that will fit the glass roundel, start by using a pencil to draw around the rim of the roundel on to a piece of paper.

2 Trace the sun motif template from the back of the book and transfer it to the plain paper, enlarging to the size required.

4 Trace over the black lines using gold contour paste. Leave to dry.

5 Colour in the central sun motif using the orange and yellow glass paints. Leave to dry. Clean the brush between colours as recommended by the paint manufacturer.

3 Place the circle of glass over the template and trace the design on to the glass using a felt-tipped pen.

6 Fill in the rest of the design using red and blue glass paints. Leave to dry.

7 Wrap the length of chain around the edge of the glass and cut to size. Rejoin the links by squeezing firmly together with pliers.

8 Cut an 8cm/3¼in length of chain, open the links at each end, and attach it to the chain circle by squeezing with pliers. Glue the chain circle around the circumference of the glass roundel using epoxy glue.

This picture frame is simply decorated using a gold marker and glass paints. The design is inspired by the devotional art and the remarkable patterns that adorn the Alhambra Palace in Granada, southern Spain.

Alhambra Picture Frame

you will need
clip-frame, with cleaned glass
gold permanent felt-tipped pen
fine artist's paintbrush
glass paints: crimson, turquoise and deep blue
piece of glass
scissors
kitchen sponge
paper towel

1 Enlarge the template at the back of the book to fit the clip-frame. Remove the glass from the frame and place it over the design. Trace it on to the glass with a gold permanent felt-tipped pen.

2 Turn the sheet of glass over. Using a fine paintbrush, paint over the diamond shapes with the crimson glass paints. Leave a white border between the crimson and the gold outline.

3 Pour a little turquoise and a little deep blue paint on to a piece of glass. Cut a kitchen sponge into sections. Press the sponge into the paint and then apply it to the glass with a light, dabbing motion to colour in the border. Clean up any overspill with a paper towel and leave to dry.

This is a magical way to transform a plain glass vase into something stylish and utterly original. When you have etched the vase, make sure that it is evenly frosted before you peel off the leaves.

Frosted Vase

you will need

coloured glass vase

tracing paper

pencil

thin cardboard or paper

scissors

self-adhesive vinyl

etching paste

medium artist's paintbrush

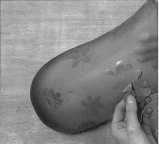

1 Wash and dry the vase. Draw a leaf pattern, then trace it on to a piece of thin cardboard or paper. Cut them out. Draw around the templates on to the backing of the vinyl and draw small circles freehand.

2 Cut out the shapes and peel off the backing paper. Arrange the shapes all over the vase. Smooth them down carefully to avoid any wrinkles. Paint etching paste over the vase and leave it in a warm place to dry, following the manufacturer's instructions.

3 Wash the vase in warm water to remove the paste. If the frosting looks smooth, you can remove the shapes. If not, repeat the process with another coat of etching paste, then wash and remove the shapes.

This jazzy painted bottle will really brighten up a bathroom shelf. It is decorated with a fun bubble pattern in blues and greens, but you can experiment with designs to complement the shape of your bottle.

Patterned Bathroom Bottle

you will need

clean glass bottle with a cork

felt-tipped pen

paper

black contour paste

glass paints: blue, green, violet and turquoise

fine artist's paintbrushes

ultraviolet glue

turquoise glass nugget

bubble bath

1 Decide on the pattern you think would look best for your bottle, then sketch your design to scale on a piece of paper.

2 Wash and thoroughly dry the bottle you have chosen. Then, using a felt-tipped pen, copy your design carefully on to the bottle.

3 Trace the felt-tipped pen design on one side of the bottle with the black contour paste. Leave the contour paste to dry completely.

4 Turn the bottle over and add contour paste circles to the other side. Leave to dry as before.

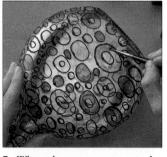

5 When the contour paste is dry, paint inside the circle motifs using blue, green and violet glass paints. Clean all the paintbrushes thoroughly between colours, as recommended by the paint manufacturer.

6 Once the circles are dry, paint the surrounding area using turquoise glass paint. Leave to dry.

7 Using ultraviolet glue, stick a glass nugget to the top of the cork.

8 Fill the bottle with your favourite bubble bath and replace the cork.

Ordinary glass jars make useful windproof containers for candles to light the garden during summer evenings; using glass paints, you can turn them into magical lanterns.

Coloured Glass Lantern

1 Clean the outside of the glass jar carefully to remove traces of grease and fingermarks, then stand it upside down and draw all around the base using the black relief outliner.

2 Measure 2cm/¾in up from the base of the glass and mark this level using a chinagraph pencil. Use the outliner to draw a horizontal line around the jar following the reference mark. Draw two more horizontal lines at 2cm/¾in intervals.

3 Measure around the jar and mark 2cm/¾in intervals with the chinagraph pencil. Referring to these marks, draw vertical lines with the outliner to divide the rings into squares. Leave to dry thoroughly.

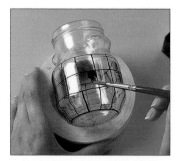

4 Support the jar on its side on a tape reel to stop it from rolling around as you work. Paint one of the squares with red paint. Using the end of a fine paintbrush or a toothpick, etch a small star through the centre of the red square. Wipe the paint off the brush after each stroke.

5 Paint the next square orange and etch a star as before. Paint and decorate all the squares, alternating the colours. Work only on the uppermost area so that the paint does not run, and wait for the paint to dry before turning the jar to continue. Bake the glass to harden the paint as required.

6 Cut a 30cm/12in length of wire and thread the beads on to it. Use a pair of round-nosed pliers to bend each end of the wire into a small loop.

7 Cut a second wire 3cm/1¼in longer than the circumference of the jar. Thread it through the loops in the handle and wrap it around the jar.

8 Bend one wire end into a loop and and thread the other end through it. Pull it tight, then bend it back and squeeze the hooks closed.

A flurry of butterflies and flowers covers the surface of this stunning bowl. They are painted freehand, with a few brush strokes forming each wing or petal, and the details are etched into the wet paint.

Butterfly Bowl

you will need
clear glass bowl
nail polish remover or glass cleaner
paper towels
tape measure
chinagraph pencil
rounded medium and fine paintbrushes
glass paints: grey, violet, mauve, bright
pink, pale blue and jade green
toothpick
cotton buds (swabs)

1 Clean the bowl. Measure 5.5cm/ 2¼in down from the rim and mark the edge of the border with a chinagraph pencil. Divide the border into equal sections, 5.5cm/2¼in wide.

2 To paint a butterfly just below the border, use a rounded paintbrush for the body and apply a single brush stroke in grey paint. Use a fine paintbrush to paint the antennae.

3 Using violet paint, paint a pair of wings on each side of the body. While the paint is still wet, use a toothpick to etch a simple design on the wings. Paint butterflies at random all over the bowl below the border, using mauve paint for some of the wings.

4 To paint the flowers for the border area, start with the centres. Paint a small circle in the middle of each of the measured sections with the mauve glass paint.

5 Use the medium paintbrush to paint five petals radiating out from one mauve flower centre, using the bright pink glass paint. Proceed to the next step before adding the remaining flower petals.

6 Etch a line along each petal, using a toothpick. Paint the rest of the petals and leave to dry.

7 Below the border, fill in the areas between the butterflies with swirls of pale blue paint. Leave to dry.

8 Rub off the pencil with cotton buds. Paint waves between the flowers using jade. Set the paint.

Stems of French lavender, with their picturesque winged flowerheads, criss-cross over the front of this beautiful vase. Opaque paints give the flowers solidity and impact against the clear glass.

French-lavender Flower Vase

you will need

tracing paper

felt-tipped pen

straight-sided glass vase

scissors

masking tape

nail polish remover or glass cleaner

paper towels

high-density synthetic sponge

opaque ceramic paints: gold, white, purple, crimson and green

paint palette

medium and fine artist's paintbrushes

1 Trace the template at the back of the book, enlarging it as necessary to fit the vase. Using masking tape, attach the tracing to the inside of the glass. Clean the outside of the vase thoroughly to remove any traces of grease and fingermarks.

2 Draw a shallow curve along a length of masking tape and cut along it. Stick the two parts to the vase, following one of the stems on the template and leaving a 3mm/⅛in space between them. Sponge gold paint along the stem and leave to dry. Peel off the tape and repeat for the other stems.

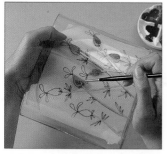

3 Mix white with purple paint and fill in the teardrop shapes for the flowerheads in light purple. Add darker shades of purple and crimson towards the bottom end of each flower shape, stippling the paint to create texture.

4 Paint the three petals at the top of each flower in pale purple, using long, loose brush strokes. Leave the paint to dry. Indicate the individual florets on each flowerhead with small ovals in dark purple. Leave the paint to dry.

5 Using a fine paintbrush, draw spiky leaves along the stems in two or three shades of dusky green. Leave to dry completely, and then bake the vase to harden the paint if necessary, following the manufacturer's instructions.

Some bottles are too beautiful to discard. This elegantly shaped blue one has been recycled with a decoration inspired by a 19th-century original found in an antique shop.

Bohemian Bottle

you will need

tracing paper

pencil

scissors

blue bottle

nail polish remover or glass cleaner

paper towels

masking tape

chinagraph pencil

ceramic paints: gold, white, green, red and yellow

medium and fine artist's paintbrushes

paint palette

1 Trace the template at the back of the book and cut out the bold centre section. Clean the bottle to remove any grease and fingermarks. Tape the template to the bottle and draw all around it using a chinagraph pencil.

2 Fill in the shape with several coats of gold paint, stippling it on to create a textured effect. Leave the paint to dry. Using white paint and a fine brush, outline the shape and add swirls along the top edge.

3 Mix white with a little green paint and shade the border design with touches of pale green.

4 Paint the green leaves with loose brush strokes, and add highlights in pale green. Draw in the red and yellow dots along the curves of the border as well as for the flower centres.

5 Paint in the daisy petals around the red flower centres using white paint. Add three small hearts and one or two small yellow flowers to the design for decorative detail.

This vase evokes the work of the designer Charles Rennie Mackintosh. Self-adhesive lead is used to create the effect of leaded glasswork and is simply pressed on to the glass surface for a decorative effect.

Cherry Blossom Vase

you will need

paper

pencil

vase

reusable putty adhesive

self-adhesive lead, 3mm/⅛in and

4mm/³⁄₁₆in wide

scissors or craft (utility) knife

fid or wooden peg

glass paints: white and pink

matt (flat) varnish

paint-mixing palette

fine artist's paintbrush

1 Enlarge the template from the back of the book to fit your vase. Stick it to the inside of the vase with reusable putty adhesive. Using the template as a guide, bend and stick the pieces of 3mm/⅛in-wide self-adhesive lead down over all of the bold lines on the template. Use scissors or a strong craft knife to trim the ends.

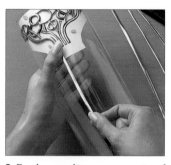

2 For the stem lines, cut two strips of 3mm/⅛in-wide self-adhesive lead the same length as your vase, and a further two 4mm/³⁄₁₆in-wide lead strips. Press the end of each into place to join the stems on the upper design and then run them down the length of the vase.

3 Splay the ends slightly at the base, and trim them so that they all end at the same point.

4 Cut a piece of 4mm/³⁄₁₆in-wide lead long enough to go around the vase with a little spare. Press it around the vase, just overlapping the edges of the stem lines. To smooth the joins, rub over with a fid or wooden peg.

5 Mix a little white paint with matt varnish. Do the same with a little pink paint. Apply the white paint sparingly to fill the blossom shapes, adding just a touch of pink to each area.

This cabinet uses opaque enamels rather than transparent glass paints, in the tradition of Eastern European folk art. Folk art relies on basic colour combinations and simple brushwork.

Folk Art Cabinet

you will need
small, glass-fronted display cabinet
reusable putty adhesive
fine artist's paintbrush
acrylic enamel paints: white, light
green, deep green, red,
raw sienna, yellow
paint palette

1 Enlarge the template from the back of the book and stick it to the back of the glass door with reusable putty adhesive. Paint the design on to the front of the glass using white acrylic enamel paint. Leave to dry.

2 Remove the template from the back of the glass. Paint over the leaves with the light green enamel paint, and leave to dry.

3 Paint a line of deep green paint along the lower edge of each of the light green leaves.

4 Paint the flowers with the red paint and then carefully blend in a little white towards the tips.

5 Paint over the stalk lines, half with raw sienna and half with yellow. Leave to dry.

The etched glass panels on this old door have been painted with coloured glass paints and finished with stick-on lead strips. The finished effect has a lighter look than genuine stained glass.

Leaded Door Panels

you will need
door with two sandblasted glass panels
tape measure
paper
pencil
ruler
black felt-tipped pen
scissors
masking tape
indelible black felt-tipped pen
self-adhesive lead, 1cm/⅜in wide
craft (utility) knife
self-healing cutting mat
boning peg
glass paints: turquoise, green, yellow and light green
turpentine
fine artist's paintbrushes

1 Measure the glass panels with a tape measure. With a pencil, draw them to scale on a piece of paper. Using a ruler, draw your design within the panel area, including 1cm/⅜in wide dividing lines to allow for the leading. Trace over the design in felt-tipped pen, cross-hatching the lead lines.

2 Cut out this paper pattern carefully with scissors and then stick it to the reverse of one of the glass panels by applying lengths of masking tape around the edges.

3 Trace the design from the pattern on to the sandblasted side of the glass with an indelible black felt-tipped pen. When the tracing is complete, remove the paper pattern.

4 Stretch the lead by gently pulling it. Cut four lengths to fit around the edge of the glass panel, using a sharp craft knife. Remove the backing paper and stick the lead in place.

5 Measure the lead needed for the inner framework and cut with a craft knife using a side-to-side rocking motion. Keep the blade at a 90° angle to the lead to ensure a straight cut. Cut and stick longer lengths of lead first, then work the smaller pieces.

6 With the edges butted closely together, remove the backing paper from the lead and press into place with your fingertips. Then press firmly along the length of the lead with a boning peg to seal it to the glass. Press around the outer edges of the lead lines with the pointed end of the boning peg in order to create a neat, watertight finish.

7 Dilute the glass paints with 30 per cent turpentine to create a subtle, watercolour feel to the paint. Use a small paintbrush to colour in the small areas between the leading. Clean the brushes with turpentine between the different colours.

8 Once the intricate areas are coloured in, paint the remainder of the design, leaving the centre of the glass panel unpainted. Alternatively, you could paint the whole area if you prefer. Repeat for the other panel.

This enchanting perfume bottle, with its swags of little dots and pretty little gilded flowers, is reminiscent of 19th-century Italian enamelled glassware. Use opaque ceramic paints for this project.

Venetian Perfume Bottle

you will need
round clear glass bottle with stopper
nail polish remover or glass cleaner
paper towels
tracing paper
pencil
scrap paper
scissors
chinagraph pencil
opaque ceramic paints: white,
red and gold
fine artist's paintbrush
paint palette
cotton buds (swabs)

1 Clean the bottle. Trace the template at the back of the book, adjusting it to fit eight times around the bottle, then cut out the scallops.

4 Using the template design as a guide, paint a four-petalled flower in gold paint between each scallop in the first round. Then fill in the centres of the daisies in gold paint.

2 Use a chinagraph pencil to draw around scallop A eight times, fitting it close to the neck of the bottle. Draw in the curls, then draw around scallop B, fitting it between the first scallops.

5 Using the fine paintbrush, add tiny dots of white, gold and pink paint in delicate swags and lines to link the flowers. Fill in the gold ovals, and pink and white dots at the top of each heart, then complete the design with two small gold dots at the base of each pink daisy. Extend the design with rows of tiny dots up the neck of the perfume bottle.

3 Using white, paint a six-petalled daisy at the base of each upper scallop. Mix a little red paint with white, and paint eight pink daisies at the base of each lower scallop.

6 Paint a large pink daisy exactly in the centre of the bottle stopper and add a gold centre to the daisy shape, as well as rows of tiny white dots radiating from the petals. Leave the paint to dry completely, then rub off the pencil marks using a cotton bud. Bake the bottle and stopper to harden the paint, if necesary, following the manufacturer's instructions.

The type of paintwork used in this unusual window decoration is not very easy to control, and it is precisely this free-flowing quality that gives the style its appeal.

Window Hanging

you will need
paper and pencil
glass, 3mm/⅛in thick
glass cutter
cutting oil
scythe stone
5mm/¼in self-adhesive copper foil tape
fid
red glass nuggets
flux and flux brush
solder and soldering iron
1mm/½sin tinned copper wire
round-nosed pliers
straight-nosed (snub-nosed) pliers
black contour paste
paint-mixing palette
glass paints: blue, turquoise, red, yellow, violet and white
clear varnish
fine artist's paintbrush

1 Enlarge the template at the back of the book to a size that is suitable for the window you wish to hang the pieces in. Lay a sheet of glass on the template and cut out five sections. (Have a glazier do this if you are not confident in cutting glass.)

2 Wash all of the pieces to remove any traces of cutting oil. Remove any sharp edges with a scythe stone, then press self-adhesive copper foil tape over all of the edges. Press the foil down with a fid.

4 Brush all of the copper-foiled edges with flux. Melt a bead of solder on to your soldering iron, and run the bead along the edge of each piece of glass to "tin" it with a thin coating of solder. Repeat as necessary until all of the edges are equally coated. Cut ten pieces of tinned copper wire 5cm/2in long for the hanging loops.

5 With round-nosed pliers, bend the ends down to form an upside-down "U". With straight-nosed pliers, grip each arm of the "U" and bend it up to form a 90-degree angle. Grip with round-nosed pliers while you bend the two arms downwards. Touch-solder the loops on the top of the glass pieces. Wash the pieces.

3 Using a scythe stone, lightly abrade the edge of each glass nugget. Wrap each nugget in copper foil tape.

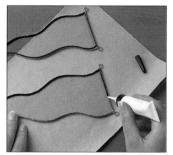

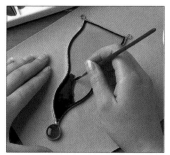

6 Apply flux to the end of one of the sections and one of the nuggets. Melt a bead of solder on to the iron and then solder the nugget in place. Melt on some more solder to ensure the nugget is secure.

7 Apply a line of black contour paste around the edge of each of the glass pieces in order to contain the glass paint solution.

8 In a mixing palette, prepare the colours you wish to use. Mix each with equal parts of clear varnish and opaque white paint. Apply the colours thickly and freely, allowing them to blend into each other. Leave to dry for at least 24 hours.

This plaque is made from pieces of stained glass and glass nuggets. Nuggets come in a wide range of colours and can add bright spots of colour among the crazy patchwork of glass.

Door Number Plaque

you will need
circle cutter
cutting oil
30cm/12in square of 3mm/⅛in clear glass
piece of carpet or blanket
glass cutter
tracing paper
pencil
paper
indelible black felt-tipped pen
pieces of stained glass
scythe stone
glass nuggets
ultraviolet glue
lead came
lead knife
bradawl, awl or drill
2mm/¹⁄₁₆in copper wire
round-nosed (snub-nosed) pliers
flux and flux brush
solder
soldering iron
black acrylic paint
tiling grout
grout spreader
clean cotton rag

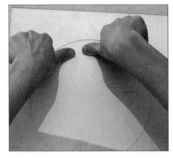

1 Set a circle cutter to cut a 20cm/8in diameter circle. Dip the cutter in oil, centre it in the glass square and score the circle in one sweep. Turn the glass over and place it on a piece of carpet or blanket on a work surface. Press down with both thumbs just inside the scoreline until the line begins to break. Repeat until the scoreline is broken all the way around.

2 Use a glass cutter to score a line in from each corner of the glass square, stopping just before you reach the circle. With the ball of the glass cutter, tap behind each scored line until the glass cracks up to the circle. The side sections will fall away, releasing the circle.

3 Trace the required numbers from the back of the book, enlarging them to the size required. Draw around the circle of glass on to plain paper and write your own door number centrally using the template as a guide.

4 Score pieces of stained glass for the numerals. Break the glass by tapping behind the scoreline with the ball of the glass cutter. Remove any rough edges with a scythe stone. Centre the glass circle over the template.

5 Arrange the numerals on the glass circle and place glass nuggets around them. Cut pieces of glass in contrasting colours to fill the spaces. Working away from sunlight, apply ultraviolet glue to the back of each piece and press it into place. This glue sets when it is exposed to ultraviolet light or sunlight. When all of the pieces are glued, check the position of each and slide them into place.

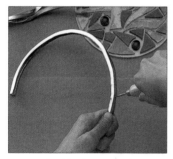

6 Use a lead knife to cut a length of lead came approximately 70cm/28in long. Use a bradawl, awl or drill to make a small hole in the centre of the strip of came.

7 Cut a 10cm/4in length of copper wire. With a pair of round-nosed pliers, bend a hanging loop. Thread the ends through the hole in the came and bend them up to lock the loop in place. Wrap the came around the glass with the hanging loop at the top.

8 Trim off any excess lead came with the lead knife. Flux the joint and then lightly solder the ends together.

9 Mix some black paint with grout. Spread it over the surface, into the spaces between the glass. Remove any excess with a rag. Leave to dry, then polish with a clean cotton rag.

Mosaic

Mosaic is a craft achievable by complete beginners. Essentially, it is painting-by-numbers but with pieces of glass or ceramic, known as tesserae, instead of paint. The skill lies in combining colours together in a pleasing way, and in producing a representative pictorial image. To start with, draw simple stylized shapes freehand or mark out geometric patterns on a plywood base, then fill in the designs with coloured tesserae.

The main materials used in mosaic are the individual pieces, known as tesserae, which can be ceramic, glass, china or any solid material. The other important material to consider is the base, which should be rigid.

Materials

Adhesives

There are several ways of attaching tesserae to a background. Cement-based tile adhesive is the most well known, and it can also be used to grout between the tesserae once the design is complete. For a wood base, use PVA (white) glue. For a glass base, use a silicone-based or a clear, all-purpose adhesive; to stick glass to metal, use epoxy resin. PVA is also used to prime a wooden base to make a suitable surface for the mosaic.

Admix

This is added to tile adhesive for extra adhesion.

Bases

Mosaic can be made on top of almost any rigid and pre-treated surface. One of the most popular bases is plywood.

Brown paper

This is used as backing for mosaics created by the semi-indirect method. Use the heaviest available.

Grout

Specialist grouts are smoother than tile adhesive and are available in a variety of colours.

Shellac

Use this to seal finished mosaics, especially those for outside use.

Tesserae

Mosaic material is described as tesserae.

1 *Ceramic tiles* – These are available in a range of colours and textures, glazed or unglazed. Household tiles can be cut to size using a hammer, or tile nippers for precise shapes.

2 *China* – Old china makes unusual tesserae. It creates an uneven surface, so is suitable for decorative projects rather than flat, functional surfaces. Break up china using a hammer.

3 *Marble* – Marble can be bought pre-cut into small squares; to cut it with accuracy you need specialist tools.

4 *Mirror glass* – Shards of mirror add a reflective sparkle to a mosaic. Mirror can be cut with tile nippers or glass cutters, or broken with a hammer.

5 *Smalti* – This is opaque glass that has been cut into regular chunks. It has a softly reflective surface.

6 *Vitreous glass tesserae* – These are glass squares which are corrugated on the back to accommodate tile adhesive. They are hardwearing and thus perfect for outdoor projects.

Many of the tools needed to make mosaics are ordinary household equipment; the rest can be purchased in a good hardware store. A pair of tile nippers is the main piece of specialist equipment you will need.

Equipment

Protective face mask
Wear a mask when mixing powdered grout, sanding the finished mosaic, and cleaning with hydrochloric acid.

Protective goggles
Wear safety goggles when you cut or smash tiles, and when working with hydrochloric acid.

Sacking (heavy cloth)
Use to wrap up tiles before breaking them with a hammer.

Saw
Use to cut wooden base material. Use a hacksaw for basic shapes, and a jigsaw for more complicated designs.

Spatula/Spreader/Squeegee
Used for spreading glue or other smooth adhesives, such as cellulose filler, on to your base material.

Abrasive paper
Use coarse-grade sandpaper to prepare wood. Wear a mask.

Clamps or bench vice
These are needed when cutting out the wooden base for projects.

Dilute hydrochloric acid
Use to clean cement-based grout from the finished mosaic if necessary. Always wear protective clothing, and work in a well-ventilated area.

Drill
Mosaic is heavy and a drilled hole for a wallplug will be needed to hold hanging projects securely.

Glass cutter
Use to score or cut awkward shapes in glass tesserae.

Paint scraper
This is used to remove awkward pieces of dried tile adhesive or grout from the surface of a completed mosaic.

Tile nippers
These are invaluable for cutting shaped tiles, especially curves.

You will also find the following items useful: bradawl or awl, chalk, craft (utility) knife, flexible knife, rubber gloves, hammer, felt-tipped pen, masking tape, mixing container, nailbrush, paintbrushes, pencil, plastic spray bottle, pliers, ruler, scissors, set square, sponge, tape measure.

Read the instructions below carefully before beginning a mosaic project and choose the methods most appropriate to the design that you are creating. Remember to wear protective clothing.

Mosaic Techniques

Cutting tesserae
There are two methods of cutting tesserae, one using tile nippers and one using a hammer. Choose the method depending on the shape of tesserae you require. Always wear protective goggles.

1 Using tile nippers hold a tessera between the nippers, and squeeze the handles together. It should break along the line of impact. To cut a specific shape, nibble at the edges.

2 Use a hammer to break up larger pieces such as household tiles and china, where regular shapes are not required. Remember to wear protective goggles.

3 When working with a hammer it is also advisable to wrap each tile or plate in a piece of sacking or heavy cloth to prevent flying shards.

Cutting glass
This technique requires practice and is potentially more dangerous. Wear protective goggles and follow the instructions below.

2 Applying firm, even pressure, score a line across in a single movement, without a break. You can either push the cutter away from you or pull it towards you. Don't score over the same line; if you make a mistake, try again on another part of the glass.

3 Hold the scored piece of glass in one hand. With your working hand, place pliers along the scored line and grip them firmly.

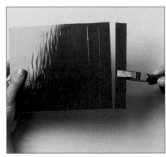

1 Holding the glass cutter, rest your index finger along the top. Hold the cutter at a 90-degree angle to the glass.

4 Angle the tip of the pliers up and pull down. The glass should break cleanly in two along the scored line.

Direct method   This is a popular technique, in which the tesserae are stuck, face up, on to the base and grouted into place. On a three-dimensional object or uneven surface this may be the only suitable method.

1 Cover the base with adhesive. Press the tesserae into it, cover with grout, leave to dry, then clean.

2 If you are following a design drawn on the base as a guide, apply a thin layer of tile adhesive on to the wrong side of each individual tessera and stick it into place.

3 If the tesserae are reflective, such as mirror glass or gold or silver smalti, try placing them at slightly different angles on a three-dimensional surface, to catch the light.

Semi-indirect method   With this method the tesserae are glued to the design off-site, but are then set into the tile adhesive in the final position.

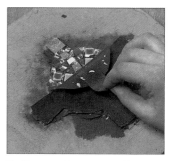

1 Draw a design on to brown paper. Adhere the tesserae right side down on to the paper using PVA (white) glue and a brush or palette knife.

2 Spread tile adhesive over the area designated for the mosaic. Press the mosaic into the adhesive, paper side up. Leave to dry for at least 24 hours.

3 Dampen the paper with a wet sponge and peel it off. The mosaic is now ready to be grouted and cleaned.

Indirect method This technique originated as a way of making large mosaics off-site so that they could be transported ready-made. The design is divided into manageable sections which are fitted together on-site.

1 Make a wooden frame to the size required, securing the corners with 2.5cm/1in screws. Make a brown paper template of the inside of the frame. Draw a design on the design area of the paper, leaving a 5mm/¼in margin all around. Grease the inside of the frame with petroleum jelly.

2 Wearing protective goggles and gloves, cut the tesserae as required. Glue them right side down on the brown paper, using water-soluble adhesive and following the design. Leave to dry.

3 Place the wooden frame carefully over the mosaic, then sprinkle dry sand over the mosaic, using a soft brush to spread it into the crevices between the tesserae.

4 Wearing a face mask, on a surface that cannot be damaged, mix 3 parts sand with 1 part cement. Make a well in the centre, add water and mix it with a trowel until you have a firm consistency. Gradually add more water, if necessary, until the mortar is pliable but not runny.

5 Half-fill the frame with mortar, pressing it into the corners. Cut a square of chicken wire a little smaller than the frame. Place it on top of the mortar so that the wire does not touch the frame. Fill the rest of the frame with mortar, then smooth the surface. Cover with damp newspaper, then heavy plastic sheeting, and leave to dry thoroughly for 5–6 days.

6 Turn the frame over. Dampen the brown paper with a wet sponge and then carefully peel it off. Loosen the screws and remove the frame from the mosaic. The mosaic is now ready to be grouted and cleaned.

Grouting

Mosaics are grouted to give them extra strength and a smoother finish. Grout binds the tesserae together. Coloured grout is often used to unify the design; this can either be purchased as ready-made powder, or you can add dye or acrylic paint to plain grout.

1 When grouting three-dimensional objects or uneven surfaces, it is easiest to spread the grout with a flexible knife or spreader.

2 Rub the grout deep into the crevices in between the tesserae. Always wear rubber (latex) gloves when you are handling grout directly.

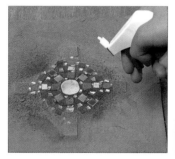

3 To grout large, flat mosaics, you can use powdered tile adhesive. Spoon it on to the surface, then spread it with a soft brush to fill all the crevices between the tesserae.

4 When you have completed the grouting process, spray the adhesive with water from a plastic spray bottle. You may need to repeat the process to achieve a smooth finish.

Cleaning

It is advisable to get rid of most of the excess grout while it is still wet. Wipe off the excess with a sponge before leaving to dry.

Purpose-made grouts

Once dry, most purpose-made grouts can be scrubbed from the surface using a stiff-bristled nailbrush and then polished off.

Cement-based adhesives

Cement mortars and cement-based adhesives need rougher treatment, and you will probably need to use abrasive paper. A fast alternative is to dilute hydrochloric acid and then paint it on to the surface to dissolve the excess cement. The process should be done outside, as it gives off toxic fumes. When the excess cement has fizzed away, wash off the residue of acid from the mosaic with plenty of water. Remember to wear a face mask when sanding, and a face mask, goggles and gloves when using hydrochloric acid.

Fragments of plain and patterned broken tile have been incorporated into the design of these plant pots. Collect your materials by looking in junk shops for old china in contrasting and complementary patterns.

Plant Pots

you will need

terracotta flower pots
PVA (white) glue and brush (optional)
mixing container
acrylic paint
paintbrush
chalk or wax crayon
plain and patterned ceramic tiles
tile nippers
rubber gloves
flexible knife
tile adhesive
powdered waterproof tile grout
cement dye
cloth
nailbrush
lint-free, soft cloth

1 If the pots are not frost-resistant and they are intended for outdoor use, treat inside and out by sealing with a coat of diluted PVA glue. Allow to dry. Paint the inside of all the pots with acrylic paint in your chosen colour. Leave to dry. Using chalk or a wax crayon, roughly sketch out the design for the tile pieces.

2 Snip small pieces of ceramic tile to fit within your chosen design. Using a flexible knife, spread tile adhesive on to small areas of the design at a time. Press the tile pieces in place, working on the outlines first, and then filling in the background.

3 Mix powdered grout with water and a little cement dye. Spread the grout over the pot, filling all the cracks between the tile pieces. Allow the surface to dry thoroughly.

4 Brush off any excess with a nailbrush. Allow to dry thoroughly for at least 48 hours, and then polish with a dry, soft cloth.

Personal letters and correspondence often have a tendency to be lost or misplaced in a busy household. This simple design for a letter rack could be the solution.

Love Letter Rack

you will need
3mm/⅛in and 1.5cm/½in MDF
(medium-density fiberboard)
or plywood
pencil
jigsaw (saber saw)
PVA (white) glue
paintbrushes
wood glue
panel pins (brads)
pin hammer
vitreous glass tesserae
tile nippers
white cellulose filler
grout spreader or flexible knife
sponge
abrasive paper
red acrylic paint

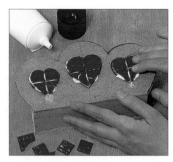

1 Draw the shapes of the components of the rack on to both pieces of MDF or plywood. Cut them out with a jigsaw. Prime the surfaces with diluted PVA glue. When dry, draw the pattern on to the front panel. Stick the pieces together with wood glue and secure with panel pins. Leave to dry overnight.

2 Select two tones of red vitreous glass tesserae to tile the heart motifs. Using tile nippers, nibble the tesserae into precise shapes to fit your design. Fix the tesserae in position on the front panel of the letter rack with white cellulose filler.

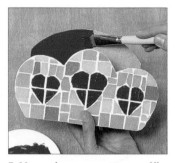

3 Select the colours of vitreous glass to tile around the hearts. Trim the tesserae to fit snugly around the heart motif and within the edges of the letter rack. Fix them to the base. Leave the rack to dry overnight.

4 Smooth more filler over the mosaic using a grout spreader or flexible knife. Rub the filler into all of the gaps with your fingers. Rub off any excess filler with a damp sponge and leave to dry.

5 Use sandpaper to remove any filler that has dried on the surface of the mosaic and to neaten the edges. Paint the parts of the letter rack that are not covered with mosaic with red acrylic paint. Leave to dry.

For this flowerpot, which combines both functional and decorative qualities of mosaic, the design and colours reflect the flowers which might be planted in it. Squares of mirror add reflections.

Part-tiled Flowerpot

you will need
ready-glazed, high-fired
terracotta flowerpot
chalk or wax crayon
selection of china
tile nippers
tile adhesive
flexible knife
tile grout
cement stain
nailbrush
soft cloth

1 Draw a simple design on the pot, using chalk or a wax crayon. Cut appropriate shapes from the china using tile nippers. Use tile adhesive to fix the tesserae to the pot, spreading it with a flexible knife. Work first on the main lines and detailed areas, applying the adhesive to small areas at a time so you can follow the lines of the design.

2 Fill in the larger areas of the design using tesserae in a plain colour. When these areas are complete, leave the pot to dry for 24 hours.

3 Mix the tile grout with a little cement stain, then spread the grout over the pot with your fingers, filling all the cracks between the tesserae. Allow the surface to dry, then brush off any excess grout with a nailbrush. After the pot has dried for about 48 hours polish it with a dry, soft cloth.

This sunflower mosaic is simple to make, and, if you have enough china, you could make several plaques to brighten up an outdoor wall using bright fragments of china in a harmonious blend of colours.

Sunflower Mosaic Plaques

you will need
5mm/¼in thick plywood sheet
pencil
coping saw or electric scroll saw
abrasive paper
bradawl or awl
electric cable
wire cutters
masking tape
PVA (white) glue
paintbrushes
white undercoat
china fragments
mirror strips
tile nippers
tile adhesive
tile grout
cement stain
nailbrush
soft cloth

1 Draw a sunflower on the plywood. Cut it out with a saw and sand any rough edges. Make two holes in the plywood with a bradawl or awl. Strip the cable and cut a short length of wire. Push the ends of the wire through the holes from the back and fix the ends with masking tape at the front. Seal the front with diluted PVA glue and the back with white undercoat.

2 Using tile nippers, cut the china and mirror strips into irregular shapes. Dip each fragment in the tile adhesive and stick them to the plywood. Scoop up enough of it to cover the sticking surface; the tile adhesive needs to squelch out around the edge of the mosaic to make sure that it adheres securely. Leave the adhesive to dry thoroughly overnight.

3 Mix some cement stain with the grout. Press small amounts of grout into the gaps on the mosaic with your fingers. Leave to dry for about 5 minutes, then brush off any excess with a nailbrush. Leave again for 5 minutes and then polish well with a dry, soft cloth. Leave overnight to dry.

This dramatic mosaic creates the invigorating effect of rocks sparkling with drops of water in a mountain stream. This project is quick to complete, as it does not need to be grouted.

Watery Slate Shelf

you will need

2cm/³⁄₄in thick plywood sheet
saw
bradawl or awl
PVA (white) glue
paintbrush
hammer
slate
piece of sacking (heavy cloth)
tile adhesive
black cement stain
flexible knife
pebbles
glass globules: blue, grey, white
silver smalti
tile nippers

1 Cut the piece of thick plywood to the desired size with a saw. Lightly score one side with a bradawl or awl, then prime with diluted PVA glue.

2 Using a hammer, break the slate into large chunks. It is advisable to wrap the slate in a piece of sacking to prevent injury.

3 Mix the tile adhesive with half a teaspoon of black cement stain. Mix to a thick paste with cold water.

4 Using a flexible knife, spread the tile adhesive in a thick, even layer over the scored side of the plywood. Smooth it over the front to conceal the edge.

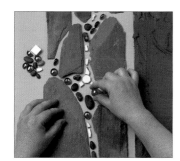

5 Arrange the broken slate, pebbles, glass globules and silver smalti on a flat surface next to the board in your chosen design, making any adjustments until you are satisfied.

6 Transfer the design, piece by piece, to the board. Tap the slate with the side of the tile nippers to settle it, but do not move any pieces once firmly positioned. Leave to dry overnight.

Mosaic is an ideal surface for decorating bathrooms and kitchens since it is waterproof and easy to wipe clean. This simple design is made of tiles in two colours, alternated to give a chequerboard effect.

Splashback Squares

you will need

12mm/¹⁄₂in thick plywood sheet, cut to fit along the top of your basin or sink and half as deep

PVA (white) glue

paintbrushes

bradawl or awl

soft dark pencil

thin-glazed ceramic household tiles in two contrasting colours

tile nippers

flexible knife

tile adhesive

damp sponge

grout spreader or cloth pad

abrasive paper

yacht varnish

4 domed mirror screws

screwdriver

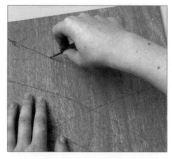

1 Prime both sides of the plywood with diluted PVA glue. Leave to dry, then score across one side with a bradawl or awl to create a key for the tile to adhere to.

2 Divide the scored side of the plywood into eight squares. Draw a simple and easily recognisable motif of your choice into each square.

3 Make a hole in each corner of the plywood, using a bradawl or awl. These will form the holes for the screws to fix the splashback to the wall in its final position behind the sink.

4 Using tile nippers, cut the tiles into random shapes. Following your drawn designs, and using a flexible knife, stick the tiles in place with PVA glue over the pencil markings on each square. Position the tiles carefully around the holes made for hanging. Wipe off any excess glue with a damp sponge before it dries. Leave until completely dry, preferably overnight.

5 Spread tile adhesive over the surface of the mosaic with a grout spreader or cloth pad, smoothing around the edges with your fingers. Wipe off any excess adhesive and re-open the hanging holes. Leave to dry overnight.

6 Carefully sand off any remaining dried adhesive on the surface of the mosaic. Paint the back of the plywood with yacht varnish to seal it and make it waterproof, and leave to dry for 1–2 hours. Fasten the splashback to the wall with domed mirror screws inserted through the holes at each corner.

Give your bathroom a new lease of life with this colourful and original fish splashback. Beads clustered together make an original addition to mosaics, and are perfect for creating intricate shapes.

Fish Splashback

you will need

pencil

paper

piece of plywood to fit splashback area

carbon paper

vitreous glass tesserae in a variety of colours

wood glue

interior filler

mixing container

spoon

acrylic paints in a variety of colours

selection of beads including:

metallic bugle beads,

frosted and metallic square beads,

large round beads and mixed beads

tile nippers

tile grout

cloth

1 Sketch a design to fit the splashback on a large sheet of paper, keeping the shapes simple and bold. Use a sheet of carbon paper to transfer the design to the plywood by drawing firmly over all the lines using a pencil.

2 Apply the mosaic border. Lay out all the tiles first, alternating the colours. Then apply wood glue to the border, a small section at a time, positioning the tiles carefully on top of the glue as you work along.

3 Following the manufacturer's instructions, mix up a small amount of interior filler, then add some green acrylic paint to colour it.

4 Spread green filler thickly over the seaweed fronds, then carefully press in metallic green bugle beads. Fill in the fish fins using green filler and metallic green square beads. Make sure all the beads are on their sides so that the holes do not show.

5 Mix up another small amount of interior filler, this time colouring it with the orange acrylic paint. Spread filler thickly over the starfish and press in orange square frosted beads. Use some darker beads for shading.

6 Glue on a large bead for the fish eye using wood glue. Mix up some white filler and spread it thickly on to a 5cm/ 2in-square section of the fish body and press in mixed beads. Repeat, working in small sections, until the fish is complete.

7 Glue on large beads for bubbles. For the background design and the rocks at the bottom of the splashback, use mosaic tile nippers to cut the mosaic tiles into 1cm/½in squares.

8 Fill in the background, varying the shades and sticking the tiles down with wood glue. Clip the edges of the tiles to fit any curves. Mix up some tile grout following the manufacturer's instructions and spread over the design. Spread lightly and carefully over the beaded areas. Wipe off with a damp cloth and leave to dry.

A step riser or skirting board is an unusual and discreet way of intro-ducing mosaic into your home. You can use a repeated design (such as this daisy), a succession of motifs, or a combination of the two.

Daisy Step Riser

you will need

skirting (base) board to fit the room

abrasive paper

PVA (white) glue

paintbrush

dark pencil

ruler

piece of sacking (heavy cloth)

selection of marble tiles

hammer

tile adhesive

flexible knife

sponge

soft cloth

1 Roughen the surface of the skirting board with coarse-grade abrasive paper, then prime with diluted PVA glue. Leave to dry.

2 Mark the skirting board into small, equally spaced sections. Using a dark pencil, draw a simple motif in each section. Here, the motif is a daisy.

3 Smash the marble tiles for the daisies into small pieces with a ham-mer. It is advisable to wrap the tiles in a piece of sacking.

4 Using a flexible knife and working on a small area at a time, spread tile adhesive along the lines of your draw-ing. Press the broken pieces of marble firmly into the adhesive. Choose tesserae in shapes that echo those of the design. The marble can be roughly shaped by tapping the edges of larger tesserae with a hammer. When each motif is tiled, wipe off any excess adhesive with a sponge and leave to dry overnight.

5 Break up the tiles in the background colour with a hammer. Working on a small area at a time, spread adhesive on to the untiled sections of skirting board and press the tesserae into it. When the surface is covered, use small pieces of the background colour to tile along the top edge of the skirting, ensuring that the tesserae do not overlap the edge. Leave to dry for 24 hours.

6 Rub more tile adhesive into the surface of the mosaic with your fingers, filling all the gaps between the tesserae. Use a flexible knife to spread the adhesive into the edge. Wipe off any excess with a damp sponge and leave overnight to dry.

7 Sand off any adhesive that has dried on the surface of the mosaic and polish the surface with a dry, soft cloth. Fix the skirting board in position.

This mosaic jewellery box was inspired by the treasures of the Aztecs and Mayas of pre-Columbian Central America, which were decorated with turquoise, coral and jade.

Aztec Box

you will need

wooden box with hinged lid
felt-tipped pen or dark pencil
PVA (white) glue
glue brush
glass nuggets backed with gold and
silver leaf
masking tape
fine artist's paintbrush
vitreous glass tesserae
tile nippers
cinca ceramic tiles
sand
cement
mixing container
black cement dye
sponge
soft cloth
plastic bag

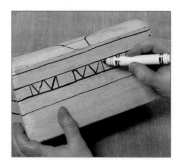

1 Draw a design on the wooden box with a felt-tipped pen or dark pencil. The design shown here represents the head of a fierce animal, and the teeth and jaws of the beast should be drawn immediately below the opening edge of the lid, using the picture as a guide.

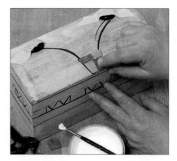

2 Using PVA glue, stick glass nuggets on the box for the eyes. Hold them in place with masking tape to dry. Cut vitreous glass tiles in coral and stick on to the nose and lips. Cut vitreous glass tiles in terracotta and pink for the lips. Use a paintbrush to apply glue to small pieces.

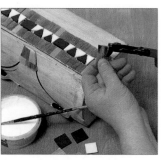

3 Cut triangular black and white tesserae into precise shapes to fit the areas marked for the teeth, then stick them in place.

4 Select tesserae in varying shades and use to define the eye sockets and the snout, cutting to fit as necessary. Include a few small nuggets positioned randomly. When tiling around the hinges, leave 1cm/½in untiled, so the box can be opened. Leave it to dry, then tile the lid in the same way.

5 Mix three parts sand with one part cement. Add some black cement dye. Add water, mixing it to the desired consistency. Rub the cement on to the box surface. Scrape off the excess, rub the box with a slightly damp sponge and polish with a dry cloth. Cover with plastic to dry slowly.

This design is simple to execute and adds a naive charm to a plain wooden tray. The semi-indirect method of mosaic used here helps to keep the surface smooth and flat.

Country Cottage Tray

you will need

scissors

brown paper

wooden tray

pencil

tracing paper (optional)

tile nippers

vitreous glass tesserae

water-soluble glue

white spirit (paint thinner)

PVA (white) glue

mixing container

old household paintbrush

bradawl or awl (with chisel edge)

or other sharp instrument

masking tape

cement-based tile adhesive

notched spreader

sponge

soft cloth

1 Cut a piece of brown paper to fit the bottom of the wooden tray. Draw a very simple picture in pencil or trace the template at the back of the book. Plan out the colour scheme for the picture and, using the tile nippers cut all of the vitreous glass tesserae into quarters.

2 Position the tiles on to the paper to check your design before going any further. Once you are satisfied with the design, apply water-soluble glue on to the paper in small areas, and stick the tiles on face down. Take care to obscure any pencil marks. Trim the tiles to fit if necessary.

3 Prepare the bottom of the tray by removing any varnish or polish with white spirit. Prime with diluted PVA glue, leave it to dry, then score it with a sharp instrument such as a bradawl or awl. Protect the sides with masking tape.

4 Mix the tile adhesive according to the manufacturer's instructions. Spread an even layer over the bottom of the tray, using a notched spreader. Cover the tray completely and spread well into the corners.

5 Place the mosaic carefully in the freshly-applied tile adhesive, paper side up. Press down firmly over the whole surface, then leave for about 30 minutes. Moisten the paper with a damp sponge and peel off. Leave the tile adhesive to dry overnight.

6 Some parts of the mosaic may need to be grouted with extra tile adhesive. Leave it to dry, then clean off any of the adhesive that may have dried on the surface with a sponge. Remove the pieces of masking tape and then polish the mosaic with a soft cloth.

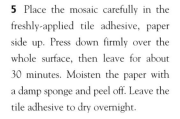

This unusual design is shown here as a mirror frame, but a similar frame could just as easily be used to frame a photograph or favourite picture. Only two colours are used, although the grouting is a third element.

Squiggle Frame

you will need
9mm/³⁄₈in thick plywood
jigsaw (saber saw)
PVA (white) glue
paintbrush
glazed ceramic household tiles:
6 blue, 10 black
dishtowel
hammer
pencils
tracing paper
tape measure
carbon paper
thick felt-tipped pen
tile adhesive
admix
tile grout
rubber spreader
sponge
soft cloth
mirror

1 Cut a sheet of plywood measuring 50 x 70cm/20 x 28in with a jigsaw. Using a large brush, prime the wood by coating it all over with diluted PVA glue. Leave it to dry for 24 hours.

2 Place two blue tiles face down on a dishtowel and fold over the edges. Using a hammer, smash the tiles repeatedly, checking from time to time until they are roughly broken into manageable fragments, keeping the blue and black pieces in separate piles.

3 Draw around the plywood sheet on a large sheet of tracing paper, then draw an inner rectangle of 39 x 60cm/16 x 24in. Sketch one scroll design on the tracing paper, then use sheets of carbon paper to transfer your design onto the plywood, flipping the tracing paper to repeat a mirror image another five times. Go over with a thick pen.

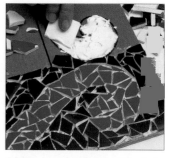

4 Mix some tile adhesive with admix, then spread it 3mm/⅛in thick over a small section of one of the scrolls, removing any excess. Working from the scroll edge out, fill in the blue tiles, and repeat until the frame is covered. Allow 24 hours for the adhesive to dry.

5 Spread some tile grout over the mosaic with a rubber spreader, using a circular motion. Continue until the grout fills all the gaps and is level with the tesserae. Sponge away any surface grout with a damp sponge. Allow to dry for 1 hour, then polish with a dry, soft cloth to rub off any residual grout. Glue the mirror in place.

In this vivid mosaic, it is important that the tesserae are accurately shaped, with no gaps between them. They are left ungrouted so that tile adhesive dust will not disturb the workings of the clock.

Cosmic Clock

you will need
40cm/16in diameter circle of wood
strip of plywood, 5mm/¹/₁₆in deeper
than the circle of wood and
130cm/52in long
hammer
tacks
black paint
paintbrush
brown paper
scissors
drill
charcoal or black felt-tipped pen
vitreous glass mosaic tiles
PVA (white) glue and brush
tile nippers
tile adhesive
admix
grout spreader
piece of flat wood
sponge
craft (utility) knife
soft cloth
double-sided tape
clock mechanism and hands
picture-hanging hook

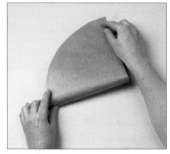

1 Position the strip of plywood around the circumference of the circle of wood, and, using a hammer and tacks, cover the edge of the circle to make a neat rim. Paint the rim black and leave to dry. Cut a circle of brown paper to fit inside the rim. Fold it in quarters to find the centre, and make a small hole.

2 Place the paper over the circle of wood and mark the centre through the hole on to the wood. Remove the paper and then drill a hole through the centre of the wood, large enough to allow the spindle of the clock mechanism to rotate freely.

3 Draw a cosmic design on the brown paper circle, using a stick of charcoal or a felt-tipped pen. (Charcoal is easier to correct.)

4 Snip the glass tiles into tesserae using tile nippers, then stick the tesserae face down on the paper, using PVA glue. Place them as close together as possible, without any gaps in between. Make any further cuts necessary to allow them to fit around the curves in your design.

5 Mix the tile adhesive and admix according to the manufacturer's instructions. Using the fine-notched edge of a grout spreader, spread this over the whole of the board, right up to the edge. Lower the mosaic on to the adhesive and press flat.

6 Smooth over the paper with a flat piece of wood, using small, circular movements. Leave for 20 minutes, then dampen the paper and gently pull it away from the mosaic. Scrape away any adhesive that has come through the tesserae with a craft knife. Leave to dry for at least 2 hours.

7 Carefully wipe any remaining glue from the surface of the mosaic with the sponge and polish with a dry, soft cloth. Using double-sided tape, attach the clock mechanism to the back of the board. Insert the spindle through the hole in the centre and fit on the hands. Fit a picture hook to the back.

In this panel, the tiles have been laid very close together to avoid the need for grout. This allows the range of tones used here to relate to one another as directly as possible, giving a luminous, glowing appearance.

Abstract Colour Panel

you will need

vitreous glass mosaic tiles in
various colours
coloured pencils to match the tiles
paper
tracing paper
tile nippers
MDF (medium-density fiberboard)
50 x 50cm/20 x 20in with frame
different coloured felt-tipped pens
wood stain
paintbrushes
PVA (white) glue
soft cloth

1 Match the proposed tile colours to the pencils to enable you to produce an accurate coloured drawing. As this scheme is fairly complex, involving boxes within boxes, and tonal colour changes, a line drawing was produced as a plan for the coloured sketch.

2 Draw an accurate coloured sketch. To get a good idea of how the different blocks of tones and shading will work, put a layer of tracing paper over the line drawing and fill in the coloured areas. Use the tile nippers to cut the mosaic tiles in your chosen colours.

3 Draw the fundamentals of the design on to the board using felt-tipped pens. It is not necessary to mark up any more detail than you see here. The segmented pattern is sketched in black, and the ladder lines in different colours. Stain the frame of the board before starting to stick down the tiles.

4 Sort your tiles into tones of greater or lesser intensity. Paint each area of the board that you are working on with a good layer of PVA glue. If the layer is too thin, the tiles will fail to adhere; if it is too thick, the glue will squeeze between the joints on to the tile face. Start by laying the coloured ladder shapes.

5 Continue working around the board, filling in the different coloured areas as you go. Wipe off any blobs of glue as you work, then wipe over the whole thing with a cloth when you have finished to remove any residual adhesive. Finally, polish with a dry, soft cloth.

This striking table has been decorated with bits of broken china and chipped decorative tiles, yet with clever colour co-ordination and a very simple design, it makes an attractive piece of garden furniture.

Garden Table

you will need

2.5cm/1in plywood, at least
122cm/4ft square
string
drawing pin (thumb tack)
pencil
jigsaw (saber saw)
wood primer
paintbrush
broken china
tile nippers
tile adhesive
mixing container
flexible knife
tile grout
grout colour (optional)
washing-up (dishwashing) brush

1 To mark a circle on the plywood, tie one end of a 60cm/2ft length of string to a drawing pin. Tie a pencil to the other end. Push the pin into the centre of the plywood, then draw the circle. Cut it out using a jigsaw. Draw your chosen design on the plywood circle, adjusting the string length to draw concentric circles.

2 Prime the plywood circle with wood primer on the front, back and around the edge. Apply a thick and even coat, and allow each side to dry before proceeding with the next. Allow the primer to dry thoroughly according to the manufacturer's instructions before proceeding further.

3 Snip pieces of the border china to fit your chosen design and arrange them on the table top.

4 Mix up the tile adhesive according to the manufacturer's instructions and spread it on to the back of each piece of china with a flexible knife before fixing it in position. Cover the whole table with the design.

5 Mix up the grout and colour it as desired, then work it into all the gaps. Using a washing-up brush, continue to work the grout in, then clean off any excess.

This unusual garden urn is decorated with modern faces but has a look that is reminiscent of Byzantine icons. A simple and naive drawing of a face can look better than realistic depictions when rendered in mosaic.

Garden Urn

you will need

large frost-resistant urn

yacht varnish

paintbrush

chalk

vitreous glass tesserae

tile nippers

cement-based tile adhesive

mixing container

flexible knife

sponge

abrasive paper

dilute hydrochloric acid (optional)

1 Paint the inside of the urn with yacht varnish, then leave to dry. Divide the pot into quarters and draw your design on each quarter with chalk. The design used here depicts four different heads and shoulders. Keep the drawing simple, sketching just the basic elements of the face.

2 Choose a dark colour from the range of tiles for the main outlines and details such as eyes and lips. Cut these into eighths using tile nippers. Mix up cement-based tile adhesive and stick the tesserae on to your drawn lines. Select a range of shades for the flesh tones and cut into quarters.

3 Working on a small area at a time, apply cement-based tile adhesive to the face and press the tesserae into it. Use a mixture of all the colours, but in areas of shade use more of the darker tesserae and in highlighted areas use more of the lighter pieces.

4 Choose colours for the area that surrounds the heads. Spread these out on a clean table to see if they work together. A mixture of blues and whites with a little green has been chosen here. Cut the pieces into quarters with tile nippers.

5 Working on a small area at a time, spread tile adhesive on to the surface and press the cut vitreous glass into it, making sure the colours are arranged randomly. Cover the outer surface of the urn with tesserae, then leave to dry for 24 hours.

6 Mix up more tile adhesive and spread it all over the surface of the mosaic. Do this thoroughly, making sure you fill all the gaps between the tesserae. This is especially important if the urn is going to be put outside. Wipe off any excess cement with a sponge and leave to dry for 24 hours.

7 Use abrasive paper to remove any cement that has dried on the surface of the mosaic. If the cement is hard to remove, dilute hydrochloric acid can be used. Wear protective clothing and a mask. Wash any acid residue from the surface with plenty of water and leave the urn to dry.

8 Finish off the urn by rubbing some more of the tile adhesive over the lip and around the inside rim of the pot. This will prevent the mosaic design from seeming to end too abruptly and will give the urn and mosaic a more unified appearance.

Sea urchins are found clinging to wild, rocky shorelines or nestling in rock pools. Their simple, pleasing shapes bring a taste of the ocean to your garden. They come in many colours, including these soft blues.

Sea Urchin Garden Seat

you will need

4 whole breezeblocks (cinderblocks) and 1 small cut piece

sand

cement

hammer

cold chisel

charcoal

vitreous glass mosaic tiles

tile adhesive

black cement stain

notched trowel

tile nippers

slate

piece of sacking (heavy cloth)

glass baubles, silver and glass circles or stones

1 Mix 3 parts sand to 1 part cement with some water. Use this mortar to join the breezeblocks into a cube formed from two L shapes, with a cut block in the centre.

2 When the mortar is dry, knock off the corners of the blocks with a hammer and cold chisel. Continue to shape the blocks into a flat dome, with the cut block at the top.

3 Using charcoal, draw a curved line on each side of the cube to give the impression of a rounded sea urchin. Draw lines radiating out from the centre. Keep your choice of colours simple and bold. Lay out the design before you start and apply the tiles to check the spacing. Vitreous glass tiles were chosen because of their suitability for outdoor work. Cut them into strips for easy lines or soak them off the mesh.

4 Add a small amount of black cement stain to the tile adhesive and trowel it directly on to the surface of the block, no more than 5mm (¼in) thick. Place each tile on the surface of the adhesive and tap it down sharply, once only, with the tile nippers. Do not adjust the tiles too much or they will lose their adhesion. Wrap the slate in a piece of sacking and break into pieces with a hammer.

5 Avoid making any sharp edges, as these will have to be filed down afterwards. Use just one dark shade of tiles for the curved line marked in step 3 to give the design visual clarity. Place the broken slate pieces on the adhesive around the square base of the seat and tap them down with the tile nippers.

6 In between the gaps on the square base of the seat, place glass baubles, silver and glass circles, blue and white cut tiles or stones in the pattern of running water. Leave to dry completely. Grout the seat with sand, cement and black stain mixed with water. Allow to dry slowly but thoroughly. To secure the seat in position, dig out a shallow base for two breezeblocks, and then mortar the seat to them.

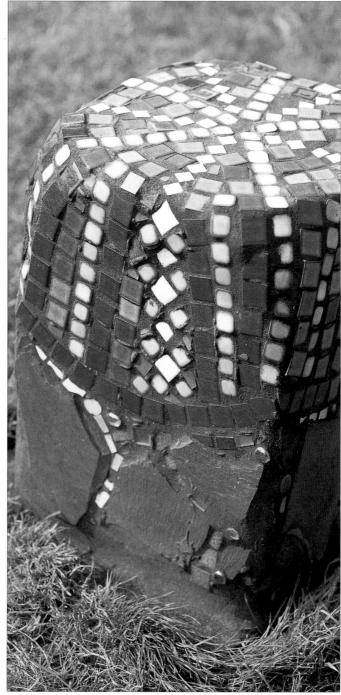

This traditional design uses the colours seen in ancient Roman mosaics to create a table top suitable for a simple metal base. Unglazed tiles are much easier than glazed tiles to cut and shape for this precise design.

Star Table

1 Follow the instructions for the Garden Table (see p. 474) to cut a circle from the plywood. Prime one side of the plywood with diluted PVA glue and leave to dry. Score with a bradawl or awl. Using a pair of compasses, draw circles 12mm/½in apart, working out from the centre, then draw a large star on top. If you wish, go over the design in felt-tipped pen.

2 Using tile nippers, cut the white tiles into neat quarters. Apply PVA glue to the base in small sections, using a fine paintbrush. Stick the tesserae on to alternate sections of the star. Keep the rows straight and the gaps between the tesserae even and to a minimum. Trim the tesserae as necessary to fit. Continue laying the tesserae until all the white sections are complete.

3 Cut up the beige tiles into neat quarters and fill in the other sections of the star in the same way as the white tiles in step 2.

4 Cut the black tiles into neat quarters and glue around the edge of the plywood. Leave until it is completely dry.

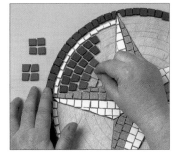

5 Glue a row of black quarter tiles around the outer edge of the table top. Cut some white quarter tiles in half and glue these inside the black circle, keeping the gaps to a minimum. Cut the terracotta tiles into quarters.

6 Using your drawn lines as a guide, fill in the rest of the background with alternating bands of colour. Lay out the tesserae before you glue them in place. Leave to dry overnight. Grout with tile adhesive, then clean the surface with a damp sponge. Leave to dry, then sand off any remaining adhesive and polish with a dry, soft cloth.

This unusual and decorative dragonfly plaque is made from plywood and pieces of old china. Try creating your own designs, based on different insects – they make a fun decoration for the garden shed.

Dragonfly Plaque

you will need

tracing paper

pencil

5mm/¼in plywood, 50cm/20in square

jigsaw (saber saw)

bradawl or awl

PVA (white) glue

paintbrush

acrylic primer

abrasive paper

dark green acrylic paint

cable strippers

electric cable

wire cutters

selection of china

tile nippers

tile adhesive

coloured tile grout

brush

cloth

1 Enlarge the template provided and transfer it on to the plywood. Cut out the dragonfly and make two small hanging holes at the top of the body with a bradawl or awl. Seal the front with diluted PVA glue and the back with acrylic primer. When dry, sand the back and paint with green acrylic paint. Strip some electric cable and cut a short length of wire. Push this through the holes from the back and twist together securely.

2 Cut the china into regular shapes using tile nippers. Dip each piece into tile adhesive, scooping up a thick layer, and press down securely on the plywood to fill in the design. Leave to dry overnight.

3 Press grout into the gaps between the china. Leave it to dry for about 5 minutes, then brush off the excess. Leave for another 5 minutes, then polish with a cloth.

With a little work and imagination, this battered old chair has been transformed into an unusual, exciting piece of furniture. This example shows the extremes to which the medium can successfully be taken.

Crazy Paving Chair

you will need

wooden chair

2cm/³⁄₄in plywood (optional)

jigsaw (saber saw) (optional)

paint or varnish stripper

coarse-grade abrasive paper

paintbrush

PVA (white) glue

wood glue

cement-based tile adhesive

admix

mixing container

flexible knife

pencil or chalk

large selection of china

tile nippers

dilute hydrochloric acid (optional)

soft cloth

1 If the chair you have chosen has a padded seat, remove it. There may be a wooden pallet beneath the padding which you can use as a base for the mosaic. If not, cut a piece of plywood to fit in its place.

2 Strip the chair of any paint or varnish and sand down with coarse-grade abrasive paper. Then paint the whole chair with diluted PVA glue to seal it.

3 When the surface is dry, stick the seat in place with a strong wood glue and fill any gaps around the edge with cement-based tile adhesive mixed with admix, which will provide extra strength and flexibility.

4 Draw a design or motifs on any large flat surfaces of the chair with a pencil or chalk. Use simple shapes that are easy to read.

5 Select china that has colours and patterns to suit the motifs you have drawn. Using tile nippers, cut the china into the appropriate shapes and sizes.

▶

6 Spread cement-based tile adhesive with admix within the areas of your design and press the cut china firmly into it.

7 Select china to cover the rest of the chair. As you are unlikely to have enough of the same pattern to cover the whole chair, choose two or three patterns that look good together.

8 Cut the china into small, varied shapes. Working on small areas at a time, tile the rest of the chair. Where one section of wood meets another, change the pattern of the china you are using.

9 Cut appropriately patterned china into thin slivers and use these to tile the edges of any thin sections of wood. Here, the edges of the back rest are covered. Leave for at least 24 hours to dry completely.

10 Mix up some more cement-based tile adhesive with the admix. Using a flexible knife, smooth this grout into the four corners of every piece of wood. Use your fingers to rub the grout over the flat surfaces. Work on a small area at a time and try to clean off most of the excess as you go. Leave overnight to dry.

11 Sand off the excess cement. This can be quite a difficult job, as there are many awkward angles. Alternatively, dilute hydrochloric acid can be used, but you must wear the appropriate protective clothing and apply it either outside or where there is good ventilation. Wash any residue from the surface with plenty of water and, when dry, polish with a soft cloth.

The ancient tradition of games, paths and puzzles in mosaic gives this simple, strong design an ageless appeal. The background is quick and easy to do, and the swirling design of the snakes uses vibrant colours.

Snakes and Ladders Floor

you will need
paper
felt-tipped pens
tape measure
scissors
clear film (plastic wrap)
fibreglass mesh
vitreous glass mosaic tiles in various
colours and matt (flat) black
tile nippers
PVA (white) glue
paintbrush
patio cleaner
black cement stain
tile adhesive
notched trowel
sand
cement
sponge

1 Draw a design for the whole board, with 100 squares. Play a game on it to make sure that it works. Measure out one of the outside paving slabs to be covered. Cut out 25 pieces of paper to fit the slab.

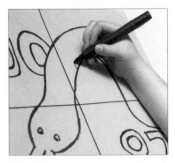

2 Fold them into quarters and mark out the sections. These are the 100 squares needed for your game. Copy out your design on to the 25 squares of paper using a thick felt-tipped pen.

3 Cover the front of each of the 25 squares with clear film and then a piece of mesh, cut to size.

4 Outline each of the 100 squares with matt black tiles, cut in half. Use PVA glue and a fine paintbrush to stick them to the mesh. Outline the numbers with quarter tiles and the snakes with both half and quarter tiles. Fill in the snakes and ladders with glossy, brightly coloured glass tiles.

5 Fill in the background squares with different colours for even and odd squares. Leave the squares to dry overnight, then turn them over, peel off the paper and the plastic film (used to prevent the tiles and mesh sticking to the paper) and leave until totally dry. Make sure all the tiles are stuck on to the fibreglass mesh, and restick any that fall off.

6 Clean all the paving slabs with patio cleaner and rinse well. Add a black cement stain to the tile adhesive, following the manufacturer's instructions, and apply a thin, even layer to each square with a notched trowel.

7 Lay on the design, one section at a time, allowing for gaps between the slabs. Mark all the pieces clearly and refer to the plan often as you work. Tamp down the squares gently and evenly. Leave to dry completely.

8 Grout the mosaic, using a mixture of sand, cement and water, with an added black stain. Wipe off the excess with a damp sponge and allow to dry slowly.

Patterns for some of the projects are given here so you can make templates. The way you copy these may depend on the materials being used, but cutting out a card template and drawing round it is often the best approach.

Templates

Tracing

Unless you have access to a photocopier, you will need to trace the printed pattern before transferring it to a piece of card for cutting out.

1 Use a pen or pencil to draw over the template. Turn the tracing over on a piece of scrap paper and use a soft pencil to rub over the lines.

2 Place the tracing, right side up, on a sheet of paper or card (stock). Using a hard pencil, draw firmly over all the lines of the design.

3 Lift off the tracing to reveal the design. Go over the lines if necessary before cutting out the template.

4 When working with fabric, it may be possible to trace the design directly using a fabric pen. Tape the drawing to a light box or window and tape the fabric over it to hold it still while you draw.

Scaling up

You may want to make a template that is larger than the printed design. Scaling up is easily done using a photocopier with an enlarging facility, but failing this you can use graph paper. For very small designs, scaling down may be required.

1 Trace the design and tape the tracing over a sheet of graph paper. Using an appropriate scale, draw the design on a second piece of graph paper, copying the shape from each small square to each larger square.

2 Lay or paste the graph paper template on a sheet of card and cut around the outline.

Stars-and-stripes Floorcloth,
pp20–1

Lino-printed Leaves, pp32–3

Mexican Motif Place Mats, p27

Summery Duvet
Cover, pp34–5

Sponge-printed
Gingham Bed
Linen, pp30–1

Summer Parasol, p46

Foam-printed Boat Towel, pp36–7

Patterned Seat Cover, pp54–5

Flowery Camisole, pp48–9

Painted Fan, p47

Poppy Painting, pp60–1

Cotton Sarong pp76–7

Indian Motif Shawl,
p56–7

Indian Motif Shawl, pp58–9

Stained-glass Silk Panel, pp62–3

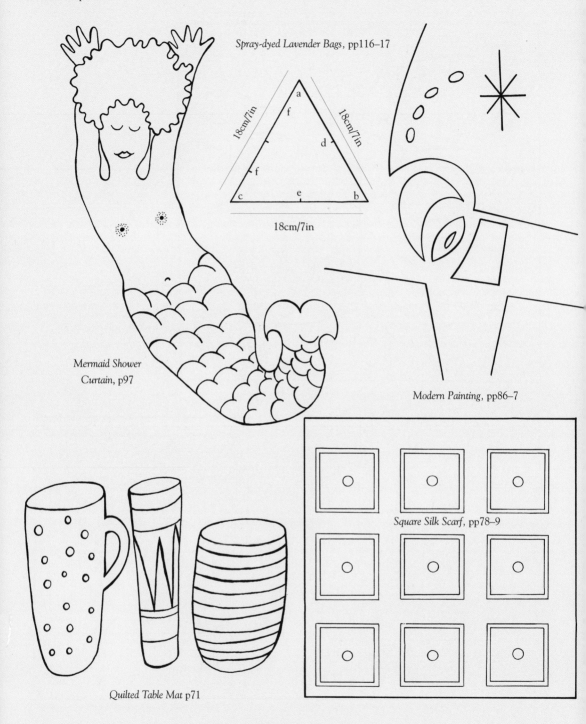

Spray-dyed Lavender Bags, pp116–17

18cm/7in

18cm/7in

18cm/7in

Mermaid Shower
Curtain, p97

Modern Painting, pp86–7

Square Silk Scarf, pp78–9

Quilted Table Mat p71

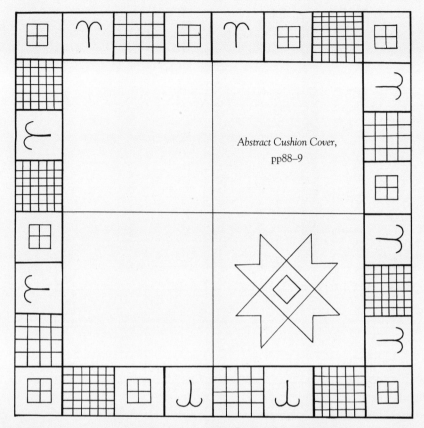

Abstract Cushion Cover,
pp88–9

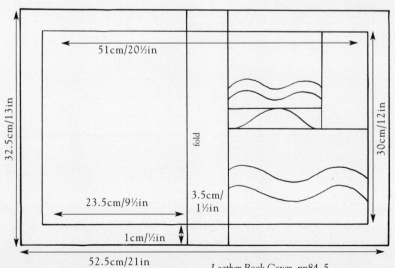

51cm/20½in

32.5cm/13in

fold

30cm/12in

23.5cm/9½in

3.5cm/
1½in

1cm/½in

52.5cm/21in

Leather Book Cover, pp84–5

Maple Leaf Table Runner,
pp80–1

Striped Bordered Scarf, pp82–3

Tea-dyed Hot Water Bottle Cover,
pp102–3

Loom-woven Choker,
pp190–1

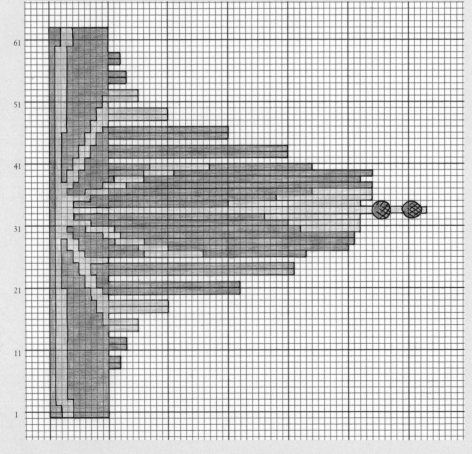

Repeat line 1
35 times
Repeat line 63
35 times

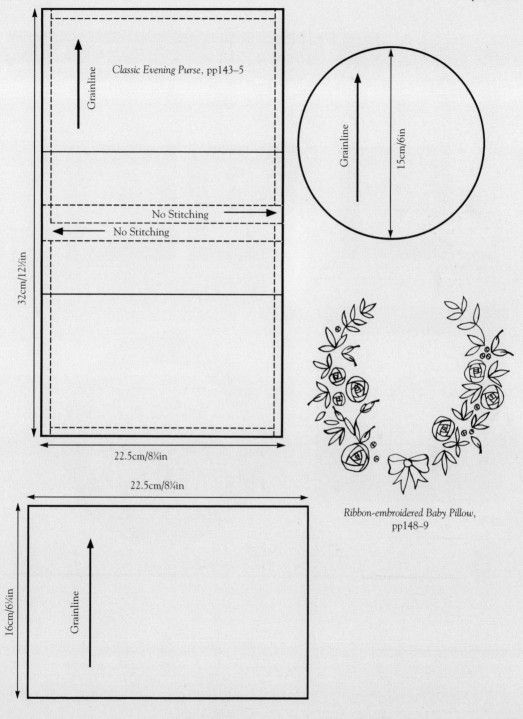

Grainline

Classic Evening Purse, pp143–5

No Stitching →

← No Stitching

32cm/12⅝in

22.5cm/8¾in

Grainline

15cm/6in

22.5cm/8¾in

16cm/6¼in

Grainline

Ribbon-embroidered Baby Pillow,
pp148–9

Bird Lapel Pin, pp210–11

Banded Ring, pp214–15

Fishy Cufflinks, pp216–17

Stargazer Earrings, pp218–19
Two alternative designs are shown here

Pet Hound Brooch, pp220–1

Flower Pendant, pp222–3

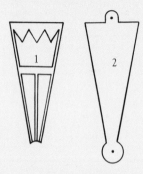

Triangular Pendant, p229

Shield Earrings, pp226–7

Cloisonné Earrings, pp224–5

ABCDEFGHIJKLM
NOPQRSTUVWXYZ

Monogrammed Clothes Hanger, pp240–1

3

4

2

Monogrammed Clothes Hanger,
pp240–1

1

Desk Accessories, pp246–7

Embossed Greetings Cards, p285

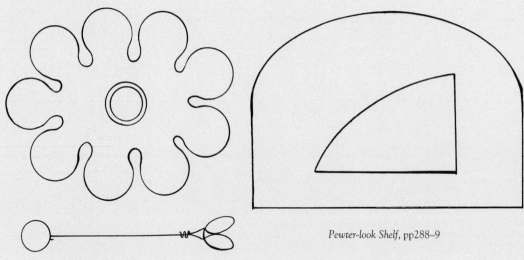

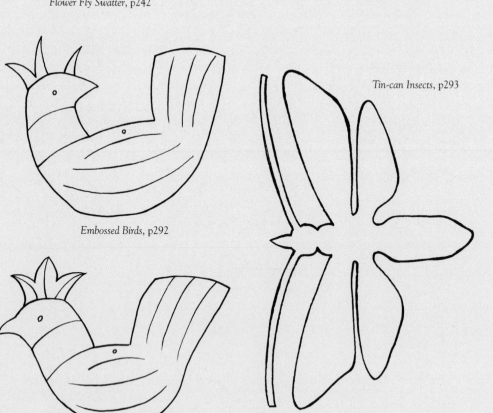

Flower Fly Swatter, p242

Pewter-look Shelf, pp288–9

Tin-can Insects, p293

Embossed Birds, p292

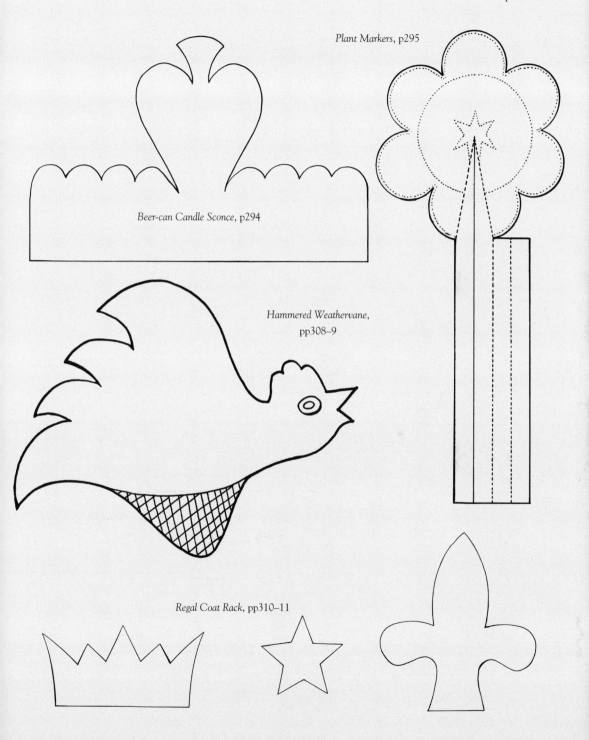

Plant Markers, p295

Beer-can Candle Sconce, p294

Hammered Weathervane,
pp308–9

Regal Coat Rack, pp310–11

Scrollwork Doorstop,
pp300–1

Treetop Angel, pp296–7

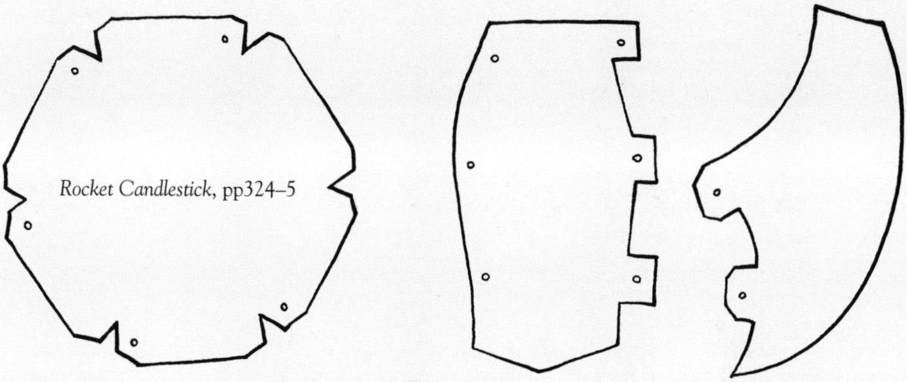

Rocket Candlestick, pp324–5

Mexican Mirror,
pp315–17

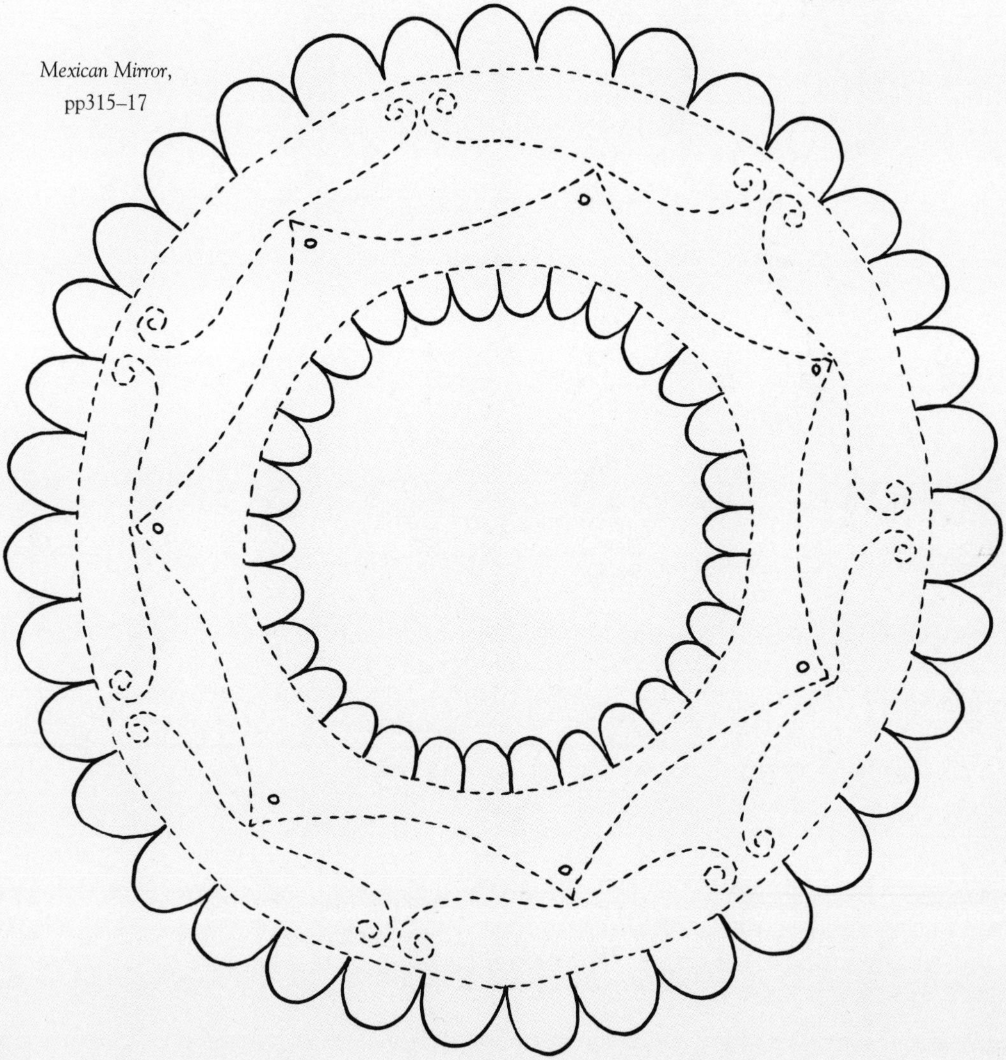

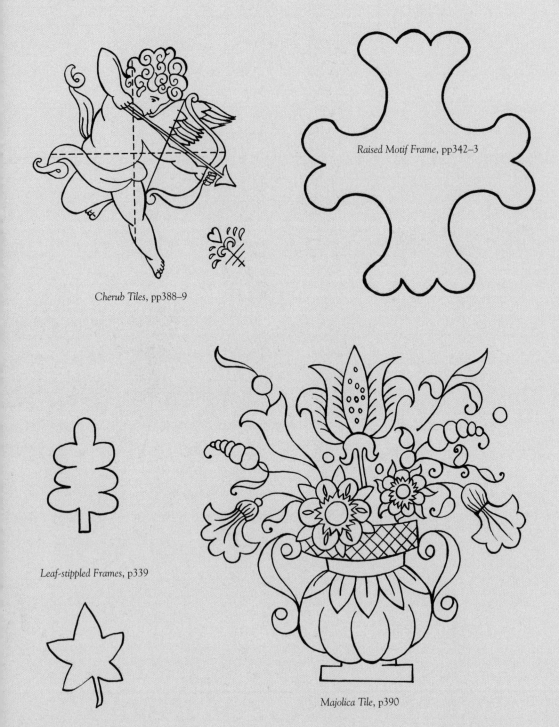

Cherub Tiles, pp388–9

Raised Motif Frame, pp342–3

Leaf-stippled Frames, p339

Majolica Tile, p390

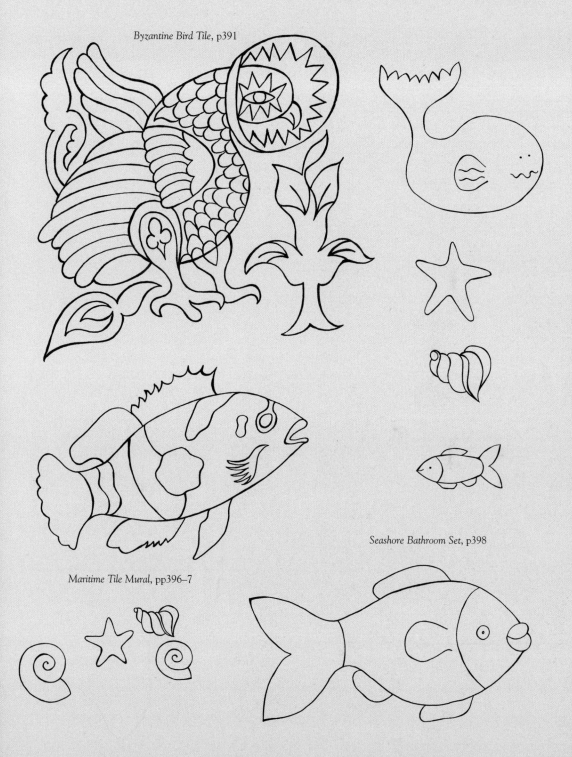

Byzantine Bird Tile, p391

Maritime Tile Mural, pp396–7

Seashore Bathroom Set, p398

Playful Fun Tea Set, pp400–1

Sunshine Jug, p399

Vegetable Storage Jars, pp402–3

Sunlight Catcher, pp416–17

Alhambra Picture Frame, p418

French-lavender Flower Vase, pp426–7

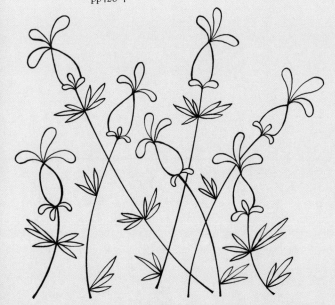

Bohemian Bottle, pp428–9

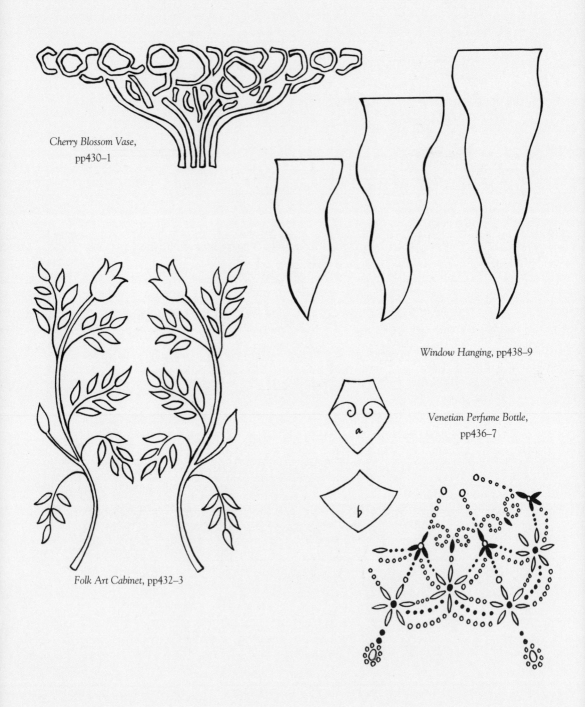

Cherry Blossom Vase,
pp430–1

Window Hanging, pp438–9

Venetian Perfume Bottle,
pp436–7

Folk Art Cabinet, pp432–3

Dragonfly
Plaque, p482

Door Number Plaque, pp440–1

Country Cottage Tray, pp466–7

Index

This edition is published by Southwater,
an imprint of Anness Publishing Ltd,
108 Great Russell Street,
London WC1B 3NA;
info@anness.com

www.southwaterbooks.com;
www.annesspublishing.com

If you like the images in this book and would
like to investigate using them for publishing,
promotions or advertising, please visit our website
www.practicalpictures.com for more information.

© Anness Publishing Ltd 2014

Publisher: Joanna Lorenz
Editorial Director: Helen Sudell
Project Editor: Simona Hill
Production Controller: Pirong Wang

Parts of this book have previously been
published in separate volumes: *Decorating Fabric,
Decorative Tin & Wirework, Make Your Own
Jewellery, Beadwork & Ribbons, Decorating Glass &
Ceramics, The Complete Book of Picture Framing
& Decorative Framework, Mosaics by Design*

PUBLISHER'S NOTE

Acknowledgements

The publishers would like to thank the following people for designing projects in this book: **Helen Baird** for the splashback squares, daisy skirting board, country cottage tray, cosmic clock, garden urn, crazy paving chair. **Michael Ball** for the Alhambra picture frame, cherry blossom vase, folk art cabinet, window hanging, door number plaque. **Evelyn Bennett** for the jewel box, tin spice rack. **Emma Biggs** for the abstract colour panel. **Petra Boase** for the flowerpot throw, leaf-stippled frames, Mexican folk art tiles, frosted vase. **Penny Boylan** for the tea-dyed hot water bottle cover, velvet-edged throw, ribbon-rose coat hangers, embossed greetings cards. **Lisa Brown** for the bead-trimmed voile jug covers, chunky bead tie-backs, silken key tassels, beaded cushion trims, pillowcase edgings, ribbon-rose coat hangers, appliquéd ribbon café curtain, tasselled tie-back, beaded wire candlesticks. **Tessa Brown** for the love letter rack. **Victoria Brown** for the decorative mouldings. **Anna-Lise De'Ath** for the sunlight catcher, patterned bathroom bottle, leaded door panels. **Stephanie Donaldson** for the mermaid shower curtain. **Marion Elliot** for the punched panel cabinet, number plaque, embossed book jacket, regal coat rack, painted mirror, tin can chandelier, photograph frame, Byzantine bird tile. **Mary Fellows** for the alphabet tiles, heart decoration. **Lucinda Ganderton** for the foam-printed boat towel, marbled spectacle case, beaded charm bracelet, beaded hatpins, silver chain belt, crystal butterfly, Majolica tile, morning sun face, French-lavender flower vase, Bohemian bottle, Venetian perfume bottle. **Andrew Gilmore** for the flower fly swatter, heart-shaped trivet, bottle carrier, toasting fork, copper bird bath, pewter-look shelf, plant markers, hammered weathervane, rocket candlestick. **Judith Gussin** for the block-printed chair pad, spray-dyed lavender bags. **Lesley Harle** for the low-relief ceramic, squiggle frame. **Helen Heery** for the cotton sarong, square silk scarf. **Karin Hossack** for the sponge-printed gingham bed linen, doughnut floor cushion, mesh place mat, woven pipe-cleaner basket. **Alison Jenkins** for the Mexican motif place mats, marbled fabric desk set, glittering window decoration, desk accessories, fabric-covered baskets. **Lindsay Kaubi** for the loom-woven choker. **Rian Kanduth** for the fabric-covered mount, colourwashed frame, raised motif frame, lime-waxed frame, woodstained frame, multi-window frame, reclaimed timber frame, framing a canvas, insetting objects into a frame, craquelure frame, verre eglomisé frame, ink penwork frame, scorched frame. **Dinah Kelly** for the crackle-glaze frame. **Christine Kingdom** for the gift boxes, ribbon table mats, ribbon lantern, ribbon-embroidered baby pillow, roll-up needlework case, classic evening purse, flower and ribbon headdress, woven ribbon waistcoat. **Mary Maguire** for the decorative candle sconce, vegetable basket, copper bowl, garden lantern, heart spice rack, utility rack, embossed heart, heart candle sconce, treetop angel, scrollwork doorstop, Mexican mirror. **Sipra Majumber** for the leather book cover. **Jane Moore** for the banded ring, fishy cufflinks, stargazer earrings, pet brooch, flower pendant. **Izzy Moreau** for the stamped spongeware, maritime tile mural. **Helen Musselwhite** for the seashore bathroom set, fun bunnies tea set, vegetable storage jars. **Cleo Mussi** for the plant pots, part-tiled flowerpot, sunflower mosaic, mosaic garden table, dragonfly plaque. **Andrew Newton-Cox** for the Rapunzel's tower. **Diedre O'Malley** for the glass lantern. **Cheryl Owen** for the butterfly bowl. **Denise Palmer** for the plique-à-jour earrings. **Sandra Partington** for the stained-glass silk panel. **Marie Perkins** for the citrus fruit bowl, kitchen herb jars. **Sue Radcliffe** for the monogrammed clothes hanger. **Alex Raphael** for the multicoloured buttons. **Ruth Rushby** for the bird lapel pin, *cloisonné* earrings, triangular pendant. **Jennie Russell** for the toothbrush holder, spiral napkin holders. **Deborah Schneebeli-Morrell** for the embossed birds, tin-can insects, beer-can candle sconce. **Isabel Stanley** for the summer parasol, flowery camisole, abstract picture frame, patterned seat cover, Indian motif shawl, little fringed bag, spiral bracelets, bead candle-holder, fringed lampshade, bead-fringed cushions, satin and velvet ribbon shade, leaf motif cup and saucer, fish splashback. **Susie Stokoe** for the lino-printed leaves, summery duvet cover, painted fan, salt-painted tie, salt-patterned greetings card, poppy painting, quilted table mat, geometric napkin, maple leaf table runner, bordered scarf, modern painting, dip-dyed lampshade, double-dyed place-mats, pleated table runner, tie-dyed patchwork cushion. **Norma Vondee** for the slate shelf, Aztec box, sea urchin garden seat, star table, snakes and ladders floor. **Liz Wagstaff** for the gilded shell frame, good as gold. **Stewart and Sally Walton** for the stars-and-stripes floorcloth, potato-printed tablecloth, rolling pin holder, kitchen hook rack, punched metal bucket, stamped star frame. **Sarah Wilson** for the shield earrings. **Dorothy Wood** for the abstract cushion cover, basic frame.

Note to Reader